# A Vision of American Law

# A VISION OF AMERICAN LAW

## *Judging* Law, Literature, and the Stories We Tell

Barry R. Schaller



PRAEGER
Westport, Connecticut
London

**Library of Congress Cataloging-in-Publication Data**

Schaller, Barry R., 1938–
A vision of American law : judging law, literature, and the stories we tell / Barry R. Schaller.
p. cm.
Includes bibliographical references and index.
ISBN 0–275–95111–1 (alk. paper)
1. Legal stories, American—History and criticism. 2. American fiction—History and criticism. 3. Lawyers in literature. 4. Law and literature. I. Title.
PS374.L34S32 1997
810.9'355—DC20 96–44683

British Library Cataloguing in Publication Data is available.



Library of Congress Catalog Card Number: 96–44683
ISBN: 0–275–95111–1

First published in 1997

Praeger Publishers, 88 Post Road West, Westport, CT 06881
An imprint of Greenwood Publishing Group, Inc.

Printed in the United States of America

The paper used in this book complies with the Permanent Paper Standard issued by the National Information Standards Organization (Z39.48–1984).

10 9 8 7 6 5 4 3 2 1

*For Carol V. C. Schaller*

# Contents

# Abbreviations

*APOE* Wendell Berry. *A Place on Earth*. New York: Harcourt, Brace & World, Inc., 1967.

*AT* Theodore Dreiser. *An American Tragedy*. New York: The New American Library, Inc., 1981.

*BM* John Dos Passos. *The Big Money*. New York: Harcourt, Brace and Company, 1936.

*CL* Richard Price. *Clockers*. New York: Avon Books, 1993.

*DL* Nathanael West. *Miss Lonelyhearts & The Day of the Locust*. New York: New Directions Publishing Corporation, 1969.

*GG* F. Scott Fitzgerald. *The Great Gatsby*. New York: Charles Scribner's Sons, 1953.

*GW* John Steinbeck. *The Grapes of Wrath*. New York: Bantam Books, Inc., 1966.

*H* Saul Bellow. *Herzog*. New York: The Viking Press, 1964.

*HF* Mark Twain. *Adventures of Huckleberry Finn*. New York: Penguin Group, 1959.

*IM* Ralph Ellison. *Invisible Man*. New York: Vintage Books, 1990.

*L* Don DeLillo. *Libra*. New York: Penguin Books, 1991.

*MGS* Stephen Crane. *Maggie: A Girl of the Streets*, in *Great Short Works of Stephen Crane*. New York: Harper & Row, 1968.

*NR* Robert Penn Warren. *Night Rider*. New York: Random House, 1939.

*O* Frank Norris. *The Octopus*. New York: The New American Library, Inc., 1964.

OV William Faulkner. ''An Odor of Verbena,'' in Malcolm Cowley, ed., *The Portable Faulkner*, rev. and exp. ed. New York: Penguin Books, 1977.

*P* James Fenimore Cooper. *The Pioneers or The Sources of the Susquehanna*. New York: Penguin Books, 1988.

PG William Faulkner. ''Percy Grimm,'' in Malcolm Cowley, ed., *The Portable Faulkner*, rev. and exp. ed. New York: Penguin Books, 1977.

*ROB* Russell Banks. *Rule of the Bone*. New York: HarperCollins, 1995.

*SL* Nathaniel Hawthorne. *The Scarlet Letter*. New York: Penguin Books, 1983.

TES William Faulkner. ''That Evening Sun,'' in Malcolm Cowley, ed., *The Portable Faulkner*, rev. and exp. ed. New York: Penguin Books, 1977.

*them* Joyce Carol Oates. *them*. New York: The Vanguard Press, 1969.

*TRM* Craig Nova. *Trombone*. New York: Ballantine Books, 1994.

*TSH* Russell Banks. *The Sweet Hereafter*. New York: HarperCollins, 1991.

*TV* Owen Wister. *The Virginian: A Horseman of the Plains*. New York: MacMillan Publishing Co., 1979.

*WOTH* James Fenimore Cooper. *The Ways of the Hour*. Upper Saddle River, N.J.: The Gregg Press, 1968.

# Preface

My purpose is to develop the idea of looking beyond the narrow confines of legal writing into the world of imaginative literature as a way of understanding more fully the role and impact of law in American society. The inspiration for this work came as a result of teaching law and literature to judges from many parts of the United States during the past decade. As I became increasingly aware of the value of using literary texts as a vehicle for discussing legal issues in their broadest sense, I recognized the need for a book that would develop in depth the treatment of legal ideas in important works of American literature. That objective quickly led to others—the discussion of law as an integral part of American culture and the need to preserve our fundamental values while, at the same time, making sure that the benefits of those values are accessible to all our citizens.

As I began to make choices about the ideas to include, I realized even more fully the relevance that works of American literature hold for today's society. Many literary texts illuminate issues that trouble Americans today. Recognizing that each text selected tells a part of the whole story of American culture, I began to search for meanings that would bring coherence and clarity to a story of law and culture. Even though the latter part of this century has seen dramatic changes in the structure and pace of society, literary texts from earlier times still contain useful insights. The forces at work today are rooted in our past. While this book broadly integrates law and literature, along with intellectual historical concepts, it is not meant to be comprehensive in all these areas. Rather, I intend to draw from each area what is necessary for the purpose of making observations and suggestions concerning our current law-related problems. My goal is to bring them together in an effort to make sense of the sometimes disturbing, fragmented world in which we live.

I believe I have found a way to highlight some of the major problems of our society today through the vehicle of American literature. In the final chapter, I offer my own suggestions as to how we can approach some of our major legal and cultural problems. In the end, however, you must be the judge.

# Acknowledgments

I thank the Quinnipiac Law Review Association for permission to reprint portions of my articles. The first is “Faulkner's Law: An Analysis of the Interaction of Law and Private Codes in William Faulkner's Short Fiction,” *Bridgeport Law Review*, vol. 12, no. 3 (Spring 1992). Copyright 1992 by the Bridgeport Law Review Association. The second is “Culturally Speaking: Equality, Responsibility and the Social Compact,” *Quinnipiac Law Review*, vol. 14, no. 3 (Fall 1994). Copyright 1994 by the Quinnipiac Law Review Association. I also thank the *Connecticut Law Tribune* for permission to reprint portions of several of my articles. They include “Law and Literature: At the Heart of American Society,” 19 *CLT* 39, October 4, 1993; “Perspectives on Family Violence: Problems and Solutions,” 21 *CLT* 3, January 16, 1995; and “Proposed Solutions to the Family Violence Problem,” 21 *CLT* 4, January 23, 1995. In addition, I thank *The National Law Journal* for permission to reprint portions of my article, “Violence in American Culture is Deeply Rooted,” 19 *NLJ* 7, October 14, 1996.

I wish to thank Christopher Jefford, Keith Marks, Thomas Langdon, Tahir Aftab, Cynthia Barlow, Christa Dommers, Lisa Fielding, Noelle Simpson, Sandra Sharr, Virginia Street, and Peter Tsimbidaros for their excellent research and editing assistance. I am especially grateful to Thomas Morawetz for his extensive and illuminating comments on an earlier draft of the manuscript, and to Aviam Soifer, who made detailed and instructive comments on portions of the manuscript. My wife, Carol V. C. Schaller, not only supported and encouraged me as I continued this project through countless weekends, but also guided me with the wisdom of her insightful comments on my thinking and writing.

My determination to write this book came from many sources, including more than two decades on the trial and appellate bench, the considerable body of scholarly writing in the law and literature field, and the inspired teaching of Cleanth Brooks and Charles Feidelson while I was a student at Yale College. The interest on the part of so many dedicated judges in law and literature seminars also contributed to my decision to produce a book on American law, literature, and culture. In addition, I remain deeply indebted to my parents, Raymond T. and Mildred M. Schaller, for their devotion to my pursuit of lifelong interests in law, literature, and government.

# Introduction

> Accountability of each individual for individual conduct lies at the core of all law—indeed, of all organized societies. . . . [I]ndividual accountability is fundamental if the structure of an organized society is not to be eroded to anarchy and impotence.[1]

> I often wonder whether we do not rest our hopes too much upon constitutions, upon laws and upon courts. These are false hopes; believe me, these are false hopes. Liberty lies in the hearts of men and women; when it dies there, no constitution, no law, no court can save it; no constitution, no law, no court can even do much to help it. While it lies there it needs no constitution, no law, no court to save it.[2]

Law and literature traditionally have played vital roles in American culture. Law has played a dominant role in the development of our society from pre-Revolutionary times to the present. Works of imaginative literature have helped to shape the thinking of Americans about our society and, in many instances, have paved the way for important societal changes. Law has been a prominent theme in much of that literature. Virtually every major writer—from Ralph Waldo Emerson to Ralph Ellison and from Herman Melville to Toni Morrison—has found law to be a compelling focal point for the narrative.

While law has an important role in most societies, it has consistently been an unusually dominant force in American society. This may be so, in part, because of the absence of other prevailing systems of moral or ethical values in the United States, and thus the need for a substitute ordering system. It may even be said that law, in all its dimensions—as a code of rules, as an institution, and as a process—is *the* binding value. Law is the force that holds our political, social, and economic structure together.

The great diversity of racial, ethnic, and religious backgrounds in our society, virtually from its beginning, has contributed to our national dependence on law as a shared value system and, therefore, as a source of unity. Ours is a nation of immigrants—past and present—largely self-selected from among the most aggressive and discontented people of the world. Those who came here from Europe in the seventeenth and eighteenth centuries, for the most part, were fleeing societies with value systems that had failed them in a religious, political, economic, or social sense. Seeking a new beginning, they hoped to create a new society based on individual opportunity and personal autonomy rather than on traditional social values. Later immigrants have come—and continue to come—for similar reasons, except that they anticipate a social system already in place to provide them economic, social, political, and religious opportunities—often as a matter of right, in fact.

The primary system of values they find is one based on law, rather than on cultural or religious traditions. The early rejection of a state-enforced religion probably is a contributing factor to this situation. Indeed, the federal Constitution possesses near-mythical status in our society. That and other important documents, which together constitute the traditional ''written text'' of American society (a category which doubtless would include, at least, the Declaration of Independence and Lincoln's Gettysburg Address), share this mythical status.

Law exercises, therefore, a powerful influence on the values, culture, historical development, and direction of American society. Recent examples of this influence are the civil rights decisions of the 1960s, the Warren Court's expansion of rights available to criminal defendants, and the U.S. Supreme Court decision in *Roe v. Wade*, which continues to reverberate to this day. Remarkably, even when lawyers, judges, and lawmakers are not held in high regard by the public, law and legal institutions retain their enormous significance for the vast majority of citizens.

The study of legal issues in society in their *macro* form misses one important dimension—the emotional content of facts and events. The imaginative literature produced by American writers adds this missing dimension. Because law has been constant as a dominant force shaping our society, it has emerged inevitably as a major theme in our imaginative literature. By incorporating legal themes and ideas in their works—either explicitly or implicitly—and by adding the missing emotional content to facts and events, American writers have had considerable impact on the shaping of American society.

Throughout this book, I refer to imaginative literature as *primary* literature, the sole purpose of which is to serve as literary art. *Secondary* literature refers to writings, such as the Constitution itself, the purpose of which is to accomplish some extrinsic goal. The impact of secondary literature is more obvious and direct since that category would include all writings done for any purpose other than literary art. My focus here, with few exceptions, is on imaginative literature. In this regard, I have chosen to use many classic works of American literature. Although some of them were written in the nineteenth and early twentieth centuries, they contain valuable points for our late-twentieth-century society. By looking at these works from our present point of view, we shed light on current issues. I have supplemented them with a selection of contemporary, late-twentieth-century texts. Although the literary stature of these texts is yet undetermined, they assist by directly addressing current issues.

In the early years of the republic, when the legal principles being developed were fundamental and far-reaching, they reflected the cultural values of the society as a whole. In his seminal work, *Law and Letters in American Culture*, Professor Robert A. Ferguson emphasizes that "The law supplied . . . a useful paradigm for order in the world."[3] As Ferguson points out, our society was in the process of developing as a culture, *and* as a republic, at the same time. In fact, until the Civil War, lawyers were not only remarkably well-read in the classics, they were important contributors to the body of fiction as well as nonfiction.

Dissident voices have spoken along the way. The words of Walt Whitman reverberate in our collective consciousness:

> (Were you looking to be held together by lawyers?
> Or by an agreement on a paper? or by arms?
> Nay, nor the world, nor any living thing, will so cohere.)[4]

Despite Whitman's prophecy, Americans continue to expect "to be held together" by law and lawyers and, in fact, continue to be informed as well as entertained by fiction based on themes of law and justice. Law and lawyers are a prominent part of popular culture, reflected in novels, movies, and television programs. The American writers who have engaged their readers with law themes—whether of crime and punishment, order and chaos, corruption and justice, guilt and remorse, or other designs in the mosaic of ideas generated by thinking about law—have, in a very real sense, reported on the currents and undercurrents of our society. Their literary storytelling explains the nature of the community as forcefully—and far more vividly—than the legal *storytelling* which performs a parallel function.

Many observers of the contemporary scene share the view that American society lacks a sense of direction as it faces myriad problems and conflicts. Indeed, many of our elected and appointed leaders seem immobilized by indecision, doubt, and uncertainty. Principled decision making in the political process is a rare commodity. Problems of urban decay, unresolved racial and ethnic tensions, and unacceptable conditions of homelessness and poverty mar our national self-image of pride and progress. Images of violence permeate our conscience and our culture, reflecting the complex constellation of contributing factors. Many of our citizens live in isolation or alienation from the main currents of society. The resulting hopelessness often breeds not merely apathy and irresponsibility, but discontent. The by-products of those conditions—self-destruction and violence—threaten our harmony and stability.

The same suffocating materialism decried by Eugene O'Neill in *The Iceman Cometh* and Arthur Miller in *Death of A Salesman*, and illustrated so vividly by F. Scott Fitzgerald in *The Great Gatsby*, continues to permeate American culture. Too often, we measure self-worth by a materialistic yardstick.

Our infatuation with power also persists. From Emerson's time, our culture has been, in the words of the late Yale president A. Bartlett Giamatti, "infected . . . with a scorn of the past. . . . [Emerson] . . . encouraged America to shake loose from any constraint on our strength and then to call the resulting power miraculous because it had no moorings."[5] As a nation, we lack a sufficiently clear and sustaining view of our past and present and often seem to have no reliable view of our future.

In addition to those problems which lie in the dimension of identity and justice, other problems of no less significance exist in the dimension of truth and reality. Some writers of fiction, notably Saul Bellow, have been heard to complain that times are difficult for imaginative writers because reality is stranger and more incredible than fiction. In fact, it becomes increasingly difficult to discern and define reality at all. In many respects, Americans seem infatuated with *virtual reality*—reality as viewed through the television screen—and, even beyond that, *portrayed or representational reality* as seen in the computer monitor. Exactly what is reality has become a puzzling question.

The news media, like the notorious courtroom trials they are drawn to cover and embellish, too often serve the goal of entertainment rather than informational reporting. In that setting, the communications industry increasingly shapes—even creates—the subject of its reporting. Subjectivism reigns supreme. Americans are fascinated in an almost cult-like way with colorful, outrageous personalities who assert boldly their polarized—and polarizing—opinions of the factual realities of our age. Truth is a scarce commodity in public as well as private life. Lying and deception are commonplace, not only in political life, but in virtually every dimension of our society.

Given the remarkable potential of the rich racial, ethnic, and religious diversity of our nation, there need not be a single, self-contained set of substantive values for our society. The concept of diversity of values itself needs protection. At a bare minimum, then, we must identify the fundamental or *primary* values that we all can share and adhere to in order to protect the *secondary* values (i.e., personal, cultural, religious, and social) that we do not necessarily share.

When we speak of the primary values that *can* be shared by all Americans, we are essentially speaking about the role of law in our society. These primary values, to be preserved, must be incorporated into the processes, codes, and institutions of law. While many of these values are provided in our constitutions and other *written texts* of society, these documents are constantly subject to interpretation and reinterpretation and constitute only the skeletal framework. One problem that results is how to maintain a value system adequate to provide harmony and order in our diverse society.

In many respects, our nation is inflicted with a continuing *identity crisis*. This condition is rooted deeply in American history. Even in the immediate post-Revolutionary period, many prominent leaders were deeply disturbed at the changes in character of a society that they had struggled to secure and stabilize. Even if we assume that our democratic society, by its nature, is committed to an ongoing process of redefinition and recommitment, the present multitude of problems often seems to obscure the guiding principles that do exist.

By reciting this litany of problems, I do not mean that we should despair about the prognosis for America. Although we must squarely face reality, we have many reasons to be hopeful about the future. The very freedom of choice, which may even foster our social problems and concomitant instability, gives us the greatest hope for the future. The possibility, as well as the means, of change and adaptation inheres in the core of our system of government. Our federal Constitution and our state constitutions allow us to review and recommit to our fundamental principles in light of our changing common experience.

Literary works can assist us in illuminating and explaining the past, clarifying and guiding the present, and providing a vision for the future.[6] Our national literature represents a living history and analysis of the universal legal themes of order and disorder, individual and community, liberty and responsibility, and their changes. The writers of imaginative literature, deeply engaged in perceiving, compressing, analyzing, and reformulating the forces at work in our society, have presented us with blueprints for our task of preserving, reconstituting, and revitalizing a free, civil, and humane society.

A study of American fiction informs us that there is nothing startling about the problems that we face today. In the important process of *re-membering* (both recalling and reassembling) the past, we learn that similar doubts, anxieties, and uncertainties have troubled this nation since its inception. The issue today is not so much that the problems exist, but that we lack a true sense of why they exist and how we can go about resolving them—for the present and the future. The nation and its leaders need to develop a vision for providing meaningful choices for individuals and communities, in addition to constructive alternatives for society as a whole—even while acknowledging that the process will go on in the future.

We benefit from realizing that the texts defining and describing this society are not only the Declaration of Independence, the Constitution, and other *founding documents*, but also the works of primary literature which have informed, analyzed, refined, illustrated and, in the process, shaped the developments in society. While we have in our founding documents the means and empowerment to reassess the nature and goals of our society, literary treatment of the development of our society is essential to that process.

The language of lawyers, legislators, and judges does not provide the sole text of society. Many voices are absent from the institutions and processes of government. Literature can help in expressing a variety of viewpoints and emotions. For example, voices representing minorities can speak convincingly.

Voices representing a feminist perspective speak clearly with the important message that the male perception of the world is not the only perception.

Imaginative works, in fact, may present a more accurate, realistic view of today's society than sources that we usually consider to be more objective and factual, such as newspapers and television. Television news, a major source of our factual information, is colored by opinion and affected by time and space limitations. The use of *sound bites* drastically affects the content of the information. In the print media, the use of bold headline type, as well as editing constraints, also affect the content. The information that we receive through these sources now may be more of a product packaged for sale to consumers than it is objective, factual reporting.

Just as the news media can distort truth and reality, so, too, can the legal system create distortion—by the fact that it is one-dimensional. The severe legal, rhetorical framework forces the complex, multidimensional human events and experiences into a narrow, rigid set of legal concepts. The evidentiary principle of relevance highly restricts the content of each adjudicatory process, for example, and reduces it to a small, often distorted, fractional part of its original self. All emotion is drained from the stuff of legal determinations. The version of the original story that is allowed to remain as the basis for decision making may be distorted indeed.

While it may be true that constraints of time and resources, similar to the time and space constraints on the news media, make it necessary that the legal system operate in this narrow and confining way, it is no less valid an obervation that the product that passes for reality and truth often bears little resemblance to actual reality. The legal system is commonly exploited in our society for personal gain by lawyers and litigants alike, as well as by the media. Some recent, highly publicized criminal trials provide striking examples of this exploitation.

For some time now, the legal system has been struggling with the effort to manage its caseload within reasonable time frames, consistent with the principles that govern the process. The system loses credibility in the eyes of the public when it fails, for example, to adjudicate criminal cases in a way that appears to fulfill legislative mandates. The court system is the institution in society to which people turn for many reasons, including prompt, fair adjudication of disputes and vindication of rights. It is increasingly difficult to perform all those roles and to meet public expectations concerning the way it should function. The demands have far outpaced the ability of the system to function fairly and effectively. The adversarial system often seems inappropriate in dealing with some of the problems with which it must contend. In many areas of law we would benefit from a more sophisticated, less confrontational manner of adjudicating disputes, just as we would benefit from the renewed use of the political process to solve complex social problems rather than excessive reliance on rights-based jurisprudence for that purpose.

In Part I, I examine some of the pervasive forces and relationships involving law in American society. What is the role of law? How does it function? How does it operate in relation to individual action and the private codes that serve as systems of rules and values for various groups within society? In this context, Chapter 1 focuses on the relationship between the individual and the state. This topic encompasses the tension and balance of power between order and freedom or authority and choice. The concept of American individualism, a concept first articulated by Alexis de Toqueville, will be closely examined with respect to its crucial role in shaping American society. The literary texts analyzed in Chapter 1 are James Fenimore Cooper's *The Pioneers* and Ralph Ellison's *Invisible Man*.

Chapter 2 deals with the relationship between private codes of communities and the law. Moral codes, codes of honor, and racial codes are among those discussed. The major literary texts used are Nathaniel Hawthorne's *The Scarlet Letter*, Owen Wister's *The Virginian*, and William Faulkner's "That Evening Sun," *Light in August*, and "An Odor of Verbena." In addition, recent works, including Russell Banks's *Rule of the Bone*, and Richard Price's *Clockers*, reveal that the private codes of underworld communities still exist.

Part II traces and examines the problems with the legal system in American society and how those problems have contributed to the fragmentation and violence existing today. A central question is how the legal system has failed to maintain authority in the face of dramatic social change in the twentieth century. Maintaining authority has always been a problem, but it has become more critical since the breakdown of social order that came to the forefront in the late 1960s.

Chapter 3 deals with the factors involved in the historical problem of violence in our society—a problem which has reached enormous proportions. The historical problems of violence are illustrated by James Fenimore Cooper's *The Last of the Mohicans* and Robert Penn Warren's *Night Rider*. In connection with my discussion of the random violence that plagues society today, I will also allude to several recent works, including Craig Nova's *Trombone*, Don DeLillo's *Libra*, Joyce Carol Oates's *them*, and Richard Bausch's *Violence*, as well as *Clockers*.

Chapter 4 attempts to identify and explain the early stages of failure and loss of confidence in the legal system, and the ideas and developments that caused the first cracks in the foundation. Theodore Dreiser's *An American Tragedy* and James Fenimore Cooper's *The Ways of the Hour* provide the literary foundation, and modern works including *Clockers, Trombone*, and Russell Banks's novel *The Sweet Hereafter* all contribute to the discussion.

Chapter 5 focuses on the lessened expectations of progress and upward mobility in American society. The main literary texts are John Dos Passos's *The Big Money* from his *U.S.A. Trilogy*, Stephen Crane's *Maggie: A Girl of the Streets*, Frank Norris's *The Octopus*, Nathanael West's *The Day of the Locust*, and F. Scott Fitzgerald's *The Great Gatsby*. I will also integrate into the discussion several of the current novels mentioned earlier, which illustrate problems of authority in society today.

Part III takes on a guardedly hopeful tone. Chapter 6 examines some of the mechanisms of change as they have operated in American society from time to time since its origin. In this chapter I draw upon such diverse works as Mark Twain's *The Adventures of Huckleberry Finn*, John Steinbeck's *The Grapes of Wrath*, Saul Bellow's *Herzog*, and Wendell Berry's *A Place on Earth*, for the power of their transforming ideas about change, renewal, and recommitment within and outside the law. Chapter 6 also contains discussions of several U.S. Supreme Court cases in terms of their guiding principles for our judicial system.

In Chapters 7 and 8, my synthesis and concluding note, I will explore some of our common goals and values. I will also warn against some of the dangers lying ahead if our society does not transform itself. In the process, I will suggest specific ways in which the law—as process and as institution—can operate in a commonsense manner to contribute to constructive change, renewal, and recommitment to our principles.

Part I

# The Law in Society: Elemental Forces

## Chapter 1

# The Individual in Society: Individual Autonomy and State Power

> If the inhabitants of democratic countries had neither the right nor the taste for uniting for political objects, their independence would run great risks. . . . [I]f they did not learn some habits of acting together in the affairs of daily life, civilization would be in peril.[1]

> Those who won our independence believed that the final end of the state was to make men free to develop their faculties, and that in its government the deliberative forces should prevail over the arbitrary. . . . They believed that . . . the greatest menace to freedom is an inert people; that public discussion is a political duty.[2]

A dominant feature of American culture is the quest to achieve selfhood and individual identity within the framework of society. The relationship of the individual to society, which is dynamic rather than static, is largely defined by law, just as so many other relationships within our society are defined by law to an extraordinary degree.[3] The nature of the relationship, however, has been subject to changing political, economic, and sociological ideas.

In expressing this relationship in terms of individual autonomy and state power, I intend the term *state* to refer to the political identity of society as a whole. The term *culture* refers to the shared way of life that includes all the attitudes, ideas, and procedures that members of the population share and transmit to each other and to future generations. In general terms, society is composed of individuals and communities. Communities are social units in which some individuals are associated by virtue of shared characteristics or values. In this regard, W. H. Auden defined various groups of people as follows: In its most basic form, a group of onlookers is a "crowd"; a "society," next, is a group of people bound together for economic reasons in a merely functional relationship. Finally, in its highest form, a "community" is formed when a group of people is united by common likes and dislikes, aversions and enthusiasms, tastes, ways of life, and moral beliefs. When agreement on these factors is substantial, the group constitutes a "community."[4] Every community is a society, but a society is not necessarily a community.

Analysis of these relationships reveals that an emphasis on individual rights—apart from individual responsibility—now dominates American society. The full significance of that observation depends upon consideration of how the present conception of rights differs from the original conception. The idea of individual rights was, of course, a vital element in the formation of the American republic. Our federal and state constitutions identify and preserve the rights that were deemed fundamental. These protected rights were seen as immunities or protections against governmental intrusion for individuals who bore responsibility for the functioning of society as a whole. Society was a network of community-based relationships where rights and responsibilities were integrated. These rights, as originally envisioned, however, had a *civic* dimension that is missing today. This civic dimension of rights has increasingly been replaced by an entitlement dimension whereby rights have become means of securing individual identity and other goals. Personal responsibility for oneself and for the well-being of society as a whole is not part of this entitlement philosophy.

While a tension exists between the desire for individual autonomy and the need for societal participation, the desire for individualism clearly prevails. America's "near-aphasia concerning responsibility, [and] its excessive homage to individual independence and self-sufficiency . . . impede development of the sort of rational political discourse that is appropriate to the needs of a mature, complex, . . . pluralistic republic."[5] One characteristic of individualism that is divorced from civic responsibility is the dependence of Americans on court decisions adjudicating asserted rights rather than on the political process for resolving their problems.[6]

## TRADITIONAL AMERICAN CONCERNS

The relationship of the individual to society has many dimensions. One dimension involves the balance of power between the individual and society. Another is the simultaneous attraction-rejection tension between the two identities of individuals—independent and conformist. One critic has suggested that the dual attraction of Americans to individualism and community is generated by four historic American concerns. Those consist of the *concern about being owned* (being controlled by or dependent on others); the *concern about falling apart* (isolation or anarchy); the *concern about winding down* (losing energy or failing to maintain progress); and the *concern about falling away* from past virtue and potential.[7] Those concerns, in fact, can be seen underlying American political discourse in nearly every era including the present.

## ASPECTS OF INDIVIDUALISM

One important aspect of the relationship of the individual to society is that in American legal history the individual is portrayed as an equal opponent of the entire society, in the form of the state. All criminal trials involve an adversarial contest between the government, on one hand, and an individual, on the other. While the resources available are rarely equal, the principle of individual justice defines the form of the adversarial contest. Criminal trials, in fact, have special significance for the people of the United States. A portion of the power of the criminal justice system is delegated to jurors along with judges and other officials in the system. Citizens traditionally have been conditioned to believe (at least, according to the rationale of the jury system) that they are as qualified (or even more qualified) as any judge to determine the guilt of an accused.

Trials within major literary works illustrate the phenomenon of individual versus society in the context of the criminal trial. Theodore Dreiser's *An American Tragedy*, Richard Wright's *Native Son*, Nathaniel Hawthorne's *The Scarlet Letter*, and James Fenimore Cooper's *The Pioneers*, for example, contain criminal trials which pit an individual against the forces of the state.

## HISTORICAL TRADITION: EMERSON AND COMPANY

A strong sense of individualism developed in America in the late eighteenth and early nineteenth centuries (or before).[8] In this regard, the social contract theory,[9] which is closely related to the natural law theory,[10] places the individual in existence prior to the state and is associated with individual rights, consent as the basis of government, and with democratic, constitutionally based institutions.[11] Emerson contributed heavily to the development of the concept of individualism, especially in his essays ''The American Scholar'' and ''Self-Reliance.''[12] Other writers, including Cooper, Owen Wister and, later, Ernest Hemingway, celebrated a type of rugged individualism that is still an important part of American character. Other versions of individualism developed in order to express the condition of the poor, and various racial and ethnic minorities whose individual rights were not fully protected in Emerson's time. Herman Melville, Walt Whitman, Ralph Ellison, and Toni Morrison all dealt with those subjects. The dynamics of American society operate to promote the idea of individualism, but they also conflict with it at various stress points. Indeed, a natural tension exists today between individual autonomy and societal values.

## INTERRELATIONSHIP AND OTHER MEANINGS

Several additional points about individualism and American society are important. First, the autonomy of individuals in our society cannot be evaluated apart from their relationship with society as a whole. Each individual is partly defined by, and partly limited by, his relationship with other individuals and with society. Similarly, no evaluation of society is complete without considering the status of all individuals composing society. The status of each individual has a bearing on the status of all others. For example, if the rights of one individual are at risk, the rights of all are on the line. A fundamental interrelationship among individuals exists naturally.

In contrast, the isolation ideal of Emerson is a false belief, suggesting a false promise, as is his notion of disconnecting American thinking from its roots in European history. The past and present are inextricably linked; the past exists in the present. The past, present, and future shape each other in a continuing and dynamic relationship. All three dimensions of time exist on a continuum. Each dimension, in turn, defines and redefines the others in a continuing cycle. For example, while we may look to historical data in an effort to understand the text of a constitution, the significance of those historical facts will be altered by the present and future development of society. Similarly, the meaning of present events varies, depending on whether they are evaluated in terms of past events or in the context of future events. In a real sense, even the original stories of a society and its predecessors are still being formed and will continue to be formed indefinitely.[13]

Individualism has different meanings, depending on the nature of the interpreter. To some, it signifies the instinct, based on natural right, to act independently of society and the law; to judge the law for oneself. It can also support the idea of civil disobedience. To others, it can mean a desperate search for identity and recognition—the kind of self-actualization that has become prevalent in contemporary society. It can relate to the protection of individual rights against society's interest or the self-centered, self-aggrandizing wish to compete economically and obtain more than a reasonable share of profit. It can mean using the forces of the state to maintain an inequitable status quo or to bring about an upheaval of the status quo for the purpose of realigning the balance of power among individuals and groups within the society. In fact, competing ideas and beliefs about individual autonomy and societal values continue to coexist in American society. The relationship between these competing interpretations continues to change.[14]

## PREVAILING MODES OF INDIVIDUALISM

In the course of American history, the concept of individualism has taken on several readily identifiable forms. While some forms may have been prominent during particular periods, all of them continue to exist in American society, even when they are no longer dominant. These various forms of individualism frequently are incompatible with one another.

The forms of individualism can be classified in a great many ways. One method, for example, identifies them as the *original* American *exploring individualism*; inward-looking or *defensive individualism; imperial individualism*; and *democratic individualism*. These categories are not all-inclusive or self-contained.[15] The past century and a half—notably the past three decades—has produced major technological, economic, and social change that deeply affected the traditional ways in which individual freedom and autonomy are measured. These changes include a decline in traditional religious belief, the disintegration of previous community and social order, the division of work and leisure life, and the fragmentation of culture pursuant to social, religious, and economic interests and prejudices. The major characteristics of each manner of defining the self follow.

**Exploring Individualism**

The idea of the exploring self stemmed from American frontier stories in which the individual was portrayed as existing in the open space of the unsettled wilderness. The individual frequently physically existed outside formal communities and had a high degree of autonomy relative to life in more structured communities. When the individual tired of the growing restrictions of society, he was able to leave the community and make his way in the unexplored lands beyond formal civilization.

This mode became highly idealized, oversimplified, and mythologized[16] because exploration was so important to American society in the eighteenth and nineteenth centuries. Frontier imagery has been used extensively in American political and literary life. The history of life on the frontier has been vastly oversimplified in the process. The development of the American West has been a complex process rather than a simple conquering of the frontier, as it has so often been portrayed.

Responsible historical scholarship sees a continuous sweep of Western American history which opens up new organizing ideas without a simple, unitary model.[17] While recognizing the validity of this scholarship, I will occasionally refer to the mythical version of the frontier which appears so frequently in literature. The novels of James Fenimore Cooper celebrated this mythical version of American individualism, which freely rejected the rules and customs of communal society. The exploring individual also appears in Ellison's *Invisible Man* and in the fiction of Jack London,[18] Ernest Hemingway,[19] and Tom Robbins.[20] The exploring self finds expression in our modern technological society, in which cyberspace is commonly referred to as a new frontier.

Although it is difficult to find a precise equivalent of the exploring self in court decisions, cases like *Sabo v. Horvath*,[21] decided by the Supreme Court of Alaska, and *Pennoyer v. Neff*,[22] a U.S. Supreme Court decision, arose out of factual situations suggesting that mode of individualism. *Sabo* involved a dispute over land obtained under the Alaska Homesite Law. A landowner, Grover Lowery, conveyed title to the same piece of land, first to the Horvaths and later to the Sabos. A dispute arose because the transfer to the Horvaths was outside the chain of title. Lowery had not yet received title from the U.S. government before he conveyed the land to the Horvaths. The Sabo deed was the first deed to be recorded within the chain. The court held that Lowery had an interest in the land upon entering it even though he had not received legal title from the U.S. government. The *exploring individualism* of Lowery, therefore, was recognized and legitimized by law in that situation.

In *Pennoyer*, a dispute over title to land granted by a U.S. patent caused the Supreme Court to define in personam jurisdiction requirements in such a way as to support the American *exploring self.* If the defendant was not available within state boundaries to be personally served, the court could not exercise jurisdiction over him, thus creating an incentive to leave for the *frontier.*

## Defensive Individualism

The defensive self represents a type of individualism that turns away from worldly pragmatic experience and looks inward in a way that promotes a false and unrealistic sense of security. The individual who embodies this form of individualism seeks relief and protection from dangers, anxieties, uncertainties, and turmoil. James Fenimore Cooper, Henry David Thoreau, Emily Dickinson, and Edgar Allan Poe all have presented this type of individual—retreating from life—in American culture. Thoreau, Dickinson, and Poe, in fact, lived out much of their lives in that manner. In contemporary times, writers like Alice Walker, Joyce Carol Oates, and Toni Morrison have portrayed women who exhibited qualities of defensive individualism.[23] While this portrayal suggests a negative characterization, the creative potential of this type of individualism has also been noted.[24] In many respects, the writings of Emerson, Whitman, and Henry James presented a transcending mode of this inward-turning individualism.

A classic example of the defensive self exists in cases involving the battered-woman's syndrome. In *State v. Kelly*,[25] the defendant, Gladys Kelly, stabbed her husband to death with a pair of scissors. According to Ms. Kelly, he had assaulted her that afternoon and she stabbed him in self-defense, fearing that he would kill her if she did not take action. The court discussed at length the various phases of the battering cycle and the immense difficulty of some women in extricating themselves from battering relationships. The court applied the law of self-defense in determining that expert testimony on battered-woman's syndrome was relevant.

## Imperial Individualism

The remaining two forms of individualism, imperial and democratic, are in direct confrontation in American society today. They differ significantly in emphasis. Imperial individualism involves an elevation of the self—beyond being merely inward-looking or seeking to escape—into a position of dominance. A classic description of this form of individualism suggests that where there is increasing estrangement between idealism and reality, the individual infuses "personal needs and wishes with a sense of universal significance and moral righteousness. . . . [S]elf-consciousness regards itself as the necessary element. It knows that it has the universal, the law, immediately within itself.''[26]

While giving the illusion of being a liberating force against a dehumanizing and oppressive reality, imperial individualism actually can be destructive in its own right. This concept is present in Cooper's writings, where his protagonist, Natty Bumppo, known as ''Leatherstocking,'' when confronted by rules and restrictions of society, acts according to his own will, rationalized as a sort of natural law, but then withdraws to the uncivilized wilderness. Other, more sinister forms of this mode can be seen in activities of individuals who belong to organizations like the Ku Klux Klan or the American Nazi Party. *The Village of Skokie v. The National Socialist Party of America*[27] concerned the activities of the Nazi Party. The issue there was whether the display of the swastika could be enjoined under the fighting-words exception to free speech. The Illinois Supreme Court, in a First Amendment decision that appeared to be a triumph of ''neutral principles,''[28] held that it could not be enjoined.

Imperial individualism also is evident in contemporary society. For example, the hate crimes prosecuted under recently enacted hate-crime laws in many jurisdictions illustrate the idea.[29] Moreover, the crime and violence resulting from gang activity occurring in urban and suburban areas, in which power is sought through violence rather than through economic or political methods, involves imperialistic activity. Literary works such as *Foxfire* by Joyce Carol Oates,[30] the subject of which is urban gangs, and *Rule of the Bone*[31] by Russell Banks, discussed in Chapter 2, illustrate this type of activity. Similarly, instances of violent vigilante activity also serve as striking examples of imperial individualism.

### Democratic Individualism

Democratic individualism, while not purely distinct from the other modes, envisions individual fulfillment as associated with society's well-being. This mode, the only one to connect the individual to society directly, reconciles itself to historical experience and understands the inseparability of private and public liberty. In Jefferson's words, this form of individualism recognizes limits by seeing ''rightful liberty as the unobstructed action according to our will within limits drawn around us by the equal rights of others . . . rather than unobstructed action according to our will''[32] that defines imperial individualism. Independence comes to mean interdependence with—rather than separation from—other individuals and groups. In this mode, citizens feel a sense of personal and social responsibility.

This ideal vision is remarkably similar to Ellison's vision of personal moral responsibility for democracy. John Steinbeck's *The Grapes of Wrath*,[33] discussed later in Chapter 6, is concerned with democratic ideas. In addition, Walt Whitman's poetry embodies his energetic version of democratic individualism. According to Henry A. Beers, a noted writer and literary scholar at Yale at the beginning of this century, Whitman was the "spokesman of democracy and of the future; full of brotherliness and hope, loving the warm, gregarious pressure of the crowd."[34]

A variation of democratic individualism appears in affirmative action cases such as *Regents of the University of California v. Bakke*,[35] *City of Richmond v. J. A. Croson*,[36] *Metro Broadcasting, Inc. v. FCC*,[37] and *Shaw v. Reno*.[38] Discrimination cases brought under the Civil Rights Act of 1964, especially *Jones v. Alfred H. Mayer Co.*,[39] which interpreted 42 U.S.C. Sec. 1982 to prohibit "all racial discrimination, private as well as public, in the sale or rental of property,"[40] involve democratic individualism, as well.

## THE LITERARY FOCUS

The complex pattern of thought concerning the relationship between the individual and society is illustrated in important American literary texts. In analyzing the texts, the discussion generally focuses on several issues. One issue is the extent to which the idea of individual autonomy appears in the governing texts of society and how the power which that autonomy represents can be exercised. Another is whether all individuals in society are equal in their opportunities to exercise and enjoy the autonomy provided. An additional issue is the role of society as a whole in protecting and defining individual autonomy. A final issue is the extent to which individual autonomy may be exercised to defy or thwart society as a whole.

## *THE PIONEERS*: NATURAL MAN

James Fenimore Cooper's nineteenth-century novel, *The Pioneers*,[41] focuses on the conflict between an individual who embodies the mythologized American ethic of exploring individualism based on natural rights and the developing civilized society which employs the rule of law as its instrument. Cooper's heart, in some sense, may have been with his exploring protagonist, Leatherstocking. Cooper, however, recognized that in a developing society natural justice had to yield to civil justice, and that the needs of the community would overcome the right of the individual to do as he pleased.[42]

The novel takes place in 1793 in Templeton, a settlement in upstate New York. Leatherstocking is a seventy-year-old, hardy, simple, upright woodsman living on the outskirts of civilization as represented by the new white settlement. Although disgusted by the wanton killing of game for sport, he insists on his own right to kill for food. In so abiding by the code of nature, and killing only what he needs to eat, he violates the new game laws. He is arrested when he openly defies the magistrate who tries to execute a warrant issued by Judge Temple, the principal citizen and landholder, to authorize the search of Leatherstocking's cabin. Leatherstocking is tried, convicted, stocked, and imprisoned for the offenses of resisting arrest and assaulting a law officer. After he is pardoned by the governor, he moves west into unsettled territory.

Leatherstocking represents the natural right of autonomy, and Judge Temple and his magistrates represent the right of the community to limit the exercise of autonomy through civil law. The story raises a question about what limits civil law should impose on an individual who claims prior natural rights. To what extent can that individual refuse to comply with the civil law?

Leatherstocking violates the game law because he does not acknowledge the legitimacy of man-made law. He has not consented to enter any voluntary social compact with the citizens of Templeton. In his view, the law enforced against him is an unwarranted invasion of his natural rights. While conceding that he committed the acts with which he is charged, he pleads not guilty. In denying the officials admission to his hut, Leatherstocking relies on natural law to defend his liberty and property.

Leatherstocking's skepticism concerning the administration of civil law in Templeton appears justified. While he is prosecuted for killing one deer out of season, other game laws directed at the seasonal netting of bass are not enforced. Moreover, no laws have been enacted to control the wholesale cutting of trees and the regular massacre of pigeons for sport by citizens, including the sheriff and the justice of the peace. The decision by the magistrates to obtain a search warrant for Leatherstocking's hut was not made for the purpose of enforcing the game law for social good, but was a ruse to satisfy their interest in discovering the location of his rumored secret silver mine so they could seize it for themselves.

Although Cooper makes a case for Leatherstocking's natural rights by presenting Leatherstocking's point of view, by the end of the novel Leatherstocking's position appears overly simplistic. Leatherstocking, for instance, is unable to evaluate whether law is necessary in a community. He criticizes all law, whether unjust or merely unjustly executed.

Cooper praises Judge Temple's mental clarity and observes that his decisions were both correct and well-reasoned. For example, the judge explains the trial and sentencing to his daughter in terms of the right of society to place limits on individual autonomy: "Society cannot exist without wholesome restraints. Those restraints cannot be inflicted, without security and respect to the persons of those who administer them. . . . [T]he laws alone remove us from the condition of the savages" (*P*, 382–383).

Leatherstocking's perception of the situation is exactly the reverse of the community's perception. In his view, he is not the law-breaker but the victim of unjust law. In the end, to maintain his commitment to natural law, he must head westward to find his place in "uncivilized" territory. His parting words reflect his commitment to natural law:

I pray that the Lord will keep you in mind—the Lord that lives in clearings as well as in the wilderness—and bless you . . . from this time, till the great day when the whites shall meet the red-skins in judgment, and justice shall be the law, and not power. (*P*, 455)

Conflicts between the individual and society similar to those presented in *The Pioneers* are visible in American society today. In many areas of law, for example, in housing, land use, and zoning controversies, as well as in many types of constitutional rights-based litigation, the exercise of individual rights frequently conflicts with identifiable interests of the community as a whole. Moreover, episodes of civil disobedience occasionally occur in contemporary society. Notable examples have been protests concerning the Vietnam War, environmental concerns, animal rights, and nuclear weapons.

Individual autonomy was protected in the society in which Leatherstocking found himself or which, in a sense, enveloped him in the wilderness. The social contract, if there could be said to be one at that point, was probably fairly limited in scope. The interests of the community, which were virtually coextensive with the society, coincided with the interests of a small, dominant group. Leatherstocking clearly was given some latitude in expressing his civil disobedience. Although consequences resulted initially, they were moderate and did not prevent Leatherstocking from departing for uncivilized territory where individual autonomy could still be exercised without societal restraint.

The brand of individualism presented in *The Pioneers* leaves little room for negotiating differences or for compromise solutions. A head-to-head confrontation occurs in which the winner takes all. This type of clash exists today in confrontations over rights. As Glendon expressed it, ''in its simple American form, the language of rights is the language of no compromise. The winner takes all and the loser has to get out of town.''[43] Rather than compromise his brand of individualism, Leatherstocking departs for the wilderness. While Cooper viewed that solution as an acceptable way of resolving the tension between individual and society in his eighteenth-century fictional world—with the availability of frontier space—it is hardly a viable way to solve problems in our complex world of the late twentieth century.

## *INVISIBLE MAN*: THE FRONTIER WITHIN

In Ralph Ellison's *Invisible Man*,[44] an individual is pitted against the power of society. The nameless individual, whom I will call simply IM, seeks, not to retain natural rights previously enjoyed, but rather to gain access to natural rights withheld. He engages in a search for personal identity and recognition within the society to acquire visibility where invisibility presently exists. While the story is concerned with social and psychological conditions, it also involves legal implications of IM's autonomy and individuality. The rights sought by the protagonist in *Invisible Man* coexist with and are congruent with the posited communal law of society, but are not extended to all its members. The issue here relates to natural rights that are exercised by some members of society and denied to others, rather than to natural rights that have become anachronistic in the developing society. Those rights are vital to an individual's position and standing in society.

In his novel, Ellison employed the *Bildungsroman*, or coming of age tradition, in which the narrator moves from faith in freedom, simplicity, and possibility to a realization of limitation and complexity. Both the Prologue and the Epilogue are set in time after the main story has taken place. IM acknowledges that while he accepts his invisibility, he is no longer blind. IM explains the title as a reference to poor sight: "That invisibility to which I refer occurs because of a peculiar disposition of the eyes of those with whom I come in contact. A matter of the construction of their *inner* eyes, those eyes with which they look through their physical eyes upon reality" (*IM*, 3). The imagery of blindness and invisibility refers to IM and the racist society in which he lives. IM lacks sight and insight into his experience and the reality of his world at the outset of his journey. The racially prejudiced world which confines him to invisibility is blind to his identity as an individual human being.

IM lives in an underground basement which he has rigged with 1,369 lights all operating by illegally obtained power from the local electric company. In the Prologue and Epilogue, the narrator gives us in capsule form his insights and ideas gained from his transforming journey through a series of events. In the course of the events, he becomes aware of the realities of the world, gains a sense of his own identity and role, and develops a vision of the ethic that should govern the individual in the journey through the chaotic universe.

The Prologue and Epilogue are designed to be considered together because, in essence, they convey similar messages. They represent the narrator's recording of his progress in the journey through the episodes related in the novel, the culmination of his experiences narrated in the twenty-five chapters. In the Prologue, the narrator tells us that "the end is in the beginning" (*IM*, 6). The final words of the novel before the Epilogue are: "The end was in the beginning" (*IM*, 571). In both sections, the narrator describes his existence in a hole; he has gone underground to discover his identity. The hole represents the underground condition in which he has always existed; he simply did not recognize his situation before.

The narrator relates his insights into his position as a black man living on the fringe of American society. While he accepts the fact that he is still invisible in the perception of those who have a central place in society, he has emerged from his personal blindness and now understands his identity and relationship to society.

The twenty-five chapters of the novel contain an account of the narrator's experiences as he engages in an odyssey in which he discovers his identity and the meaning of his social environment. Eventually, he emerges from his personal *blindness* and realizes that identity and freedom are interconnected and interdependent.[45] At one point, he becomes involved with an organization called the "Brotherhood" and finds that he is treated as an object rather than being recognized for the sake of his own identity. His activities as a worker for the Brotherhood prove personally enlightening, however, and he eventually recognizes the distinction between his old self and his public, Brotherhood self. He develops an awareness of the complexity of life as he leaves behind his former belief in frontier simplicity. Ultimately, he comes to grips with the nature of his invisibility and accepts his past along with his personal moral responsibilities. In his wholeness, he becomes the writer of his own story, the creator of his version of reality. He now realizes, however, that his version is only one of many versions of reality. Although he has formed his own plan, he must not forget the underlying chaos that persists.

In the end, IM is ready for his emergence from his underground hole. In his rebirth, he recognizes his connection with the larger community and understands that he must define his own socially responsible role. He affirms the Adamic myth of America, becoming an integrative figure, one who contains or consolidates opposing forces. He determines that something his grandfather said was an affirmation of the ''principle on which the country was built'' (*IM*, 574). An integral part of that principle is the old frontier belief in the unlimited freedom of an individual to define and live his own life. He has gone full circle: ''[L]ike almost everyone else in our country, I started out with my share of optimism. I believed in hard work and progress and action, but now, after first being 'for' society and then 'against' it, I assign myself no rank or any limit, and such an attitude is very much against the trend of the times'' (*IM*, 576).

The narrator of *Invisible Man* not only experiences his life but writes about it. As a writer, he is able to create meaning out of his painful and, in some cases, risk-filled experiences. With his creative imagination, the narrator-writer opens up infinite possibilities and creates meaning out of disorder. Imagination gives him freedom from the restrictions of the real world and enables him to shape his existence.

Ellison viewed his decision to write this novel as an opportunity and a responsibility to describe experience and to create, through writing, a conquest of the frontier. He not only contributed to literature but also sought to shape American culture. Ellison's narrator, IM, is able to conquer the frontier after discovering through his experiences an awareness of discord, complexity, community, and love. Then IM describes, through his writing, his version of reality, thus connecting himself with other heroic figures who create a positive result from apparent defeat. In determining to be socially responsible, even though invisible in the society, IM must find his own way to live his socially responsible role. He no longer shares his grandfather's belief in the Emersonian ideal of the part being connected to the whole or the fingers of the hand being separate but equal.

IM ponders his next phase. Having started with optimism and belief in hard work and progress, then experiencing a reversal of those feelings, he now finds his world to be one of ''infinite possibilities'' (*IM*, 576). He believes he has achieved an understanding of his world. He has come to accept the value of the diversity of the nation:

> Whence all this passion toward conformity anyway?—diversity is the word. . . . America is woven of many strands; I would recognize them and let it so remain. It's "winner take nothing" that is the great truth of our country or of any country. Life is to be lived, not controlled; and humanity is won by continuing to play in face of certain defeat. Our fate is to become one, and yet many—This is not prophecy, but description. (*IM*, 577)

Like Bigger in Richard Wright's novel *Native Son*, the narrator comes to reject the vision of himself as victim. Unlike Bigger, however, he decides to assume responsibility for his own destiny. Having experienced self-imposed alienation in his underground dwelling, he engages in his journey—his mission—the search for a viable moral principle for life in America. He searches externally in the communities to which his odyssey takes him, including the southern town where he was born; a college for blacks; a segregated community in the North; the northern world of industry; a revolutionary political group; and a ghetto in a northern city. He discovers that the sought-after ethic does not exist in any community; that the creation of the ethic is an individual human responsibility. After that discovery, the narrator begins his inward odyssey, into the self.

The main subject of *Invisible Man* is this journey within the self. The narrator discovers that only he can answer his own questions. The narrator concludes that the key to his reconciliation with self and society is knowledge, illumination—and truth.[46] The route to freedom is not through death or violence but through mastery of the chaotic reality that surrounds him. This discovery provides the sense of meaning to his life. His final words to the reader reflect his narrative mission—"to tell you what was really happening when your eyes were looking through[.] And it is this which frightens me: Who knows but that, on the lower frequencies, I speak for you?" (*IM*, 581). With this question, he suggests the universality of his experience and knowledge.

The mythology of the frontier which is present in *The Pioneers* is also a major theme in *Invisible Man*. In that sense, the frontier represents the *border* of civilization where the individual's desire to be completely free and the community's demand to restrict freedom are in conflict. Although Ellison set the principal locus of the novel in Harlem, he uses frontier imagery to illustrate the confrontation.

Frontier mythology involves images and values growing out of the clash between civilization and the uncivilized world. In this traditional theme in American literature, civilized society is seen as restricting individual freedom. Uncivilized society—the wilderness beyond the frontier—represents an environment without those community institutions and restrictions where the individual can be free to test himself against the forces of nature. American literature has repeatedly emphasized the theme—the civilized society/ wilderness dichotomy—of the innocent American confronting opposing forces of society. In the pattern that develops, the individual moves into the wilderness and becomes a "new Adam" in the garden.[47]

One point of view suggests that the process of transformation often requires a ritualistic hunt in which the American hunter regenerates himself "through violence and return to familial bonds of civilization with a renewed awareness of . . . [his] own individuality.''[48] While legal rules may not be dominant in uncivilized society, other rules may produce as much if not more restriction. Private codes that govern human activity, however, are always present in the wilderness.

Ellison emphasizes various other dualities, in addition to the wilderness/society conflict. Some of those dualities are central to this discussion, including order/chaos, good/evil, one/many, visible/invisible, and freedom/restriction. Ellison attempts to synthesize the conflicting ideas into a greater whole that suggests not only the variety of ideas in American society, but also the possibility of discovering unity and harmony in the diversity.

While the novel deals with universal themes of identity and search for meaning, it has at its heart an idea about the African-American experience that was first expressed by W.E.B. Du Bois in *The Souls of Black Folk*. Du Bois expressed his view about one of the confining features of American life for blacks in a well-known passage: ''It is a peculiar sensation, this double-consciousness, this sense of always looking at one's self through the eyes of others, of measuring one's soul by the tape of a world that looks on in amused contempt and pity. One ever feels his twoness,—an American, a Negro; two souls, two thoughts, two unreconciled strivings; two warring ideals in one dark body, whose dogged strength alone keeps it from being torn asunder.''[49]

Ellison recognizes the inseparable relationship between personal identity and the social conditions in the environment that generate *personal troubles*. Personal identity cannot be defined without reference to the social conditions of the community in which one lives. At the end of the novel, the narrator has reached the conclusion that he will have to leave his underground environment to return to the world in order to play a responsible role in society.

## INDIVIDUAL AND SOCIETY IN CONFRONTATION

Radically different results occur in the confrontation between individual and society in *The Pioneers* and *Invisible Man*. The difference is due primarily to the standing of the particular individual in the society and to the nature of the society itself. Leatherstocking is treated unjustly by the legal system, although he is ultimately absolved. Although unfairly treated, he is recognized as existing within the legal system—even though he rejects it. Unlike IM, he is not invisible. His beliefs about individual autonomy clash irreconcilably with the authority of the system and he chooses to leave rather than accommodate its standards. He insists on absolute freedom and absolute autonomy.

When Leatherstocking's views cannot prevail, he has a place to go. He can strike out beyond the frontier into the wilderness of the uncivilized world where his freedom will be less restricted, at least for a while, until society catches up to him and eventually consumes him and others like him. IM, however, does not have that prerogative. Existing within a more complex and oppressive society, he is invisible and without equal standing in the society. He is not free to exercise his individual autonomy as others can. The coercive force of society is used to control and limit him, rather than to protect him or his rights.

IM is wholly defined by society and that definition controls his choices and opportunities. He begins the laborious and lengthy process of ascertaining his own identity—defining himself. Once he has accomplished that task, he removes himself from society but then recognizes that he must reenter it in order to fulfill his personal and social responsibilities. He has no realistic choice but to find his place, however invisible, within society. IM's action is more mature, civilized, and socially responsible than Leatherstocking's action. IM is ready to assume a responsible position in society.

Both Leatherstocking and IM understand the importance of the self and recognize the need to define themselves apart from society. Leatherstocking and IM, however, occupy markedly different positions in their respective societies. The laws of society were exercised to control Leatherstocking's behavior but, so long as he conformed to those laws, he would be able to participate fully in the activities of the dominant society. IM, on the other hand, had no such standing or opportunity. Conform he must, but participate fully in society he could not. While society applied its law to control Leatherstocking's assertion of unlimited individual autonomy, it applied its law to exclude IM from participating in the processes of his society. Whereas Leatherstocking rejected any accommodation between himself and society, IM ultimately recognized his need to define himself within the community or society and to participate in society. IM's final insights into his grandfather's words led him to accept, validate, and affirm the principles of democratic society, despite recognizing that some individuals have corrupted the principles.

Leatherstocking engages in an irreconcilable clash with society and departs for the wilderness. IM, however, determines to remain and to synthesize his confrontation with society into a new relationship. IM also recognizes the importance of maintaining a united but pluralistic society, in which individuals are not required to give up their own identities and self-definitions in order to exist. Leatherstocking provides no useful ideas for his society because he rejects all accommodation. IM's conclusions provide useful material for inquiry into the mechanisms of change and the goals for a society committed to the idea that all individuals should have the opportunity to participate.

## CONSTITUTIONAL ARCHITECTURE

The basic framework of the relationship between individual and society is articulated in the federal and state constitutions, statutes, and administrative regulations, as interpreted by judicial decisions. The first ten amendments and the Fourteenth Amendment to the U.S. Constitution contain the best known expression of the parameters of this relationship. While these amendments cover a variety of matters, they deal primarily with limitations on the power of the government and guarantees of fairness to individuals. Modern ideas of privacy and autonomy are not attributable to the drafters. As these amendments have been interpreted, however, the right to free expression and the right to privacy and self-determination have become vital. The First Amendment is concerned with both the rights of expression and self-determination (religion and association). The remaining amendments, except for the Tenth, as interpreted and applied, all deal with some aspect of the right of privacy or autonomy.

### First Amendment Cases

A vast number of U.S. Supreme Court cases have dealt with the tension between the individual and society as manifested in the areas of free expression and privacy. Recent examples of free expression cases are *Texas v. Johnson*,[50] *Rust v. Sullivan*,[51] and *R.A.V. v. City of St. Paul, Minnesota*.[52] These cases are important because they reveal current thinking, not only about the individual-society relationship, but about the tensions in American culture generally. While these cases resulted in First Amendment claims being upheld, this certainly is not meant to be representative of the results in the full range of cases.

The burning of an American flag, our most prominent national symbol, was the subject of *Johnson*. The Court held that the defendant's act of burning an American flag during a protest rally was expressive conduct entitled to First Amendment protection. As a result, the defendant could not be prosecuted for that conduct based on the state's interest in preventing breaches of the peace or in preserving the flag as a symbol of national unity. This controversial decision by a divided Court in *Johnson* protects individual expression even though the decision infringes on an established cultural value. Congress responded to that decision by passing the Flag Protection Act of 1989. That legislation was struck down by the Court in *United States v. Eichman*.[53] Political support for a constitutional amendment was not strong enough to prevail. The public reaction to Supreme Court decisions on this issue has raised serious questions about the extent to which decisions of the U.S. Supreme Court—or any court, for that matter—reflect the values of society.

Individual expression dominated societal values in *R.A.V.* as well. In this case, the petitioner R.A.V. allegedly had burned a cross on a black family's lawn. The Court held that a bias-motivated crime ordinance prohibiting the display of a symbol which "arouses anger, alarm or resentment in others on the basis of race, color, creed, religion or gender"[54] was facially invalid under the First Amendment. The Court reasoned that the city ordinance improperly imposed special prohibitions on speakers who expressed views on disfavored subjects of race, color, creed, religion, or gender. The Court protected individual expression over social values even where those values were geared to prohibiting divisive and distasteful speech.

Individual speech rights, however, fared differently in *Rust v. Sullivan.* In this case, the Supreme Court upheld regulations that implemented Title X of the Public Health Service Act's restriction on use of federal funds by family planning clinics "where abortion is a method of family planning."[55] The regulations prohibited Title X projects from engaging in activities advocating abortion as a method of family planning. The regulations did not, the Court reasoned, violate the First Amendment rights of Title X grantees, their staffs, or their patients by imposing viewpoint-discriminatory conditions on government subsidies. The facts of this case placed free expression in conflict with another social value—the prevention of abortion. The societal value of abortion regulation prevailed over rights of individual expression.

Free expression cases[56] demonstrate how the Court has defined the limits—on a case-by-case basis—that society can place on individual rights to free expression of ideas. First Amendment cases typically deal with highly controversial speech content and generally involve conflict between fundamental values. Because the right of expression is an integral aspect of individual autonomy in American society and an important factor in political discourse, the process of defining limitations is crucial.

The relationship of individual to society has arisen in other First Amendment contexts as well. The right of free association was involved in *Lyng v. International Union,*[57] for example. The issue in that case was the constitutionality of a statute precluding households of union members from becoming eligible for food stamps if a member of the household was on strike. In holding that the statute did not infringe on the associational rights of the union members, the Court recognized that "one of the foundations of our society is the right of individuals to combine with other persons in pursuit of a common goal by lawful means."[58] Justice White, writing for the majority, also observed that "at the heart of the First Amendment is the notion that an individual should be free to believe as he will, and that in a free society one's beliefs should be shaped by his mind and his conscience rather than coerced by the State."[59] While the right to associate was supported by Justice White's language, the Court refused to expand the right under the particular circumstances of the case.[60]

If any single message can be gleaned from these First Amendment cases, it may be that the relationship between individual rights and societal values is delicate and shifts from one interest to the other depending upon the factual content of the particular controversy. Although Supreme Court justices—along with other Americans—draw upon a pool of beliefs and philosophical premises, there is no inevitable consensus as to how these beliefs and premises should be applied in any given factual situation. Because these First Amendment controversies were resolved by adjudication rather than through the political process, solutions arrived at by consensus and compromise among the competing interests were unavailable.

**Privacy, Autonomy, and Order**

Apart from First Amendment issues, the conflict between individual rights of privacy and autonomy and the societal need to maintain order arises in a wide variety of constitutional contexts, including procedural and substantive due process, equal protection, search and seizure, self-incrimination, right to speedy trial, right to counsel, habeas corpus, and cruel and unusual punishment. In these constitutional contexts, the courts generally are engaged in balancing the interests of individuals as they conflict with societal interests and determining the extent to which society may restrict autonomy or encroach on privacy in order to fulfill legitimate societal needs. It is important to note, of course, that, although these concepts are linked in our thinking today with notions of individuality and even natural rights, they appeared at different stages in the development of intellectual history.

Search and seizure cases under the Fourth Amendment have occupied a substantial amount of the U.S. Supreme Court's attention and provide a rich source of commentary on the tension between individual and societal interests. This is illustrated in *Michigan v. Long*,[61] a case well-known for its recognition of independent state constitutional interpretation. *Long* involved several issues including the constitutionality of a protective search of a motor vehicle passenger compartment during a lawful investigatory stop. Justice O'Connor, in her majority opinion, held that the protective search of the passenger compartment of the respondent's car was reasonable under the principles articulated in *Terry v. Ohio* and other decisions of the Court. Disagreeing with the majority, Justice Brennan, in dissent, addressed the various levels of intrusion and stated that an arrest is "intended to vindicate society's interest in having its laws obeyed, and it is inevitably accompanied by future interference with the individual's freedom of movement, whether or not trial or conviction ultimately follows. The protective search for weapons, on the other hand, constitutes a brief, though far from considerable, intrusion upon the sanctity of the person."[62]

The right of privacy in the home was at issue in *Payton v. New York*[63]. The Court ruled that the Fourth Amendment prohibits police from making warrantless and nonconsensual entry into a suspect's home in order to make a routine felony arrest. The Court noted that "[c]rime, even in the privacy of one's own quarters, is . . . of grave concern to society, and the law allows such crime to be reached on proper showing. The right of officers to thrust themselves into a home is also a grave concern, not only to the individual but to a society which chooses to dwell in reasonable security and freedom from surveillance."[64]

Another category of cases that has produced valuable discussion of the balancing of individual autonomy and state authority consists of cases brought under the due process and the equal protection clauses of the Fifth and Fourteenth Amendments. These cases have arisen from a wide variety of factual scenarios. *Addington v. Texas*,[65] for example, was a due process case that concerned the civil commitment of the petitioner on grounds of mental illness. The

Court determined that due process required the standard of proof in such matters to be greater than the preponderance of evidence standard, though it can be less than the reasonable doubt standard that must be met to find criminal guilt. Noting that the standard of proof reflects the value society places on individual liberty, the Court stated that "[t]he individual should not be asked to share equally with society the risk of error when the possible injury to the individual is significantly greater than any possible harm to the state."[66] In articulating its rationale for the standard of proof, the Court defined its view of society's values in this particular situation.[67]

By this method of case-by-case adjudication, the contours of the relationship between individual interests and collective societal interests are defined, established—and modified. Individual values, such as the right to legal representation and the right to be free from cruel and unusual punishment, are encompassed in our society's values as expressed in the Bill of Rights and state constitutions. One problem with the case-by-case method of decision is that the confrontation in rights and values is in absolute terms and on a "winner take all" basis, without the possible compromises of resolution in the political process.[68]

## THE BALANCE OF POWER: QUESTIONS

Many questions arise in the process of defining the balance of power between individual and societal interests. To what extent is the individual free to exercise autonomy and free choice? At what point is the exercise of individual rights constrained by intervention of the state? Whose rights are protected by the state—those of all individuals or only selected individuals? To what extent can the state intrude upon the individual in the exercise of those rights? To what extent is the individual authorized or permitted to challenge or defy the state? With what consequences? Where does the balance lie between individual rights and the *good of society*?

The historic tension[69] between individual autonomy and societal order, as reflected by these questions, continues to generate many difficult legal problems for American state and federal courts. Although the problems arise in a variety of contexts and involve different constitutional and statutory provisions, at the heart of the cases are two basic issues: (1) the extent to which individual rights should be subordinated to society's need for security and order and (2) the extent to which individual decision making should be required to conform to dominant values established by society.

The first issue is involved in Fourth Amendment search and seizure cases, First Amendment free expression cases, and cases involving such matters as the privilege against self-incrimination, right to counsel, and application of the death penalty. Cases involving the due process and equal protection clauses also typically are concerned with balancing individual rights against social order. The continuing drug and criminal violence problems that plague American society produce criminal cases that tax the resources of state and federal judicial systems. The serious social consequences of these two related problems produce pressure for more severe crime control measures, which sometimes intensifies the conflict between individual rights and social values. Moreover, when the judicial system becomes overburdened with an unmanageable caseload, pressure arises to increase the use of measures that will expedite the processing of cases. These measures, while increasing the speed and volume of case disposition, can have adverse consequences for society as a whole, and victims and defendants, in particular. For example, wholesale plea bargaining and inappropriate use of accelerated rehabilitation programs can seriously impair the effectiveness of criminal law enforcement in every respect. In that context, all defendants, whether they claim innocence or concede guilt, are encouraged to plead guilty or nolo contendere in return for greatly reduced sentences or, in the case of accelerated rehabilitation, no sentence at all.

The second issue arises in a variety of factual contexts. Two familiar contexts are abortion rights cases[70] and cases involving termination of life support systems.[71] These cases generally reflect conflicting ethical values concerning major issues of life and death. The issues are complex and are best resolved through reasoned political discourse that can take into account the multiple interests and factors involved. In adjudication, the process becomes oversimplified and lacks the ability to fashion appropriately complex solutions. These cases also represent an overlap between the two basic issues because they involve tension between individual rights and social order.

## Chapter 2

# Private Codes: Rules of the Community

> Congress shall make no law . . . abridging . . . the right of the people peaceably to assemble.[1]

> Good name in man and woman, dear my lord,
> Is the immediate jewel of their souls.[2]

Private codes, the subject of this chapter, serve as regulators of the relationships of individuals within communities that are part of the whole society. The codes—systems of *private law*—reflect the values and interests of those communities. They are independent of, but may be partly coextensive with the law of society. Although the law of society supercedes the private codes, individuals may give their primary allegiance to the codes when the codes conflict with the law.

The term *law* or *legal codes* means those authoritative systems of rules embodied in constitutions, statutes, and court decisions which are designed to govern and apply to an entire society. They are enforced in practice by the officials of government, including judges, lawyers, law enforcement officers, and the like. Law functions as an institution as well as a process.

Private codes interact with individuals, communities, and with the substantive and procedural law of society. In this context, the term *private codes* refers to the values, beliefs, and attitudes which are recognized by particular subcommunities or, in some cases, by an entire community within society, but which are not necessarily embraced by the entire society. The term also refers to the rules or conventions which make the values, beliefs, and attitudes operative. Private codes define, govern, and restrict the individuals living in particular communities. In a sense, they constitute a type of *private law* that regulates and classifies individuals within communities.

Private codes shape and govern the thought and action of members of the group with respect to other group members, as well as their relationships with individuals outside the group. The extent to which the codes affect members outside the group varies according to the relative power of the respective groups. Illustrative of these private codes are codes of honor adhered to by virtually every social class. In their extreme form, codes of honor call for revenge or retribution by violence in defense of self-respect and reputation. An extension of this code—the code duello—requires action in the event of an insult or injury for which there is no apology. The code duello, which existed in this country during the times of Alexander Hamilton, who was killed in a duel, and Andrew Jackson, who killed his man in a duel, lasted in the South longer than elsewhere in the nation.[3] The code of honor often converged with the legal code or codes of higher morality. Other important codes visible in American culture—both legal and literary—are racial[4] and ethnic classification codes, social classification codes, and codes governing economic or business conduct, particularly as adhered to by the middle class.

A higher moral code, a type of private code, is a system of values and conduct generated by religious tradition or higher ethical belief. Natural law is frequently characterized in terms of moral or ethical principles. Higher moral codes are more elusive and more difficult to identify than the other private codes. Moreover, there is often considerable overlap between moral codes and other private codes.

In the course of their interaction with other factors, such as individual autonomy, equality, rights, and law, private codes often intervene between the individual and the community's legal code, thus preventing or reducing the effectiveness of law as a regulator of conduct. The codes often take precedence over the law in a community. In some situations, the law may defer to the enforcement of the codes. William Faulkner's stories "An Odor of Verbena"[5] and "That Evening Sun"[6] provide examples of that phenomenon. In those instances, the legal system actually may authorize the code rules when the legal system is in the hands of the same individuals or groups that stand behind the codes. In other cases, where the codes control the behavior of a community that lacks power in the greater society, the codes may undermine or act in defiance of the law. Examples in today's society can be found in the cities where codes of gang conduct or youth conduct in general operate in defiance of the law. Situations where the codes were authorized or allowed existed in the South and West where lynchings or charivari[7] were common occurrences.

I do not mean to suggest that all private codes involve violence and are hierarchic or authoritarian. There are notable examples to the contrary. Consider, for example, rules and customs of the Amish community, which is strongly pacifist and egalitarian. Quaker communities have similar values. Academic communities have disciplinary codes.

The subject of community and association in America, itself, continues to be the subject of scholarly discussion. Alexis de Toqueville was one of the earliest commentators about association in American life, remarking that "Americans of all ages, all stations in life, and all types of disposition are forever forming associations."[8] Dean Aviam Soifer has recently published *Law and the Company We Keep*, a fascinating discussion of community, law, and American culture. Writers like Francis Fukuyama have written extensively on civil society and intermediate institutions.[9]

Because this book deals with several of America's societal problems, however, I have chosen to focus on communities and codes that involve violence and are disruptive of society rather than the broader topic of communities and associations. I will, however, touch on the subject of communities and mediating institutions in American life and law. Many examples of codes in action, like those in literature, tend to involve situations that impede the harmonious processes of society. In addition to the illustrations drawn from Faulkner, the discussion will touch upon Nathaniel Hawthorne's *The Scarlet Letter*,[10] Owen Wister's *The Virginian*, and Russell Banks's *Rule of the Bone*.[11] In addition, several of the novels included in Chapter 3 contain strong evidence of private codes. These include Robert Penn Warren's *Night Rider*,[12] Joyce Carol Oates's *them*,[13] and Richard Price's *Clockers*.[14]

## CODES BEFORE THE LAW

Private codes frequently conflict with the law. This conflict has been the subject of litigation in cases involving the right of parents to make medical and educational decisions with respect to their children when their decisions did not comply with existing law. In *Walker v. Superior Court*,[15] a mother who refused medical treatment for her daughter, choosing instead to treat the child's illness with prayer, was charged with involuntary manslaughter and felony child endangerment after the child died from meningitis. The defendant moved to dismiss, claiming that her conduct in making decisions about her child based on her own set of values and beliefs was protected by statute and by state and federal constitutional provisions that guarantee the free exercise of religion. The California Supreme Court held that the state's compelling interest in assuring medical care for gravely ill children prevailed over the defendant's private values.[16]

In addition to conflict between law and private codes based on religious values, other types of codes have interacted with the law. *United States v. Abel*[17] involved a criminal prosecution of the defendant and two cohorts for bank robbery. Abel's cohorts pleaded guilty but the defendant went to trial. One of Abel's cohorts, Ehle, agreed to testify against him. Abel proposed to counter Ehle's testimony with that of Mills, who would testify that Ehle intended to implicate Abel falsely in order to receive favorable treatment from the government. After Mills so testified, the prosecutor attempted to discredit Mills by recalling Ehle to testify that Abel, Mills, and Ehle were all members of a secret prison organization whose tenets or code required its members to deny its existence and to lie, steal, and kill to protect each other. After the defendant was convicted, he appealed to the Court of Appeals, which reversed on the basis that Ehle's rebuttal testimony was admitted, beyond impeachment, to show that because Mills belonged to the gang, he must be lying on the stand. The Supreme Court reinstated the verdict, holding that the evidence showing Mills's and respondent's membership in the prison gang was sufficiently probative of Mills's possible bias toward Abel to warrant its admission into evidence. The code at issue in *Abel* was a code of honor demanding certain behavior on the part of participants, including adherence to a code of silence. That type of code is commonly involved in organized crime prosecutions.

A private gang code was also featured in *Dawson v. Delaware.*[18] That case involved evidence about a prison gang with its own private code of conduct. The defendant appealed his conviction for first-degree murder which resulted in a death sentence. At the capital sentencing proceeding, evidence was admitted by stipulation of the parties that the defendant was a member of an organization called the Aryan Brotherhood, a white racist prison gang which began in the 1960s in California in response to other gangs of racial minoritics. The Court held that the First and Fourteenth Amendments prohibit the introduction of that evidence where it has no relevance to the issues being decided in the proceeding, but noted that it has held that the First Amendment protects an individual's right to join groups and associate with others holding similar beliefs. In some situations, therefore, private codes that challenge the authority of law may be protected by virtue of the constitutional right of free association.[19]

## CHARACTERISTICS OF PRIVATE CODES

Private codes that prescribe individual behavior in specified circumstances, as well as honor-based codes that promote social and racial classifications, share characteristics in common, including the following:

### Values

Codes generally involve values that stem from the need for honor or respect in the eyes of the community. The origin has a cultural or ethical basis. Natural law often is used as a rationale for the value system. Codes are given legitimacy in a cultural story. The opinion of others—public reputation within the community—is a key. For example, in the Old South, the wish that one be regarded as honest was stronger than being honest itself.[20] Personal virtues are important for their social utility. That concept of honor and respect often is defective, however, and contains inner contradictions. The reliance on shame in this context can distort human personality and individualism, forcing even good people to lower themselves to the level of the crowd. Prejudice and pride often are motivating forces, serving the symbols of honor, rather than the substance of honor. In attempting to preserve order in the community, the codes often produce violence and disorder. One inherent problem is that such codes are frequently applied to bring about a false sense of community harmony at the expense of human rights and dignity.

## Structure

The social structure embodied in the codes is hierarchical, as to both the code community and its position relative to outside communities and groups. Code communities commonly are authoritarian, based on power rather than rights. Equality of members does not usually exist. Procedures, often rigid and inflexible, are prescribed, rather than individual rights or discretion. The rules or conventions dictate ways of thinking about others as well as behavior and action in prescribed situations. Codes deal with more than mere courtesy or civility. They enter the realm of ethics, morals, and the exercise of exclusionary power, sometimes employing violent means.

## Function

Codes define the rules for members of the community and exclude outsiders. Codes are concerned with status in the larger society. They compel allegiance of members of the community that often takes precedence over the law of the larger society. Code rules apply to a community which exists within a larger society. They are not enacted into law but, if the community is powerful within the larger society, they may coexist with or be implicitly or explicitly allowed or *authorized* by the larger society. Rules of the code may also subvert or oppose the law of society. Generally, codes operate to protect the community from change or intervention by outside forces. They aim to preserve the status quo by preserving and protecting the power and authority of people high in the hierarchical structure of the community. Codes use language as well as action to control or direct thought. They attempt to restrict human choices, to bring a kind of order to chaos, although the order is a carefully confined—and confining—type of order.

Codes appear to operate differently, depending upon whether they are used by people with or without power in a community and whether the community has a strong position in the greater society. The basic premises are the same, but either the purposes for which they are used, or the effect of their use, differs, depending on the situation. Codes generally are used to preserve order and peace in a community. If applied by those with power and authority in society at large, the effect may be to preserve the stratification of society. If the community does not have a strong position, codes may simply preserve the order within a community. Even then, however, the codes may preserve dominance over other individuals, groups, or communities.

## LAW, CODES, AND THE INDIVIDUAL: FAULKNER'S WORLD

The primary purpose of this discussion is to explore the relationship between the law and private codes in the context of individual action in the stories—with particular reference to individual action that transcends the codes. The principal questions that direct the inquiry are: What is the role of the law in the narrative? Who represents the law? What codes exist which govern or affect the characters' conduct? How do the codes interact with the law? Is there individual action which transcends the limitations of the codes? What changes occur in the community or society as a result of the interaction of code and law?

## "THAT EVENING SUN": CAUGHT IN THE CROSSFIRE

''That Evening Sun'' illustrates the powerful impact of the social codes—in particular the racial code—prevalent in its Southern setting in the early 1900s. Although published as a story rather than as part of a novel, this narrative actually belongs to a series of stories dealing with the Compson children, who are best known for their central roles in *The Sound and the Fury*[21]. The story focuses on a black woman named Nancy who is a servant in the Compson household filling in for the sick Dilsey, another famous Faulkner character. The title of the story derives from the opening line of the song, ''St. Louis Blues'': ''I hates to see that evening sun go down.''[22]

Nancy hates to see that evening sun go down because she is afraid of being murdered during the night by her husband, Jesus, whom she fears will punish her for betraying him by prostituting herself to Stovall, a white man. Nancy is pregnant with the child of Stovall, who also happens to be a deacon in the local Baptist church. Although Jesus is believed to have left town, Nancy is convinced that he has returned to cut her throat. In the course of the story, narrated from the viewpoint of nine-year-old Quentin Compson, Nancy seeks the comfort and protection of the Compson children. Nancy is so afraid of the dark (and all that it signifies for her) that initially she wants to sleep in the Compson home—a wish that Mr. Compson was willing to humor, but which Mrs. Compson was not.

Eventually, Nancy lures the children to accompany her for a time. She feels protected. Perhaps there is actual protection from harm, under the racial code, while the white family members are present. Mr. Compson discovers where the children are and, after superficially reassuring Nancy and attempting unsuccessfully to persuade her to stay with another black woman, retrieves them, leaving Nancy to face her terror alone. In rejecting the idea of staying with someone besides the Compsons, Nancy says, ''Twon't do no good. . . . Putting it off won't do no good.'' When Mr. Compson asks, ''Then what do you want to do?'', Nancy replies, ''I don't know. . . . I reckon it belong to me. I reckon what I going to get ain't no more than mine'' (TES, 408).

Nancy accepts as inevitable that she will be punished for being unfaithful to Jesus. By prostituting herself to Stovall she violated the private code of honor governing their marriage relationship or, at least, affecting Jesus's self-respect. She doubtless violated the criminal and civil law of society. Once she is denied the protection of the Compsons, Nancy reasons that she may as well accept her fate. She is convinced there is nothing anyone, even the Compsons, can do to prevent Jesus's retribution from eventually occurring. The law is not mentioned by anyone as a possible avenue of protection: The private code of honor will drive Jesus to retaliate against Nancy without intervention of law.

Faulkner's Nancy has had an earlier acquaintance with the law. Arrested and en route to jail with the marshal, she passes Stovall on the street. When she confronts him about not paying her for their last three encounters, he knocks her down. When she continues to taunt him, he kicks her in the mouth with his heel. Only after that did the marshal stop Stovall and continue to the jail. Nancy is undaunted by the incident. Even while spitting out blood and teeth on the ground, she continues to laugh and repeat her charge. There is no suggestion of any official reprisal against Stovall for the assault (neither was there any great effort to prevent it in the first place). During the night, Nancy attempts suicide but is cut down by the jailer, who then beats her.

After these events occur, when Jesus is warned by Mr. Compson to stay away from the Compson house, Jesus confirms his understanding of the racial code: ''I can't hang around white man's kitchen. . . . But white man can hang around mine. White man can come into my house, but I can't stop him. When white man want to come in my house, I ain't got no house. I can't stop him [then, asserting his will], . . . but he can't kick me outen it. He can't do that'' (TES, 394).

Here, both private codes—the racial code and the code of honor—operate to permit, even demand, vengeance against Nancy. Nancy is, in a sense, caught in the *crossfire* between these two codes. Given her status in society, she has no escape route and no protection. The evidence indicates that the representatives of the law elect not to intervene for the purpose of assisting or delivering Nancy from harm at the hand of Jesus. The law tolerates, perhaps even reinforces, the private codes in the community. Whatever the reason, the law proves to be impotent to protect Nancy when her life is jeopardized.

The characters clearly do not transcend the private codes; the codes control the people and their actions. Nancy looked to the Compsons for help and they did not rise to meet the standard of higher moral responsibility that she requested of them. Perhaps she knew all along that they would not protect her from the consequences of her violation of the code of honor in her relationship with Jesus. She tested the hearts of the Compsons and they failed her test.

## "PERCY GRIMM": AGENT OF REVENGE

"Percy Grimm" is contained in Chapter 19 of *Light in August*.[23] Although two stories are told in the novel, involving the same people, the two principal characters never actually meet. The story of Percy Grimm, a young captain in the State National Guard, occurs late in the action of the novel, at a point where the principal protagonist, Joe Christmas, has been arrested for the murder of his paramour, Joanna Burden.

While the story of Joe Christmas is fascinating, his life need not be covered here. Because his life intersects with Grimm's, it is enough, for these purposes, to know that Joe appeared in Jefferson, the principal city in Faulkner's mythical Yoknapatawpha[24] County, Mississippi, as an alienated soul engaged in a search for his human identity. Belonging to no community, appearing white but believing that he may have had black ancestry, he lives outside the law and any private code. He is rejected by all.

All the characters in the novel, in their own ways, are searching for some form of identity; all of them, to a greater or lesser extent, are alienated from their respective communities. Each major character either never had, or had lost, a vital connection to the community. Joe never had a connection, thus completing his ultimate separation. The Reverend Mr. Hightower, ousted from his church but insisting on remaining in Jefferson—contrary to the wishes of his former parishioners—is searching for his own sense of moral responsibility. He comes close to finding it after Joe seeks refuge in his home, the event that brings Grimm into the picture.

Grimm presents a particularly interesting case. Far from being a major player in the story, he enters near the end of the novel as the representative of the law. He, too, has been searching for identity, which previously depended upon his "scars of . . . battle" (PG, 622) received during a fight with a soldier over an unpatriotic remark the soldier had made. Grimm always regretted that he had not served in the military.

Faulkner, when asked about Grimm by students at the University of Virginia, remarked: "I wrote that book in 1932 before I'd ever heard of Hitler's Storm Troopers, what he was was a Nazi Storm Trooper, but then I'd never heard of one then, and he's not prevalent but he's everywhere."[25] Although his type may not have been prevalent in Jefferson when the events of the story take place, Grimm manages to enlist enough of his type "to compose a fair platoon" for the sake of protecting "order . . . [and the] course of justice" (PG, 624).

At the point in the story where Grimm enters, Joe has been captured and arrested. He is in the custody of the Jefferson sheriff. Grimm, in an effort to place himself in the center of the action, undertakes a campaign to establish himself as the law official in charge. By a series of Grimm-orchestrated deceptions combined with misunderstandings on the part of others, he manages to convince even the sheriff to allow him to become *the law*—in charge of maintaining order and peace in the community and preventing anyone from interfering in the legal process. In Grimm's words: ''We got to preserve order. . . . We must let the law take its course. The law, the nation. It is the right of no civilian to sentence a man to death. And we, the soldiers in Jefferson, are the ones to see to that'' (PG, 623).

To this point in the narrative, the private codes—racial, class, and honor—have defined and limited the characters and their actions. The dynamics change, however; the balance is shifted and thrown off center. Grimm, the representative of the codes, by pretense and deception, has become the representative of the law. Grimm even cloaks himself in his National Guard uniform, although he is not authorized to do so. He is acting as an individual without official authority. Moreover, the force of Grimm's individual will, in its excess, overreaches the constraints of both the law and the codes. Although this is the first instance in the story where *the law* has attempted to assume control, it does so through an illegitimate representative, Grimm. The legitimate representative, the sheriff, takes no part in the jihad of Grimm and his platoon of self-appointed storm troopers.

Word spreads throughout the square that the special Grand Jury will be meeting the next day to deliberate charges against Joe. Faulkner tells us: ''Somehow the very sound of the two words with their evocation, secret and irrevocable and something of a hidden and unsleeping and omnipotent eye watching the doings of men, began to reassure Grimm's men in their own makebelieve'' (PG, 627).

When Joe escapes from the jail, in an attempt to fulfill the dictates of his own private code of honor and regain his freedom, Grimm takes up the pursuit and, on a bicycle which he forcibly takes from a passerby, proceeds relentlessly to follow Joe through the streets. Finally, Grimm, the emotionless mechanism of the law, corners Joe at Hightower's house. Mindlessly driven, Grimm casts Hightower aside, rejecting his late attempt to provide an alibi defense for Joe. Flinging the old man aside, Grimm bursts into a room where Joe has taken cover behind a table. Although Joe offers no resistance in the moment that follows, Grimm opens fire at Joe, intending to inflict mortal wounds. Then, in one of the most dramatic moments of the book, Grimm brutally and ruthlessly mutilates the dying Joe. While Grimm commits this lawless act, to the utter revulsion of the other men who enter the room, one of whom is sickened, he repeats his reasons: '' 'Now you'll let white women alone, even in hell,' he said'' (PG, 633). Grimm, then, has taken his revenge on Joe for allegedly violating the racial code in carrying on an affair with Joanna Burden.

The law has retreated from any pretense of neutrality, fairness, or purpose. It has, instead, plunged into an abyss: the blind fury of revenge, consistent with a severe and irrational enforcement of the racial code of white against black. The brutality of Grimm's assault is devastating and, Faulkner tells us, memorable for all who witness it. After this event, Joe seems to undergo a Christ-like ascension with a suggestion of later resurrection:''[T]he man seemed to rise soaring into their memories forever and ever. They [the other men, watching] are not to lose it, in whatever peaceful valleys, beside whatever placid and reassuring streams of old age. . . . It will be there, musing, quiet, steadfast, not fading and not particularly threatful, but of itself alone serene, of itself alone triumphant'' (PG, 634).

The meaning of Faulkner's religious imagery in this story is an important subject in its own right. The perception of Joe's *ascension*, however, is significant for its suggestion that Joe, for all his failings, has somehow transcended the limitations of the codes and the law and, most certainly, the ruthless private revenge on Grimm's part.

Grimm has degraded the law to one of the lowest points narrated in Faulkner's fiction—utter lawlessness executed by the law's representative. By committing not only murder, but also mutilation, Grimm has separated himself from the community, notwithstanding the private racial code in Jefferson. The revulsion of Grimm's men at seeing his depraved act supports this interpretation. The act of murder, itself, represents, for Faulkner, the ultimate antisocial act—the complete separation from the community and society.

In this episode of *Light in August*, as in ''That Evening Sun,'' one sees the domination of events and relationships by the individual will, directed in large part by the private codes of the community. The actions of the characters, for the most part, fail to transcend those self-limiting views of human nature and human capacity. Instead, Faulkner's characters predictably act in concert with the private codes to which they adhere—even to excess, as in Grimm's case—even if this entails disregarding the law.

While it is not accurate to conclude that all private codes necessarily exert a negative influence on community or society, it is fair to say that many codes embody a narrow perspective and restrict human potential by subjecting it to limits which do not permit growth and change. In doing so, codes also may fragment society and discourage meaningful interaction among individuals within society. Both the racial code and the honor codes stratify society into socioeconomic classes and fragment society. Although there are exceptions, many codes that rely on exclusion of outsiders as a fundamental tenet produce that result. The illustrations drawn from the experience in the Old South and the codes involved in the cases discussed earlier support the view of codes as negative forces.

## ''AN ODOR OF VERBENA'': TRANSCENDING THE CODES

''An Odor of Verbena,'' which is the concluding section of the novel *The Unvanquished*,[26] embraces several forces central to the theme of this chapter: the private code of revenge and the occurrence of human action transcending the limits of the codes, thereby forcing a reexamination of the standards of the community. The full significance of the narrative depends on the context of the loosely knit novel, but it is a story in itself.

The events take place in Jefferson, shortly after the Civil War, perhaps in

1874. Bayard Sartoris tells the story as a young man of twenty-four. Bayard's father, Colonel John Sartoris, a violent and ambitious man in the tradition of the Old South, has had a long-standing quarrel with his business partner, Ben Redmond. Colonel Sartoris has struggled his way up from poverty to a position of power and wealth in the community. He has a second wife, Drusilla, a much younger woman who is only a few years older than Bayard. She and Bayard have become attracted to each other, a discovery which has become apparent just before the critical events of the story.

Bayard is a law student and resides with a Professor Wilkins at the university where he is reading law. In this way, Faulkner portrays Bayard as the law's representative. As the narrative begins, Bayard learns that his father has been killed by Redmond. A duel between the two had seemed inevitable because of Sartoris's constant provocation of Redmond. Sartoris had told his son, when they were last together, that he had wearied of killing and that he intended to confront Redmond unarmed.

Professor Wilkins provides Bayard with a horse and—ironically, for a man of law—offers Bayard a pistol which he fully expects Bayard will need. It is apparent from this story that the code of honor requires revenge for a killing of this sort. This applies not only to the white plantation class, but to the lower class of whites as well. All elements of the Jefferson community expect Bayard to comply with this code of honor. Although Colonel Sartoris did not draw his weapon in the encounter with Redmond, he was armed with his concealed Derringer, contrary to his statement to Bayard. Because the colonel was armed, the community pronounced the fight a fair duel.

Bayard, as he departs from the Wilkins household, can almost hear the professor saying:"Ah, this unhappy land, not ten years recovered from the fever yet still men must kill one another, still we must pay Cain's price in his own coin" (*OV*, 161). Bayard also imagines that Mrs. Wilkins, who reminds him of his *Granny*, is thinking: *"Who lives by the sword shall die by it"* (OV, 161), just as his grandmother would have thought. Bayard, himself, is weighing his moral dilemma:

> I was beginning to realize, to become aware of that which I still had no yardstick to measure save that one consisting of what, despite myself, despite my raising and background (or maybe because of them) I had for some time known I was becoming and had feared the test of it; *At least this will be my chance to find out if I am what I think I am or if I just hope; if I am going to do what I have taught myself is right or if I am just going to wish I were.* (OV, 162)

Bayard wrestles here with the conflict between the private codes which govern life in Jefferson, on one hand, and the law to which he has committed himself and higher religious morality, on the other. As he continues his preparations for departure, he wonders:

> [I] thought for a second how if I told him what I was going to do, since we had talked about it, about how if there was anything at all in the Book, anything of hope and peace for His blind and bewildered spawn which He had chosen above all others to offer immortality. *Thou shalt not kill* must be it, since maybe he [Wilkins] even believed that he had taught it to me, except that he had not, nobody had, not even myself, since it went further than just having been learned. (OV, 163)

In addition to the law, Bayard obviously is moved by the existence of a higher moral code based on some kind of religious beliefs. Bayard's dilemma reveals the intersection of law, private codes of honor, and higher moral codes of right and wrong. The pressure increases on Bayard to continue the revenge cycle. Virtually everyone in the community encourages him to avenge his father's murder, especially his stepmother, Drusilla, who is the very embodiment of the code of honor. Drusilla, in fact, tells Bayard how fortunate he is to be the chosen avenger of his father's death.

As she kisses Bayard's right hand, she senses immediately that Bayard does not intend to kill Redmond. Repulsed by the realization, she screams in horror and has to be taken to her bedroom. Bayard's Aunt Jenny assures Bayard that it is all right for him to decide not to kill Redmond and that he must abide by his own principles. Like Drusilla, George Wyatt, one of the colonel's *old troop*, knows instinctively that Bayard does not intend to use the pistol which he offers to Bayard by means of "something communicated by touch straight to the simple code by which he lived . . . so that he too stood suddenly back, the pistol in his hand, staring at me with his pale outraged eyes" (OV, 187).

The next day, Bayard proceeds to Redmond's office unarmed, intending to confront, but not to kill, Redmond. Bayard enters Redmond's office and walks toward the desk where Redmond is seated. Redmond, expecting him, raises his pistol, fires twice—deliberately missing Bayard—rises from his desk and leaves the office. Although the townspeople outside believe he has killed Bayard, they allow Redmond to leave town. He boards a train and departs, never to return again to Jefferson.

When Bayard's brave action is revealed—and understood—it is accepted and admired. Even Drusilla, who departs before Bayard returns to the house, has left behind a reminder (a single sprig of verbena, her emblem) that she has accepted his action. Not only was Bayard principled and brave, he was also very fortunate; fortunate that Redmond, like himself, had decided to end the revenge cycle and did not attempt to kill him. Redmond, too, acted courageously. He obviously expected to be killed and had prepared himself for that likelihood. He is described as clean-shaven and freshly dressed with tragic appearance. When he realized that Bayard was not armed, he deliberately fired both shots to miss Bayard.

Bayard did not merely reject the old code of honor; he transcended it.[27] He did everything required of him in risking his life and confronting his father's killer courageously. But he apparently decided from the outset not to kill Redmond and, for a multitude of reasons—including law, morality, and reason—he adhered to his principles in the face of community disapproval and a real likelihood of death.

Bayard, the law student, acted in accord with the law and with higher moral standards. In contrast, the entire community at that point had placed the private code of honor above all else, even the law. No mention was made of the role of criminal law or punishment for murder. It was as though the law remained suspended so long as the dictates of the code were followed. Even though there was general sentiment that a killing by Redmond of young Bayard would not have been as fair and justified as the killing of Sartoris, the community was ready to accept it. In fact, the members of the community actually demonstrated their acceptance of (what they had every reason to believe was) the murder of Bayard, by permitting Redmond to leave town without any attempt to apprehend him.

In rejecting the revenge cycle, Bayard demonstrated that he had his own standards. Bayard's act of principle and bravery substantially elevated the role of the law in the Jefferson community. Although the private codes would continue to exist, they would be accorded less deference in light of Bayard's action which undermined their hold on the community. It is apparent that the force of law was not potent. Throughout the events leading to the confrontation, no representative of the law intervened. Apart from Bayard's own reliance on his devotion to the law, the law was not an active participant in the drama that occurred, despite the likelihood that murder was about to take place in Jefferson. Nonetheless, the decisions and actions of Redmond and the colonel, as well as those of Bayard, suggest that the private code of honor—at least insofar as it requires revenge—has been exposed. Human potential has expanded and the community's standards have changed.

Faulkner has highlighted the private code of honor as the destructive force that it is and has shown what can happen when human will and human action combine to transcend the confinement of the code, elevating morality and law. As in all Faulkner's fiction, here "the human heart [has been] in conflict with itself"[28] and has prevailed, thrusting change upon the community.

Language plays an important role in directing Bayard's actions. Unlike the other characters—including Drusilla and George Wyatt, who operate based on their intuitive knowledge of the old code of honor and revenge—the language of morality and law resonate in Bayard's mind as he prepares for the encounter. He wonders, for example, whether he can follow what he has taught himself is right, as well as what he knows is right from the higher morality embodied in "the Book," (OV, 163). Rather than react instinctively to the powerful demands of the code of honor, he disciplines himself to act according to the principles that he has intellectualized from law and higher morality. In rejecting the insistent demands of everyone except his wise Aunt Jenny, who understood all the dimensions of the situation, he maintains his convictions in addition to risking his life by facing Redmond unarmed. Bayard's actions were deeply affected by language. Through his unshakable commitment and courage, he transformed the prevailing standard of his society from violence to law and morality.

## *THE SCARLET LETTER*: A NEW ENGLAND PRIMER

The role of the code of honor is illustrated in *The Scarlet Letter* by Nathaniel Hawthorne.[29] This novel involves the interaction of law, codes of honor, and morality in the context of individual courage, cowardice, and vengeance. At this time in history, 1642, legal and moral codes were virtually indistinguishable in colonial society. As the novel opens, Hester Prynne, a young woman of the community, has been found guilty of adultery and sentenced to wear a scarlet "A" on the bodice of her dress. She must also stand on the scaffold for three hours to receive the scorn of the other citizens. Hester's good reputation influenced the judges' decision to grant her what they considered leniency in their sentence. Hester is subject to permanent ostracism and exclusion from the community—a kind of exile or shunning often found in religious communities.

Hester's circumstances placed her in a difficult situation. Her marriage to Chillingworth, an older, slightly deformed physician, was arranged by her parents after they lost their wealth. The couple lived in Amsterdam before deciding to settle in the American colonies. Hester arrived in Boston alone, sent ahead by her husband. When Chillingworth failed to appear, most people assumed he had been lost at sea. At the time of the punishment, she had been in New England two years. During that time, she had an affair with the local minister, the Reverend Arthur Dimmesdale. A female child, Pearl, was the fruit of the adulterous relationship.

While Hester is serving her time on the scaffold, she recognizes her husband in the crowd. When Chillingworth, the embodiment of dark malevolence, learns the story about Hester, he is angry, not only about the disgrace, but about Hester's refusal to disclose the name of Pearl's father. Hester agrees, however, to Chillingworth's demand that she not reveal his identity either. Dimmesdale, for his part, lacks the courage to reveal himself and bear the scorn of the community.

In addition to the legal code, several codes operate in the story. The religious-based moral code, closely linked to the law and to the community's code of conventional morality, bears down on Hester alone. The honor code of silence to which she subscribes—a commonly invoked code, as we have seen—prevents her from disclosing Dimmesdale's role. Dimmesdale's concern for the community code, and the consequences of violation, prevent him from acknowledging his fault. Chillingworth's honor is damaged by Hester's disgrace. He, in turn, pledges revenge against the anonymous lover as the code of honor allows. Hester, no doubt, bears the full weight of community disapproval, not only because she had no choice except to acknowledge her failing, but also because of her gender.

As events develop in the story, Hester maintains her code of honor and remains true to her pledge of secrecy. By virtue of her fine qualities and spirit, she regains the respect and admiration of the community despite her mark of censure. Dimmesdale suffers loss of his health, partly due to his guilt and cowardice, partly due to Chillingworth's insidious undermining of his physical and mental well-being. Finally, however, Dimmesdale confesses publicly to an astonished gathering, tearing away the ministerial band from his chest and revealing "a SCARLET LETTER—the very semblance of that worn by Hester Prynne—imprinted in the flesh" (*SL*, 270). Before he dies, he tells Hester: "The law we broke!—the sin here so awfully revealed! . . . It may be, that, when we forgot our God,—when we violated our reverence each for the other's soul,—it was thenceforth vain to hope that we could meet hereafter, in an everlasting and pure reunion. God knows; and He is merciful! . . . His will be done!" (*SL*, 269).

Chillingworth repeats aloud: "Thou hast escaped me!" (*SL*, 268). Without his object of obsessive hate and revenge, he dies soon after. In Dimmesdale's view, Chillingworth's "revenge has been blacker than my sin. He has violated, in cold blood, the sanctity of a human heart" (*SL*, 212).

The actions of Hawthorne's characters, played out against the backdrop of this New England Puritan community, reveal the operation of private codes and law. Justice is represented, not as an abstract principle or fair procedure, but as public retribution. The legitimacy of the moral-legal system and its pronouncements are questioned by no one. The rules and the consequences are fully accepted by all members of the community save, perhaps, the young Pearl—a lively, precocious, irreverent creature who becomes wealthy by virtue of Chillingworth's legacy.

At the heart of the code of honor lies community public opinion—evaluation of the individual by the public. In that sense, honor has three well-defined facets.[30] The first is the inner conviction of self-worth. In *The Scarlet Letter*, Hester alone possesses that type of inner strength. The second facet is the public assertion of that self-worth. Hester, for example, insists on making that assertion and, by her actions, eventually convinces the community of her inner value. Chillingworth and Dimmesdale fail utterly in this respect. Both are unwilling or unable to acknowledge the truth about themselves to the public. Both withhold grave secrets. In the final chapter, the narrator comments that one of the morals of the minister's experience is: "Be true! Be true! Show freely to the world, if not your worst, yet some trait whereby the worst may be inferred!" (*SL*, 271). The final facet is the evaluation of the assertion of self-worth by the public, the community, on the basis of the actions of the individual. In the perception of the community, honor is difficult to distinguish from reputation.

Honor is both internal and external. It is internal to the individual in terms of understanding one's place in the order of society; it is external because only the response of the community can reveal that place. In some communities, such as the fictitious New England community about which Hawthorne was writing, personal values held by individuals are in accord with the moral and social conventions imposed by the community.

Apart from those general statements, several variations of the code of honor are apparent in the story. Chillingworth adheres to the honor code that prohibits unfaithfulness on the part of his wife. He feels justified in pursuing any means of punishment against those who have violated his honor. Chillingworth, however, declines to reveal his identity and insists that Hester join him in acting according to the code of silence. He pursues in secret the one whom he believes has wronged him. When the wrongdoer—Dimmesdale—finally reveals himself as he is dying, the secret vengeance is thwarted. Chillingworth violated the code of honor himself by failing to reveal his identity and his knowledge about the violation so that community action could take place.

Dimmesdale has violated the code of honor in several ways. He first betrayed his ministerial office and community trust. He also violated the sanctity of the marriage relationship (such as it was in Hester and Chillingworth's case.) In addition, rather than being forthcoming and truthful, he invoked the code of silence instead of revealing his violations. That dereliction, ironically, caused his downfall. He opened himself to Chillingworth's insidious revenge and conspired in the destruction of his own soul and body.

Hester, alone, accepted and submitted to the community law and code of honor except that she refused to reveal the identities of either her lover or her husband, thereby depriving the community of its rightful knowledge and proper role in enforcing the code of honor. The community, however, was satisfied to punish the female participant alone. Yet, Hester ultimately prevails over all the codes and all the offenders by virtue of her personal strength and courage.

## *THE VIRGINIAN*: EAST MEETS WEST

Wister was a wealthy, Harvard Law School–educated easterner who went west in 1885 to escape an urban career in favor of living a physically strenuous life. A protégé and lifelong friend of Oliver Wendell Holmes, Wister wrote into American literary mythology the story of a vigilante campaign in Wyoming in which a group of ranchers (the Wyoming Stock-Growers' Association, "WSGA") used private violence in an ongoing struggle against a group of rustlers. The term "vigilantism," applied to this struggle, has been used to describe a wide variety of local efforts that share the common factor of use of extralegal force and violence by a group of citizens to extinguish what they consider to be *criminal* threats to the peace and prosperity of a community.[31] This organized activity has some of the characteristics of a violent private code.[32]

The novel represents an attitude of distrust of judicial systems. The central event of the story is a hanging of two rustlers who have been captured after an extended, well-organized pursuit and held overnight before their unlawful execution. The Virginian of the story was born in poverty but rose through social ranks by the exercise of his unusual skills and highly admired character. He is educated and successful in business as his qualities are recognized. In the novel, the primary element of social and moral superiority is not nobility but virility. The Virginian possesses that quality in abundance. Through a series of challenges, the Virginian proves himself. His actions are seen through the eyes of several characters—Judge Henry, a former federal judge, a rancher and the Virginian's employer; Molly Stark Wood, who came west as a schoolteacher; and the narrator, who purports to be a gentleman visiting the west for recreation.

Judge Henry is the principal apologist for the unofficial *justice* which the group of vigilantes led by the Virginian bestows on the rustlers. Confronted by Molly, the Judge asserts his belief that there is a distinction between "burning Southern Negroes in public and hanging Wyoming horse-thieves in private" (*TV*, 374).

These are the hands into which ordinary citizens have put the law. So . . . when they lynch they only take back what they once gave. . . . [I]n the South they take a negro from jail where he was waiting to be duly hung. The South has never claimed that the law would let him go. But in Wyoming the law has been letting our cattle-thieves go for two years. . . . The courts, or rather the juries, into whose hands we have put the law, are not dealing the law. . . . And so when your ordinary citizen sees this, and sees that he has placed justice in a dead hand, he must take justice back into his own hands where it was once. . . . Call this primitive, if you will. But so far from being a *defiance* of the law, it is an *assertion* of it—the fundamental assertion of self-governing men, upon whom our whole social fabric is based. (*TV*, 375–376)

The judge is referring to the fact that the juries were controlled by the local farmers. Because the farmers hated the cattlemen, whose practices were incompatible with farming, the juries constantly refused to convict the rustlers. The cattlemen, for their part, turned to vigilante violence in taking matters into their own hands and hanging rustlers.

Wister presents an unusual twist on the concept of equality. He informs the reader that the country is divided into two classes—the quality and the equality.

It was through the Declaration of Independence that we acknowledged the *eternal inequality* of man. For by it we abolished a cut-and-dried aristocracy. We had seen little men artificially held down in low places, and our own justice-loving hearts abhorred this violence to human nature. Therefore, we decreed that every man should thenceforth have equal liberty to find his own level. By this very decree we acknowledged and gave freedom to true aristocracy, saying, "Let the best man win! That is America's word. That is true democracy. And true democracy and true aristocracy are one and the same thing." (*TV*, 125)

By this reasoning, equality is not a right or goal of the democratic system in itself, but merely the starting point—the means by which the natural aristocracy works its way to the position of control by virtue of natural superiority. The ability to use violence when expedient and to prevail in contests of will or physical strength are crucial. Success in prevailing over others apparently proves superiority and resolves the moral questions. The ability to prevail establishes the virtue of the one who prevails—a true, self-proving system. Violence, therefore, is justified in this process. With respect to the earlier discussion of individualism, Wister is advocating a brand of imperial individualism, rather than democratic individualism.

Judge Henry's apology for lynch law arose from an actual tradition of support by judges and lawyers for the practice of lynching. In the latter part of the nineteenth century, many leading members of the legal profession, along with other prominent Americans, actually participated in vigilante movements and lynchings.[33] Those members of the legal profession vigorously supported the idea of law and order. Their conception of law and order, however, emphasized control of crime and criminals to the point of subverting due process of law. Rather than suppression of the extralegal lynchings, they supported the idea of reforming the legal system to allow greater leeway for vigilantism. Similar reasoning occurs from time to time in contemporary society. Because of the increase in societal violence and the resulting feelings of anxiety and insecurity of many Americans, the concept of self-help in dealing with criminals and the exonerating of individuals who kill or injure criminals while protecting themselves continues to be an important theme both in criminal justice matters and in the entertainment media.

## URBAN CODE OF THE STREETS

A modern variation of the code of honor is thriving in urban areas that are scenes of frequent and widespread violence. This street code of honor has evolved largely as part of urban gang culture. It consists of a set of unwritten rules governing interpersonal behavior in public and provides for the use of violence when necessary. The code specifies both proper comportment and proper response when challenged. The rules of the code further attempt to regulate the use of violence by specifying the ways in which violence may be precipitated by those who wish to do so.[34]

Central to this urban code is the issue of being treated with proper respect. In this sense, the modern-day honor code closely resembles the code of honor of the Old South. The street code is a body of rules that purport to regulate public conduct. They prescribe when and how violence may be used. There are, however, some important differences.

The contemporary urban environment is far removed from the rural atmosphere of the South. Many modern city-dwellers have lost control of their environment and are uncertain about what treatment they should expect from others. As a consequence, some of them—particularly young males—become highly sensitive to advances and slights, thereby increasing the potential for violence. Respect is constantly in jeopardy. The presence of guns and drugs produces a situation of high volatility and great danger of violence and death.[35]

This late-twentieth-century version of the honor code results in part from the sense of alienation of many urban residents from mainstream society and its institutions. Several contemporary novels, including *Rule of the Bone* and *Clockers*, illustrate this type of honor code.

## *CLOCKERS*: WAR ON DRUGS

*Clockers* purports to tell the real story of the *war on drugs* as it is played out on the streets of a major New Jersey city. The story is narrated from the alternating points of view of Strike, a drug dealer with an ulcer and a conscience (a rare commodity on the streets), and Rocco Klein, an alcoholic yet basically decent homicide detective. The lives of the two characters intersect in the course of a homicide investigation of a young drug dealer's death. Strike is a middle-level player in a drug organization, charged with supervising the lowest-level dealers, called ''clockers.'' The world of the dealers, their customers, and the narcotics officers is sordid, corrupt, humiliating, and violent. The street trade in drugs is only mildly inconvenienced by the ineffective police efforts to contain it.

In addition to the aspects of violence, which will be discussed in Chapter 3, the elements of the urban honor code are starkly illustrated. The language of the drug and criminal world is adopted by police and drug dealers alike. For example, the terms ''clockers'' (street-level dealers who must operate rapidly in order to avoid arrest), ''muscle'' (bodyguard of a high-level dealer), and ''knockos'' (narcotics police) are in common usage. The street people give descriptive code names (like Duck, Thumper, and Big Chief) to the narcotics police officers and most of the officers adopt the names. Respect and disrespect—''dis'' for short—lie at the heart of much of the violence on the part of the drug people, and the police as well. On one occasion, for example, Thumper, a police officer, explains how the honor code works:

> You know, I'll tell you what the whole shouting match came down to. *Dis*. It was all about *dis*. The kid disrespected me by raising up in my face. I dissed him by throwing him up against the fence. . . . He dissed me by walking off. I dissed him by flicking his hat in front of his people. He dissed me by giving me a shove. The mother comes along, she disses me by snatching the keys. I dis her by making fun of her wheeze. Everything's *dis*. Because, you know, out there all you got to your name is your heart. You got a crowd around you, you got to show *heart*. Not just them but us too. . . . The whole thing's a trap. You got a crowd on you, you best got to act the part or you're *nothing*. It's unfortunate, but them's the rules. (*CL*, 368–369)

In another instance, Strike observes with some concern his boss, Rodney, a high-level dealer, *dis* the ''Delaware boys'' who amble into his store ''wearing their gold'':

> Carlton put his hand out to Rodney, who let it hang in the air for a few seconds, . . . finally shaking it after he'd gotten across who was on top.
>
> Strike saw Carlton stiffen over Rodney's little power play but then quickly recover, shrugging it off. . . . And as he walked off, . . . Strike thought about how swiftly this new guy had put Rodney's disrespect behind him. He tried to decide: should he feel impressed or worried? (*CL*, 549)

The complex rules of respect/disrespect constitute the governing code of the streets. They regulate and bring a kind of order to the daily transactions. In some ways, they are more important than the rules of law that purport to distinguish and control the legal and illegal activities. The meaning of *respect* in this context deserves mention because I will later refer to the value in our society of respect for the dignity of every individual. *Respect* in street terms refers to individual autonomy in the sense of power and assertion rather than individual autonomy in the sense of inherent human dignity and worth of individuals (which I advocate should be the core of our judicial and political processes). The intimidating and violent activities on the streets in furtherance of the code of respect are the very antithesis of respect for human dignity. The street code embodies values that are diametrically opposed to the values needed to maintain our judicial and political processes.

## *RULE OF THE BONE*

In this novel about adolescence and the contemporary drug culture, the protagonist, Chappie, takes on a new identity as ''Bone'' after he acquires a crossed bones tattoo. Once again, the street codes govern the various subcultures he enters. As the story begins, Chappie is a teenager living with his mother and abusive stepfather. He is already deeply embedded in petty crime and drug addiction. Essentially rejected by his mother, earlier abandoned by his natural father (a cocaine addict whom Bone later rejoins, then leaves, in Jamaica), and already a school dropout, Chappie seeks refuge in various crash pads and malls. At one point, while he is living with a group of drug-addicted and criminal bikers, there is a fire. He escapes, leaving the impression that he has been killed in the fire. His journey in general, and this episode in particular, bring to mind the story of Huck Finn, to be discussed in Chapter 6. Bone, in fact, like Huck, is a literalist, interpreting the chaotic reality around him in a simplistic, direct manner.

Bone believes that a change in outward appearance can produce internal changes in outlook and feelings. Once he has taken on his new identity, rejecting the child identity imposed on him by adults, he is reborn and empowered to direct his own life. He directs his own life disastrously, first taking up with violent bikers, then breaking into and senselessly trashing a vacation home. At that point, he declares that the Bone rules. Ultimately, he meets up with I-Man, an illegal alien from Jamaica, who guides him with his Rastafarian wisdom and gentle nature—not to mention his generous supply of marijuana, which I-Man (perhaps a contemporary version of Ellison's IM) consumes and sells. The language and rules of the drug culture prevail. The central rule of the adolescent drug culture is "don't bother your parents and don't bother the cops or one of them will sic the other on you" (*ROB*, 49).

This story about teenagers surviving on the fringes of society ends on a hopeful note, despite the bleakness of the world Banks portrays. Bone manages to free himself from the corrupt and violent people with whom he has connected, including his stepfather, the bikers, the Rastafarian drug gang, his "coke head" father, and a predatory pedophile. He concludes that he must rely on himself alone. No adults are worthy of trust or reliance, except the murdered I-Man, whose spirit we are led to believe will somehow continue to guide Bone.

## SUMMING UP

Action and reaction based on the requirements of street codes of conduct clearly are unsatisfactory and potentially destructive ways to vindicate breaches or personal wrongs. That type of confrontation is not capable of producing positive solutions to social or personal problems. The rights-based, confrontational litigation that appears to dominate American society also has deficiencies, although it is, of course, an approved method of resolving differences and vindicating wrongs. As an alternative to street action, reliance on the criminal justice system is the obvious alternative but, of course, the system must be effective and credible in order to maintain public confidence. The problems involved in meeting these standards are, in part, the subjects of later chapters on violence, authority, and change. It is noteworthy, in passing, that an obvious alternative in the civil law of our society to secure compensation for damage to reputation—*loss of respect*—lies in the law of defamation which involves the idea of reputation as property. [36] One problem with that field of law, however, is that the nature of reputation is mysterious and has "intricate and varied social foundations."[37] Although plaintiffs are sometimes successful, this type of litigation is a virtual minefield of problems and juries are not easily persuaded to award damages for injury to reputation.

The discussion thus far has focused on private codes that interfere with the operation of law. Conceivably, when not negating or subverting law or impeding individual growth, creativity, and freedom, codes could be neutral in effect, or even beneficial. The liberal code described by Robin West in Twain's *Pudd'nhead Wilson* is an example.[38] Religious or social community codes are not necessarily limiting. Although codes purport to be based on values of honor and respect, many codes actually serve the exercise of power. Society has to find other ways to preserve individual autonomy, apart from codes preserving power through violence. Codes can be beneficial only when promoting growth and freedom to make choices. While it may be a human need to bring order and reduce choices, this must be done without excluding and suppressing the individual autonomy necessary for freedom and growth.

Early in this chapter, I discussed several cases involving private codes that were in conflict with law. Those codes prescribed conduct that was required of members of various religious and criminal communities existing within American society. As I will emphasize later, the practice of individuals joining together in communities has always been, and still is, a vital part of our culture. Alexis de Toqueville was one of the earliest observers of this phenomenon when he wrote: ''In democratic countries knowledge of how to combine is the mother of all other forms of knowledge; on its progress depends that of all the others.''[39] Dean Aviam Soifer recently wrote, in his study of the different aspects of association in American law and culture: ''Various associations create and continue to anchor our deepest instincts. The law is impoverished when it seeks to marginalize the role of groups.''[40] Although the freedom to associate is protected by our federal Constitution, not all forms of association or community are beneficial to our society. The discussion of legal and literary texts in this chapter has focused on community codes that impede our democratic processes by isolating community members, excluding outsiders, and overriding the law. The structure, function, and inherent values of these negative community codes operate to impede and frustrate our judicial process as well as our political processes.

The subject of the next chapter is the cultural basis of another force that overrides the law in American society—violence. Violence, which continues to pervade American society, involves at its essence rituals of antisocial behavior which are, in part, manifestations of private codes. In particular, in addition to various honor codes, Americans tend to celebrate the code of redemption through violence.

Part II

# Systemic Problems: Violence, Authority, and the American Dream

Chapter 3

# The Roots of Violence: The Breakdown of Social Structure

> It was the best of times, it was the worst of times, it was the age of wisdom, it was the age of foolishness, it was the epoch of belief, . . . it was the season of Darkness, it was the spring of hope, it was the winter of despair, we had everything before us, we had nothing before us, we were all going direct to Heaven, we were all going direct the other way.[1]

> Violence . . . is distinguished by its instrumental character. . . . [I]t is close to strength, since the implements of violence, like all other tools, are designed and used for the purpose of multiplying natural strength until, in the last stage of their development, they can substitute for it.[2]

Crime is behavior that reflects the character, personality, and culture of a people.[3] Committing a crime signifies that a lesson of society was disregarded or a rebellious act performed. Both criminal actions and the responses to crime are generated by society. ''[T]he story of crime and punishment . . . is a story of social changes, character changes, personality changes; changes in culture; changes in the structure of society; and ultimately, changes in the economic, technological, and social orders.''[4]

American society today is deeply troubled by frequent and widespread episodes of violence that affect the daily lives of its citizens and drain the resources of the criminal justice system on both the state and federal levels. As violent crimes occupy the attention of the criminal justice system, other types of crimes go ignored and other types of litigation, such as family and civil controversies, fail to receive appropriate attention. While the problem of violence is deeply embedded in American history and culture and, repeatedly, has occupied our attention in the past, the anxiety and insecurity concerning the present levels of violence have a grip of almost unparalleled proportions on the American psyche.

The intense impact of violence in modern society is due, in part, to the nature of the violence, which is unquestionably different from prior types of violence. The contemporary violence that threatens the peace and security of Americans tends to be random and spontaneous, as contrasted with the more *structured* historical types that prevailed in the American West and the Old South, for example. The causes are undoubtedly different, as well. Present forms of violence probably result more from the *indifference* of community and society rather than from the absence of governmental structure, as in the West, or an established pattern of hierarchy, as in the South. Despite the differences in genre, however, certain recognizable patterns and common factors exist, linking past and present violence in American society. The very fact that violence of one sort or another has continuously played a central role in American life is a commentary on American society. The discussion that follows, which focuses on individual violence rather than any form of institutional violence, will illustrate common features of American violence.

The literary works that follow cover a great deal of historical territory. Some illustrate historically significant features of violence. *The Last of the Mohicans*,[5] for example, deals with the idea of regeneration through violence, a concept that still permeates some aspects of modern violence. *Night Rider* concerns itself with vigilantism. Following these traditional treatments of violence, I turn to contemporary novels that illustrate the modern, random violence. These include Richard Bausch's *Violence*, Don DeLillo's *Libra*, Craig Nova's *Trombone*, Joyce Carol Oates's *them*, and Richard Price's *Clockers*.

As the American people search for reasons and cures for the violence problem, in addition to pressing forward with necessary measures of crime control in order to guarantee the personal security and freedom of citizens, the inquiry should turn to possible causes inhering in the social, economic, cultural, and political elements of society. Probing questions arise: Why is there so much serious crime? Why are there so many violators—people who take other people's property, intrude in their homes, assault their bodies, and even take their lives? What is it about American society that breeds this epidemic of violent crime? Other questions relate to the consequences of violent crime. For example, to what extent does poverty cause crime or crime cause poverty?

## OUR ECLECTIC VIOLENCE

Violence has long been a pervasive element of American society. The nation has a history of violent behavior. Violence, of course, is not distinctively American. While many societies have considerably less violence, others are far more dominated by institutional or organized violence. America is still relatively free of governmental violence and terrorism, although recent dramatic events remind us that we are not immune. Historian Richard Hofstadter contends that America does not have a tradition of violence. He explains the distinction between having a *history* or a *tradition* of violence. In his view, the distinction is that, while violence has occurred frequently, voluminously, and commonly throughout American history, violence in America has had neither an ideological nor a geographical center. The violence has not been uniform or cohesive. "[I]t has been too various, diffuse, and spontaneous to be forged into a single, sustained, inveterate hatred shared by entire social classes."[6] Although some American violence occasionally has appeared in the form of "organized crime" or group activity like that of the Ku Klux Klan, criminal violence, for the most part, has not had an institutional or ideological nature. In that sense, it has been "unorganized"—a kind of *eclectic* violence. The patterns of American violence, however, are sufficiently clear and distinct to warrant describing American violence as a historical feature of American culture.[7]

My focus here is solely on *domestic* or *internal* violence—violence occurring within the country involving, for the most part, individuals, and, to some extent, groups or communities—as opposed to *external* violence involving, for example, military action against another country or its citizens. Two general types of violence are involved—*crime-related* and *situational*. Crime-related violence is violence linked to the commission of crimes such as burglary, assault, and robbery. Violence in that context escalates the degree of the crime. Situational violence consists of violence occurring in the course of ordinary events where people are in conflict. Examples of this type of violence can be seen in family affairs, gang disputes, and other human relationships. Although situational acts of violence may also constitute crimes, that violence does not originate in the course of committing a specific crime but arises coincidentally in the course of a confrontation.

It is important to differentiate between crime-related and situational violence in order to appreciate the full impact of the current problem. Violence in America is not limited to crimes and to people whom we commonly think of as "criminals." Violent behavior stains the entire fabric of American life. Many more everyday confrontations now involve violence. The current perception of most Americans is that the level of violence has increased in both respects in recent years.

Moreover, "we have a remarkable lack of memory where violence is concerned and have left most of our excesses a part of our buried history."[8] In addition to the inclination of Americans to display a certain amnesia concerning the violence at home, historians have had a difficult time coping with the subject of American violence. This may be because it has so often involved isolated individuals, small groups, large mobs, and a variety of purposes—or none at all.

Although studies of the violence problem have been undertaken periodically in the history of the nation, the scope and complexity of the problem have eluded meaningful definition and explanation. The difficulty, in part, lies in the fact that the nature and dimension of the violence problem undergoes constant change in every important respect, including cause, incidence, and manifestation.

## IDENTIFYING THE COMPONENTS

The objectives of this chapter are: first, to identify four major components of American violence; second, to explain the substance of the two cultural factors; and, finally, to examine literary works that assist in illuminating those factors both in their historical context and in the context of the modern type of random violence. In using the term "culture," I refer to the entire way of life—material, intellectual, and spiritual—of American society.

A complex cluster of factors peculiar to American society has produced intermittent violence throughout our history. Clearly, more than one way exists of identifying the factors involved. Parviz Saney, for example, in writing of the cultural causes of crime in the United States, obviously a closely related problem, focuses on three major cultural conditions: the presence of deviance-inducing values, a continuing crisis of legitimacy of law, and a diminishing of control-reducing values.[9]

Of the four contributing factors that can be readily identified, two can best be classified as sociological or technological and two can be termed cultural. The two sociological factors are the decreasing *stake in conformity* to society's laws and standards, and the *explosive change* that has characterized the development of the nation. The two cultural factors are the level of *cultural inhibition* (sometimes expressed instead as the level of *cultural approval*) and the *ideological resistance to change*. Although these factors can be located to some extent in all the historical forms of violence, they have special significance in analyzing modern forms of violence.

### Stake in Conformity

Stake in conformity, the first of the noncultural factors, involves the extent to which people in a society feel connected to the society so that they voluntarily conform to its laws and cultural norms. Some observers believe that the level of stake in conformity on the part of many Americans is declining because of the perceived loss of social, economic, and political opportunity available. This factor may be linked to the declining influence of mediating institutions—family, church, and neighborhood—on individuals. As the influence of those mediating institutions decreases, and as technological changes occur in the information/entertainment media network, individuals increasingly avoid interpersonal contacts. As a result, they tend to become more isolated and separated from the community and society.

### Explosive Change

Explosive technological, economic, and social changes have played a major role in disrupting family and community ties. The explosive change factor emerges from the economic and social system in addition to the advances in technology that have characterized the development of the United States virtually from the beginning. This factor is related to the idea of discontinuity in tradition and history that appeared in the writings of Emerson and others. Together, these aspects of change have created a situation conducive to violence by corroding cooperative values. Some government social and economic policy, in welfare programs, for example, may well have contributed to conditions that lead to significant increases in violence.[10]

Movement toward a national policy of federal centralization or decentralization seems to fluctuate periodically but always within a tight framework. While it may not be easy to envision dramatic change in the fundamental parameters of American political culture, there is ample room for rethinking and reshaping policies and priorities. As the society has changed from within, so the manner of governing and directing the future course of society can change. Because social, economic, and technological changes can be expected to continue transforming the American scene, federal and state government policy can work in combination with market forces to shape and direct the force of those changes.

## Cultural Approval and Ideological Resistance

The two cultural factors that provide a foundation for the high level of violence in the United States are cultural approval of violence and ideological resistance to violence control. Both of these factors encompass a multitude of ideas. They are also interrelated: cultural approval operates to encourage or permit violence to be part of American life, while ideological resistance operates to obstruct measures designed to prevent violence from occurring.

These two factors stand in close relation with the law-related concepts that were the focus of the preceding two chapters: individualism and private codes. The use of violence, realistically and symbolically, suggests the existence of a private *code of violence* that prescribes the parameters and conditions under which violent means may be used by private individuals in contravention of the law.

### *Cultural Approval*

Three aspects of violence are present in American society. These are: (1) the actual occurrence of violence; (2) the symbolic representation of violence; and (3) the political use or exploitation of that symbolic representation.[11] Although the distinctions separating these three aspects are often blurred, each is important in its own right. As to the first aspect, enough actual violence has occurred in the course of American history to warrant the widely held belief that America has been a distinctly violent country. It may be slightly reassuring, however, to recognize that most of the American forms of violence have also occurred widely in numerous other countries, as well, and that, for the most part, ‘‘[t]he mass genocides of modern times belong not to the history of the Americas, but to Europe, Asia, and Africa.''[12]

Turning to the second two factors, ''[w]hat is distinctively American is not necessarily the amount or kind of violence that characterizes our history but the mythic significance we have assigned to the kinds of violence we have actually experienced, the forms of symbolic violence we imagine or invent, and the political uses to which we put that symbolism.''[13] The processes of translating the violence into symbolism or myth and implementing that symbolism for political or other purposes produce the cultural approval of violence.

The incidence of violence in American society is well-documented. Realistically speaking, violence has been present at virtually every stage of our history. The nation was born in violence. The violence occurring in the course of the Revolution, which became enshrined in our tradition and history, was justified by the ''operational philosophy that the end justifies the means.''[14] The example of the violence employed in resisting the Crown served as a ''grand model for later . . . actions by Americans in behalf of any cause . . . deemed good and proper. . . . [I]t has been the instrument not merely of the criminal and disorderly but of the most upright and honorable.''[15]

Violence was employed in saving the nation during the era of the Civil War and the Reconstruction period. The violence which accompanied the remainder of the nineteenth century may have been, in many ways, a product of the Civil War itself. The Ku Klux Klan, lynch mobs and other vigilantes, night riders, and feuding families were among the purveyors of violence tracing their origins to events surrounding the Civil War. Many of these practices served as means of enforcing the slave code and its postwar form, the racial code.

In addition to the institution of slavery, another tradition of the Old South, the code of personal honor, contributed to the level of violence. Violence was a characteristic aspect of Southern life. Violence was central to maintaining personal honor; men were expected to be willing to risk their lives in duels. As noted, the confrontations that result from the codes of the streets prevailing in urban areas today resemble the earlier dueling practices. With the abandonment of dueling, an activity that involved many political figures, political assassination became an instrument of violent change after the Civil War. It is well-known that security concerns arising because of assassinations and attempted assassinations in the second half of this century have had a great impact on our political life. The specter of assassination has dramatically transformed the security measures taken by public figures and, as a result, their personal accessibility to the public.

The tradition of vigilantism, including lynch mobs, was not confined to the South. It also played an active role in the development of the American West where it developed as part of the ''frontier culture.'' That culture has survived myriad reincarnations during the course of American history; it has been present in Theodore Roosevelt's expansionist policies, John F. Kennedy's ''New Frontier'' vision, the various Vietnam strategies, and in some of the political rationale for the Gulf War.[16]

To this litany of violent patterns running through the history of the nation can be added urban riots representing group violence exhibited for social, economic, or political reasons. Another example is police misconduct, a form of violence that seriously undermines public confidence in the criminal justice system. That misconduct is often celebrated for its entertainment value. The entertainment industry is replete with fictitious folk heroes who use excessive violence to subdue criminals. This phenomenon occurs despite, or perhaps because of, the public anxiety about criminal violence. Americans, in fact, have typically displayed ambivalence toward crime. Official condemnation of criminals has been accompanied by fascination with, and even admiration of, criminals. Even the large-scale and powerful organized crime networks continue to fascinate the public. All forms of criminal activity seem to provide rich material for audiences of the entertainment media.

At various times during our history (especially the present) we have been anxious, and anguished, about violence. For example, we commissioned a national study after the wave of political assassinations occurring in the 1960s. Although our entertainment and even serious writing is suffused with violence, we are unusual in our ability to persuade ourselves how well-behaved we are, perhaps because we do not have the record of wholesale violence committed by some of the totalitarian states. ''What is impressive . . . is its extraordinary frequency, its sheer commonplaceness in our history, its persistence into very recent and contemporary times, and its rather abrupt contrast with our pretensions to singular national virtue. What must also be observed about . . . [American violence], however, is the circumscribed character and the small scale of the typical violent incident.''[17]

Violence has not only accompanied negative aspects of our history, such as criminal activity, political assassination, and racial conflict, but has also played a central role in the most positive developments. Examples of the latter are the gaining of independence, freeing the slaves and preserving the union, and occupying and stabilizing the West. While Americans may not acknowledge violence as part of our value system, violence is a conspicuous feature of our national identity.

### *Ideological Resistance*

Hofstadter theorizes that elements of the ethnic, religious, and racial mixture are fundamental determinants of American violence. These are exacerbated by other national circumstances, including weak government, localism, diffusion of authority and power, rapid urban growth, migrations, and rapid social change. Hofstadter also points to the development, in the nineteenth century, of a type of socially unchecked industrial baron, lording it over a distant and heterogeneous *alien* working force with which he felt no ethnic, institutional, social or religious ties. He also notes the continuing unwillingness of urban Americans to give up their gun culture.[18]

Hofstadter's analysis has touched upon a vital part of the ideological factor, that is, the reference to limited government, localism, and diffusion of authority and power. To these factors we must add the commitment to individual rights and self-determination. These factors influence and control both the resistance to crime-related and situational violence, on one hand, and the motivation to provide solutions for the causes of violence, on the other.

In addition to these factors, the lack of significant vertical authority in the political structure has led to frustration and disappointment at the results of experiments aimed at containing violence and solving other social problems. Short-range goals demanding immediate gratification are characteristic of a political process where success is measured principally by securing reelection. That aspect of the process sometimes leads to reliance on *band-aid* approaches to deep-seated problems, and results in inadequate and incomplete experimentation with programs and policies. Policies are often summarily abandoned in favor of new programs and policies that, in turn, receive the very same treatment. The ideological resistance factor operates to impede or prevent remedial action with respect to the existing violence. Before change can occur in this sphere, a change in attitude toward the ideological postures in this society would be required.

Examination of American literature reveals rich illustration of the factors involved in American violence, in its present form as well as its historical forms. Several of the texts discussed in earlier chapters deal directly with the problem. For example, violence plays a major role in Ellison's *Invisible Man*, and Faulkner's ''An Odor of Verbena.'' Beyond these literary texts, cultural approval of violence features prominently in other major works of American literature.

The discussion will focus on two manifestations of the idea. The first involves two aspects of the idea of *regeneration through violence* as illustrated in James Fenimore Cooper's *The Last of the Mohicans*.[19] The second manifestation is the idea of vigilante justice, derived from the frontier myth and the myth of virility, as it appears in Robert Penn Warren's novel *Night Rider*.[20] Owen Wister's novel *The Virginian* provides an additional illustration of that concept. The regeneration theme and the vigilante theme have elements in common with the dueling theme illustrated in ''An Odor of Verbena.'' These common elements include the idea of honor or self-respect in the eyes of the community, the concept of manliness or virility—concepts closely related to and dependent upon a brand of physical courage in the face of danger—and the use of violence as a means of securing the object of the quest. Elements of these themes continue on into the present-day forms of violence. The discussion will also embrace the current novels, referred to earlier, that deal more directly with aspects of the modern random violence that plagues today's society.

## *THE LAST OF THE MOHICANS:* THE WESTERN FRONTIER

*The Last of the Mohicans* is the second title published in a series of five novels entitled collectively the ''Leatherstocking Tales.'' After the success of *The Pioneers*, in which Natty Bumppo was in his seventies, Cooper moved back in time to Natty's early thirties in *The Last of the Mohicans*, in which Natty is called ''Hawkeye.'' The story recounts the classic American frontier myth embodying the idea of regeneration through violence. The narrative events take place against the backdrop of the wilderness/civilization, Indian/White border. The white American crosses beyond the wilderness into the Indian territory and regresses into a more primitive and natural state. He leaves behind the false values of the civilized world, and opens up the promise of a new and superior social contract.

Although the Indians and the wilderness are enemies of the frontier people, they also provide the means of purification and regeneration. According to Professor Slotkin, the heroes of this quest must know Indians as well as civilization. They exist on both sides of the frontier. Because

> the border between savagery and civilization runs through their moral center, the Indian wars are, for these heroes, a spiritual or psychological struggle which they win by learning to discipline or suppress the savage or ''dark'' side of their own human nature. Thus they are mediators of a double kind who can teach civilized men how to defeat savagery on its native grounds—the natural wilderness, and the wilderness of the human soul.[21]

Using violence to subdue the darker manifestations of human nature, the individuals and their society undergo a process of regeneration.

According to Slotkin, the frontier myth developed in two parts against that moral landscape. The first was the ''captivity narrative,'' modeled on a popular personal account written in 1682. The hero of that narrative is a white woman or minister who is captured by Indians in the course of a ''savage war.'' The victim represents values of Christianity and civilization that are imperiled in the frontier struggle. The victim's captivity is akin to entry into a ''spiritual darkness.'' By resisting the physical danger and spiritual temptation presented by the ''savages,'' the victim exemplifies a triumph of both moral character and civilized values.[22]

The second part of the traditional narrative developed somewhat later. In this phase, modeled after the exploits of Daniel Boone, the redemption through suffering of the first phase is changed into redemption through violence as the hunter/warrior subdues the Indians and rescues the victim. The hero generally knows and thinks like the Indians, is capable of violence, and turns their own methods against them. In its most extreme form, the hero is as savage as those he is trying to defeat. He becomes committed to destroying all his enemies.

Slotkin suggests that this mythology has been used in military operations in the course of our history.

Carrying out this general theme, in *The Last of the Mohicans*, two young women, traveling in the New York Colony wilderness in 1757, are captured by a group of Hurons as a result of the treachery of a Huron guide. Hawkeye and his two Delaware tribe friends, who fall in with the party, defeat the Hurons and rescue the women. Later in the story, after a series of adventures, including the capture and release of Hawkeye by the French soldiers, and a massacre of women and children by the Iroquois, the two women are recaptured by the Hurons. Once again, Hawkeye conducts a rescue and saves them through his cleverness and power. One of the women and the noble Uncas, the last of the Mohicans, are killed in the course of events.

An aside to the topic of Cooper's rendition of the frontier myth is Theodore Roosevelt's interest in *Deerslayer*, one of the other stories in the Leatherstocking series. Roosevelt believed hunting operates "as preparation for the higher function of the warrior."[23] This discussion is related to the subject of the hunt as a rebirth or regeneration through violence.[24]

## VIGILANTE JUSTICE

Another important variation of cultural approval of violence in the American tradition is the concept of vigilante justice, derived from the myths of the frontier and the myth of virility. This idea and these myths are also related to the regeneration-through-violence concept and the extralegal tradition which remains a part of the American scene today. The threat of crime and violence, no longer confined to urban areas, has caused a resurgence of the idea of defending the security of person and property.

In the mid-1980s, the case of Bernard Goetz attracted a great deal of attention as an example of a victim striking back at violence.[25] The Goetz case touched on several themes including public justice, rights of victims, police authority, and race relations. Goetz was a passenger on a New York subway when he was approached by a group of youths. One of the group asked Goetz for $5. Goetz felt intimidated and believed that he was going to be attacked. Instead of handing over the money or attempting to retreat, he pulled a pistol from inside his jacket and shot at each of them. Prior to the subway incident, Goetz had been robbed in the city. In a confession given in New Hampshire where he surrendered to the police after eluding arrest for nine days, he told police that he was afraid he was going to be beaten and he wanted to kill his assailants and make them suffer.[26] Goetz was convicted of a weapons charge but was acquitted of attempted murder and assault charges. The case was highly controversial and polarized public opinion concerning his motivations and actions.[27]

Another instance of highly controversial retaliatory action by a victim was the killing in California of Latasha Harlins, a sixteen-year-old African-American girl, by Soon Ja Du, a Korean merchant, who believed Harlins intended to shoplift a bottle of orange juice.[28] Soon Ja Du and her husband owned and operated a liquor store in 1991. They had been threatened previously by gang members and had experienced a great deal of shoplifting activity in their store. Harlins entered the store, placed a bottle of orange juice in her backpack and approached the counter with $2 or $3 in her hand. Based on her past experience with the patterns of shoplifting behavior, Soon Ja Du assumed that Harlins was shoplifting despite the visibility of the bottle and Harlins's protests. A sharp verbal exchange was followed by a scuffle between the two. Harlins placed the juice on the counter and turned toward the door. Soon Ja Du shot Harlins in the back of the head, killing her instantly. Soon Ja Du was arrested and tried for voluntary manslaughter. She was convicted and sentenced to ten years in state prison, with the sentence suspended and the defendant placed on probation. The state's petition for a writ of mandate claiming review of the probation order was denied by the appeals court.[29] Besides being a contemporary example of vigilantism, this incident was one more in a series of violent exchanges between African Americans and Korean Americans.[30]

Turning to the literary treatment of vigilantism, Wister's *The Virginian*, discussed in Chapter 2, provides a notable example of that concept, as does Warren's *Night Rider*. In Wister's novel, two aspects of cultural approval of violence are illustrated. First, violence may be used to produce "popular justice" when the legal system fails regularly. Second, violence may be used in meeting the standards of the male code of honor.

## *NIGHT RIDER*: ASSOCIATION IN VIOLENCE

Robert Penn Warren's novel *Night Rider* provides a striking example of the interaction of extralegal violence with the law. The novel was, in Warren's words, "suggested" by historical events that occurred in Kentucky in the early years of the twentieth century (*NR*, Preface). Like *The Virginian* and Frank Norris's, *The Octopus*, the narrative concerns a struggle outside the law between groups of men representing competing economic interests, in this case, tobacco growers and the powerful tobacco companies that controlled prices paid for tobacco crops. The story revolves around the life of Percy Munn, a lawyer trained in the East, whose sympathy for the tobacco farmers' position grows in the course of the events. The farmers feel oppressed because the large tobacco companies have divided up the territory and, without competition, have the power to offer unreasonably low prices for the crops.

A group of men organizes an association for the purpose of acquiring bargaining strength, but they discover that they need to coerce reluctant farmers to join in order to acquire enough strength to affect the negotiations. Munn, who is in Bardsville to undertake the criminal defense in a murder case, is drawn into the association activities and rises in prominence after he delivers an impassioned speech.

Munn soon becomes deeply involved in the extralegal vigilante activities of the night riders, the enforcing arm of the association. The activities of the night riders escalate into personal violence as well as destruction of the crops of noncooperating farmers. In order to join the night riders, Munn is required to take a solemn oath of loyalty to the association. He swears that he will be loyal to the Free Farmers' Brotherhood of Protection and Control and that he will support whatever measures may be deemed advisable. He agrees to a code of silence which prohibits speaking to anyone including his wife.

The violence breeds more and more violence of all types. The crowds become mobs when the shaky courage of the individual men is bolstered by the anonymity of the group and the encouragement of their peers. Warren offers an explanation of the dynamics of mob violence: "They say a ship can burn for days and not much harm done until somebody opens a hatch and the air strikes. A leader is like that, he just opens a hatch. . . . [T]here is no telling what a chance word of random violence or exaggerated feeling might start" (*NR,* 111–112).

Munn resists and even thwarts some of the personal violence. As he becomes more deeply mired in the enterprise, however, he begins to accept the violence and even commits personal violence himself. He is involved in the killing of Trevelyan, the very man whose life he saved when he defended him from the murder charge. The tobacco companies and local law enforcement agencies finally manage to secure the assistance of military forces which arrive to restore order. The racist-motivated burnings of properties, including Munn's own home, continue, however.

When Munn receives a threatening note, he learns what it is like to be victimized by unknown assassins. One of the other night riders shot and killed a prosecution witness from Munn's law office window and Munn is accused of murder. When Munn learns that he is about to be arrested, he flees. In hiding, he reflects on the events that changed the course of his life, that transformed him from lawyer, under oath to uphold the law, to lawbreaker, under oath to employ whatever expedient means are required to secure the elusive *justice* sought by the tobacco farmers.

Munn's final destruction comes about as the result of an ironic twist of fate. The nighttime conversation in his room between Munn and Lucille Christian, a woman with whom he had an affair, was detected by Sylvestus, an inhabitant of the ranch where Munn is hiding out. The presence of an unmarried woman in the room of an unmarried man apparently was a serious violation of the social code of honor. Sylvestus not only informs the owner of the ranch, but also, Munn realizes, informs the law enforcement authorities. The factor that moves Sylvestus to betray him was not the outstanding murder charge or the violence, but his breach of the code of honor which imposed special restrictions on female behavior. Munn leaves the home of the Senator a ruined man, having failed to carry out his mission of killing the Senator. He fails because he looks at the Senator face-to-face. He tries to escape the lawmen but is shot and killed by the posse which has come for him.

Many elements of violence appear in this novel. As in *The Virginian* and *The Octopus*, an inequitable situation existed which the tobacco growers believed could not be solved through legal means. While there is no suggestion that the law officials were corrupt or biased, the tobacco farmers lacked confidence that law had the means or power to solve their problem. In their perception, they could not turn to law to remedy the injustice which they suffered. They depended upon their bargaining strength and, to maximize it, they believed they had to coerce recalcitrant farmers to join. Given the chemistry of the situation, violence was sure to erupt.

The matter of honor was involved, in addition. A type of honor code governing male behavior in this *frontier* environment—where the legal authority clearly was weak—prevailed. The oath, secrecy, pride, arbitrary rules, insistence on paramilitary organizational authority, and the ritualistic initiation procedure were factors reflecting the honor code. The men believed that not only natural rights theory, but also religious morality, justified and reinforced their endeavor. Absolute loyalty to the association and the vow of silence were self-protective measures—of a delusional nature. Insulating the enterprise from outside knowledge, to insure secrecy, prevents confrontation, exposure, reasoned evaluation, and assessment of the activities.

As in *The Virginian*, the men purported to *take back* the authority and rights previously given to the government. They saw the desperate situation as justifying the use of extralegal means. The counterviolence initiated by the racists shows the similarity of both types of vigilante violence. The ignorant, inarticulate threats and promises of violence arose out of the same source, the illusion of honor and natural rights.

In the end, the violence accomplished nothing but to relieve the sense of helplessness of the men. Those who participated were tainted and, for the most part, destroyed by the device they created. Initially, the men justified the violence as a necessary coercive measure to build the strength of the association. The violence became retributional when it was used to punish individuals who refused to join. It ultimately spiraled out of control, spawning more and more violence. The lawmen and the soldiers used their own brand of violence. Munn ultimately received his punishment, but not by process of law. The lawyer turned lawless was killed *outside the law* in the fields, trying to escape, the victim of vigilante justice similar to his own vigilante justice. The novel produces insights into the way violence can erupt when a catalyst is introduced into its chemistry.

The vigilante violence of the night riders clearly had cultural approval, although law enforcement officials ultimately moved in to eliminate it. That action, however, probably was more a response to the economic power of the tobacco buyers and the particular threat to the security of the communities than it was a disapproval of violence. The violence arose out of a situation where there was a gross economic imbalance in bargaining positions. This may be seen as a potential cause of violence, when one group is pressed to the limit and believes that it cannot prevent disaster by nonviolent means. The group then has a diminished stake in conforming to the rule of law. Additionally, *Night Rider* reveals the absence of ideological resistance to the culturally approved violence. The existence of a weak government and law enforcement structure, combined with strong support for a type of frontier individualism, plus adherence to the male code of honor, all contributed to the inability of the community to avoid the extralegal use of violence.

Vigilante activity has continued to receive significant approval in our culture to this day. Strong public sentiment often supports the right of ordinary citizens to resist street crimes, as well as intrusions into private property, by using force. The issue of self-help arises frequently in the context of family violence crimes, where women who are victims of abuse kill abusive spouses. Issues including whether traditional self-defense law should be applied to those situations or whether new or expanded definitions of important terms like *imminent danger* should be applied under the special circumstances are currently under discussion.[31]

## CONTEMPORARY LITERARY PERSPECTIVES

Countless literary works illustrate the varieties of violence present in modern American life. I have selected five novels that demonstrate aspects of the random violence that threatens the peace and security of virtually all Americans. These literary examples do not purport to illustrate all forms of contemporary violence. Rather, they typify the qualities of such violence.

## *LIBRA*: ASSASSINATION REVISITED

It may be said that the assassination of John F. Kennedy on November 22, 1963 was a violent act that shook the whole of society and had a serious and lasting impact on the American psyche. The event was one of the dramatic events of the 1960s that triggered a significant increase in disillusionment pervading American society. The story has been told and examined countless times since that November day. Delillo's fictional account[32] which puts a credible conspiratorial gloss on the incident brings to light the darkest aspects of the American character.

DeLillo has constructed in his work of historical fiction a theory that the assassination came about as the result of a conspiracy involving two CIA operatives, an organization of Cuban exiles disgruntled by Kennedy's failure to give full support to the Bay of Pigs invasion, together with an assorted group of fringe individuals including Oswald. The original plot envisioned a deliberately unsuccessful attempt on Kennedy's life, carefully designed to be attributable to Castro. The reaction was expected to bring about military action to retake Cuba. Oswald was selected as the ideal assassin because of his military and political background. At some point, the plan was converted to carrying out a real attempt on the president's life.

The conspirators are presented as individuals fully committed to using violence as a political instrument. Oswald is carefully drawn as the mentally unbalanced, violent, politically confused individual that he was. He reportedly carried out the unsuccessful attempt on General Edwin Walker's life not long before the assassination. The story leaves few people unblemished, including the various government agencies charged with protecting the president.

Violence is portrayed in various ways in this historically based narrative. Violence is viewed, for example, as a legitimate instrument of political action. It stands as a force that draws together the wide assortment of individuals who perceive the government as an enemy with secrets that give it power over the American people. The government, itself, is seen as a vast, conspiratorial enterprise that must be dealt with on the same basis. The scene of the ultimate crime, Dallas, is portrayed as a city brimming with hatred and potential violence. The repercussions of the violent act in Dallas continue to be felt despite the decades that have elapsed. The assassination had direct impact on events in Oates's *them*, another novel focusing on the emptiness and violence of some American lives.

## *them*: AN EVERYDAY MATTER

The possibility of assassinating another president, Lyndon Johnson, arises in this narrative about Detroit life in the 1960s.[33] The discussion takes place during the course of the Detroit race riot of 1967, a historical event which is fictionalized in the story.[34] The riot is not central to the novel except insofar as it represents the misery and rage of some inhabitants of the city. It is significant mainly because it provides the context in which a major character, Jules Wendall, is provoked to an extreme act of violence.

*them* focuses mainly on the lives of the Wendalls, a family whose lives are pervaded by violence and guided by the struggle to survive. The novel opens with the murder of Loretta Wendall's lover Bernie, by her brother Brock. Loretta's discovery of the body beside her in bed is followed quickly by her rape by the investigating policeman, Howard Wendall, whom she ultimately marries. Loretta proves to be a survivor but her life is filled with hardships, including her father's insanity and institutionalization, and Howard's death which occurs when he is crushed to death at work. Her children Maureen and Jules have difficult lives. Maureen becomes a prostitute and suffers severe beatings at the hands of her stepfather. Jules, who murders a policeman during the riot, is shot earlier in the story by his former wife. After her marriage to Howard, Loretta longs for change to be over and life to be stable; that longing is an impossibility, of course, and never comes close to fulfillment.

*them* is a novel about the violence of everyday life. There is an unquestioning acceptance of violence by the characters in the story. Early in Jules's life, he is caught smoking cigarettes by a Sister at his school. She strikes him several times and tells him that a certain number of boys will die in the electric chair.

She suggests that the Devil in him is planning that he will be one of them. According to Jules, ''Violence can't be singled out from an ordinary day! . . . Everyone must live through it again and again, there's no end to it, no land to get to, no clearing in the midst of the cities'' (*them*, 503).

The ''them'' of the story are those people who are trapped within the contingencies of their lives, those who can't escape the emptiness, loneliness, and futility. Jules is not one of them; he escapes the consequences of the events, even the commission of murder. He has a sense of his own autonomy and departs for California. His sister Maureen cannot escape, however, except into mental illness for a time. She questions: ''How can I live my life if the world is like this?'' (*them*, 330). She wonders what lasts and what doesn't and concludes that neither love, nor marriage, nor money lasts.

Presented by the author as historical fiction, *them* is a complex study of the causes and effects of violence in everyday lives. A tension exists among many factors including love, materialism, power, spirituality, and violence. The events suggest that violence results from the struggle to exercise will or power—instead of love—in human relationships. Rollo May has identified three components of violence.[35] They include a need for meaning and significance, a desire for ecstasy or fascination, and an impulse to risk all. Violence, he said, results from powerlessness and is used to overcome impotence. Violence is an instrument of power by virtue of the fact that it can augment or multiply strength. Violence, however, can also destroy power because it quickly exceeds its immediate provocation. Gains produced by violent means are not permanent because they do not change the underlying condition in any lasting way.[36]

Jacob Bronowski produced interesting observations about violence in *The Face of Violence: An Essay with a Play*, where he related that ''at the heart of our violence . . . lies our wish to show ourselves men of will. Since society is an instrument for controlling our chaotic wills, the gesture of violence we make is anti-social; we invent a symbol for the forces of society, obscure and impersonal, which shall be our scapegoat. . . . We fear that society disregards us. In the wilderness of the cities, we look for respect.''[37]

Violence in the wilderness of the cities occurs in several other recent novels, as well, including *Trombone*[38] by Craig Nova, which will be discussed shortly. The relationship of respect to violence brings to mind the emphasis on respect in *Clockers*, discussed in the preceding chapter. The events of that novel are pervaded by violence of a different sort than the violence of *them*.

## *CLOCKERS*: STREET SCENES

The street violence that characterizes the action in this realistic novel about life in the drug world of our cities often appears random and senseless. This novel illustrates the urban condition that has driven law-abiding citizens from the cities. All the violence is related to the drug trade so, in that sense, it is purposeful. When the violence spills over and destroys the lives of outsiders to the drug scene, however, it takes on a random and senseless aspect. The violence is necessary because the drug trade relies for its continued existence on intimidation, exploitation, and corruption. The events of this novel, encompassing the street sales to cocaine users, the organizational machinations of the drug merchants, wholesale and retail, and the corrupt activities of the drug warriors—the police—all reflect a sordid, hopeless, utterly degraded environment. Violence, danger, and humiliation lie in wait for all participants of whatever strata. Murder, beatings, and AIDS—"the Virus" (*CL*, 226)—stalk everyone. Truth and conscience have no role on the streets. The urban environment represents decay and despair.

The brutal reality presented in this fictional account shows law and law enforcers to be essentially ineffective and virtually irrelevant to the criminal activities. All the characters, whatever their identities, are merely players in a drama that points to a final act that involves money, drugs, and death. A few characters have redeeming qualities and some hope exists at the end that escape is possible. Whether they can escape the trap of the city, however, remains questionable.

## *TROMBONE*: THE EDUCATED ARSONIST

The violence portrayed in this novel about the lives of two arsonists in Bakersfield, California, a small town in the Greater Los Angeles area, accompanies the arson for profit of a father/son team. The damage that results from their activities has multiple aspects, similar to the violence portrayed in *them*. Violence is a part of their everyday lives and, to an extent, provides a release from the routine of their existence. Ray Gollancz, the protagonist, wants life to be ordinary. In fact, he pursues his education dream and, for a time, attends college in the East before being drawn back into the criminal world of his father. His father, Dean, is a printer by trade and a part-time arsonist for profit. He does occasional fires for an organized criminal type, Mr. Mei, who operates out of Los Angeles. Dean takes great pride in his "night job," stating: "It's a way of getting free for a minute" (*TRM*, 117). Ray concludes that arson is an antidote to "a claustrophobia that came from the lack of possibilities and the certainty of being trapped" (*TRM*, 144).

Dean draws Ray into his enterprise and Ray readily goes along with the activity. He also tries to protect his father from self-destruction and from destruction at the hands of the husband of the married woman with whom Dean is carrying on one of his many affairs. The story of their pathetic lives is set against a crimson backdrop, first, of the glow of the atomic bomb tests in Yucca Flats, which father and son previously watched together; and, second, of the many fires in empty buildings which they have set.

Dean's arson activities are brought to a close by his arrest. In the end, however, his ultimate punishment occurs at the hand of the jealous husband. Ray, however, escapes disaster as well as legal responsibility for his numerous crimes.

He tracks down Iris, with whom he is obsessed and, by an act of grace on the part of his organized crime boss, he is allowed to depart the state to begin again. The reader is led to believe that the new territory for Ray and Iris will be found by heading east. The law is presented as basically ineffectual and irrelevant to the lives of the characters. Their lives appear barren and futile and lacking in spiritual dimension. The novel portrays contemporary life as essentially lacking in meaning, corrupt, and dangerous. Ray has a decent side and occasionally follows his conscience. At one point, he connects with Milton Schlage, an individual who represents uncontrolled, senseless violence. Ray saves a hitchhiking girl from Schlage's violent nature and prevents Schlage from conducting what would probably have been a violent convenience store robbery.

## *VIOLENCE*: PURE FICTION?

*Violence*[39] concerns the modern brand of random, senseless violence. The protagonist, Charles Connally, a late-night customer in a convenience store, is unable to prevent a robbery from occurring. He manages, however, to take action which others interpret as heroic. In the course of the robbery, three victims plus one of the robbers are killed. The trauma of the incident changes the course of his life, along with that of his pregnant wife. Although their relationship was strained prior to the incident, their lives were relatively normal. After the incident, Connally is fearful about his own potential for violence. Finally, he is able to uncover the reason, his childhood abuse by his own father. The novel effectively portrays the potential impact of the modern random violence which threatens our lives in American society today.

## VIOLENCE IN OUR LIVES

The problem of violence in American society, illustrated in part in the novels discussed above, produces a multitude of unresolved legal issues that are the subject of continued debate. This is so even apart from the criminal law and constitutional criminal procedural issues that they obviously involve. Most of these problems have generated legislative action. While that is a highly appropriate societal response, statutory law is not within the purview of this book, which focuses on judge-made law.

One category of issues generated by the problem of violence in American society involves *threshold* problems. They include how to treat violence within the family and violence occurring in the course of civil disturbances, problems of perceived violence versus actual violence, statistical problems in measuring violent crimes (and crimes in general), and violence in the civil disturbance context. Underlying all these problems lies the fundamental gap between perception and reality. One or two highly publicized incidents can have great impact on the perception of violence. [40] Another issue concerns *solutions* which raise a variety of problems, including First Amendment issues, in efforts to control portrayed violence in the information/entertainment media.

## THRESHOLD ISSUES

A major definitional issue is the extent to which particular types of violence should be prosecuted in the criminal justice system. The following discussion addresses several aspects of this issue.

### Family Violence

Violence within the family, while being a deeply rooted problem in American society, has received appropriate attention from the criminal justice system only within the past decade or so.[41] A case arising in Connecticut, *Thurman v. City of Torrrington*,[42] brought the issue into national prominence. The plaintiff, an abused spouse, brought a successful civil rights action against the City of Torrington and individual police officers for failure to respond properly to her complaints concerning threatened violence by her estranged husband. After her numerous complaints—including one telephoned in 15 minutes before the critical incident—were ignored, her estranged husband stabbed her repeatedly and caused her life-threatening injuries. Partly as a result of the widespread interest in this case, family violence has received more attention. Many states, including Connecticut, adopted family violence statutes which explicitly define the treatment to be given to violent incidents arising within the family context.[43]

Family violence laws brought a severe and widespread form of violence within criminal justice system protection. Despite that advance, however, the problem continues to be a serious one attracting the attention of the public. While the definitional issue is resolved, the problem of family violence continues in full force. A related problem arising out of the family context is parental kidnapping. Like spousal abuse, this activity was traditionally overlooked by the criminal justice system.[44] In recent years, it has received legislative attention and recognition in the system.

### Drugs and Guns

The factors involved in violent crime are the subject of endless debate and discussion. These factors include drugs, guns, poverty, gender, and race. The debate encompasses attempts to uncover the causes of violence and efforts to shape appropriate solutions. The relationship of drug abuse and firearms use in violent crime is common knowledge.[45] What to do about either of these problems, however, is the source of intense disagreement. Whether to intensify efforts to control the sale and possession of illegal drugs or to suspend or abandon enforcement efforts with respect to some substances is at issue. Whether to control the sale and possession by anyone of certain types of firearms or whether to concentrate upon firearms used in connection with crimes or the illegitimate firearms market is vigorously debated.

The correlation, or causal effect, of poverty and other socioeconomic factors is also widely discussed, as are the gender and racial overtones in violence. With respect to the firearms issue, however, efforts have been made to control the involvement of guns in drug transactions. In *Smith v. United States*,[46] the U.S. Supreme Court upheld an enhanced sentence for offering to exchange an automatic weapon for cocaine. The sentence was imposed pursuant to a federal law, 18 U.S.C.A. S. 924, which provided for enhanced penalties when firearms actually or potentially facilitate the commission of a drug trafficking crime.

The subject of firearms in schools was the subject of a recent Supreme Court case, as well, the result of which was to protect the role of the states in the area of education. In *United States v. Lopez*,[47] a majority of the Court held that the Gun-Free School Zones Act of 1990 prohibiting possession of firearms in school zones exceeded the authority of Congress to regulate commerce under the commerce clause of the federal constitution. The case, decided in a five-to-four decision, involved a twelfth-grade student who carried a concealed handgun into his high school. I will return to Justice Anthony Kennedy's *Lopez* opinion in Chapter 6 as an example of principled decision-making.

## Gangs: Criminal Association

Gang violence continues to receive a great amount of attention from the police, the media, and sociologists, as well as community and political leaders. This is true primarily because gangs are thought to be heavily involved with drug trafficking and they account for many of the dramatic incidents of urban—and, increasingly, suburban—violence. The structure of the contemporary version of urban gangs is complex, as is the relationship of gangs to their communities and to society at large.[48] Some cities in the Northeast, notably Bridgeport, Hartford, and New Haven, Connecticut, have seen extensive police activity directed at gangs in recent years. When murder rates decline, there is even speculation that the extensive arrests and convictions of gang leaders are at least partially responsible. As some commentators point out, gangs will doubtless continue to exist as an integral part of the community structure. Determination as to whether the court system can have a demonstrable impact on gang violence depends upon more information and analysis.

## Violence in the Workplace

This is a related problem because it often involves violence among participants in existing relationships. Workplace violence has become a serious public problem. In 1992, for example, more than 110,000 incidents of workplace violence occurred. In the decade of the 1980s, homicide was the third leading cause of death from injury in the workplace and the leading cause of occupational death for women.[49]

### Riots and Civil Disturbances

The problem of collective violence occurring during the course of civil disturbances poses unusual difficulties. While incidents of this sort do not occur regularly in American life, they can cause enormous loss of property and life and have far-reaching social repercussions. The Miami Riot of 1980 was one major example.[50] The Los Angeles riot following the verdict in the criminal proceeding that arose out of the beating of Rodney King was another. On March 3, 1991, Rodney King was involved in a physical confrontation with police officers during his arrest following a high-speed chase. The event was videotaped by a neighborhood resident and was broadcast widely on national television. Four police officers were tried in state court on charges of assault with a deadly weapon and excessive use of force. The officers were acquitted on all charges except for one count of excessive force against a single officer. A mistrial was declared on that count.[51]

The criminal trial in which the defendant police officers were acquitted was followed by a federal civil rights trial in which two of the officers were convicted of civil rights violations during the King arrest. On appeal, the convictions were affirmed but remanded for resentencing.[52] Interpreting the underlying causes of these incidents is problematical. Moreover, in the case of riots, the police have difficulty enforcing criminal laws because of the involvement of numerous unidentified offenders.[53] Although this country has been largely free of ideologically based political violence on a massive scale, these occasional riot problems can be devastating in effect and pose difficulties in attempting to find adequate solutions to the underlying problems.

## SOLUTIONS

Many difficulties arise in the course of considering possible solutions. One current issue is whether portrayal of violence in the media, particularly the visual media (including television, videos, and movies), should be controlled and, if so, whether that can be done in any meaningful way without violating the rights of free expression guaranteed by the federal and state constitutions. The ''V'' (for violence) chip is one proposal for a means by which parents could exclude portrayal of violence from their homes by programming their television sets. Many prominent public figures have strongly criticized the sometimes vulgar and tasteless talk shows as a factor contributing to the debasement of American culture. Government regulation of violence portrayed on television is a delicate matter involving serious problems of definition and categorization. A fundamental problem at the outset is establishing a causal link between the portrayed violence and violent behavior. Beyond that, determining the amount and types of violence to be regulated is difficult. Since the material to be regulated is a form of speech that has constitutional protection, the government must clearly define what it proposes to regulate, and regulate it narrowly in order to achieve the specified objectives. While such regulation need not be ruled out, the possibility of self-regulation should be fully explored and encouraged in the meantime.[54]

The subject of how to deal with the violence problem is the source of debate in virtually every state and federal political campaign in recent years, and of ongoing debate in state legislatures and Congress. The debate encompasses potential solutions lying within social, educational, and economic spheres and solutions involving increased crime control measures. The cultural context of American violence often does not receive adequate attention in political debates, which tend to focus mainly on measures that appeal to the immediate concerns of the electorate. While that is a legitimate priority, it is unwise to ignore investigating causes of violence toward the end of reducing the amount of crime and violence. The most appropriate place to consider the overall causes of crime is in legislatures, rather than, for example, in the course of criminal proceedings, where attention must be given to adjudicating the specific cases at hand.

Societal policies dealing with crime fluctuate widely and reflect little consistency in approach over the years. When the favored method is enhanced criminal legislation, more police enforcement, and increased penalties, the pressure on the criminal justice system, particularly the courts and correctional institutions, is intensified, often to the point of diminishing returns. The formidable problem that remains for the court system to solve is how to deliver timely and efficient criminal trials, and, in the case of convictions, predictable and effective punishment for violent crimes. Whether we are any closer to that goal—or farther from it—at the present time, is questionable.

The solution probably lies in combined approaches dealing—in the legislative and executive arena—with the underlying social, economic, educational, and political causes, along with carefully designed and executed crime control measures. These measures should target specific types of criminal activity and must be supported by adequate funding of support services, including court facilities, personnel, correctional facilities, and postincarceration control resources, such as probation and parole personnel. A long-term approach to the problem, involving cooperative, multidisciplinary efforts involving the public and private sectors, is essential. At the same time, all the factors contributing to violence discussed earlier in this chapter need to be considered.[55]

Many of the literary texts discussed in this chapter, in addition to illustrating and illuminating the cultural roots as well as the historical and present forms of violence in American society, provide examples of a phenomenon that is the subject of the next chapter—loss of authority of the legal system as a whole and courts in particular. Loss of authority stems, in part, from a failure to meet the needs of society. That failure flows from many causes, some of them attributable to the violence in American society. The inability of the judicial system to adjudicate and, where appropriate, to sentence swiftly and surely undermines public confidence in the system. The apparent inability to render effective and consistent punishment is another cause for disenchantment with the judicial system. The pervading fear and anxiety of citizens—especially citizens of urban areas—heightens the reaction of anger and skepticism. The fear and anxiety that result from real risk have a devastating effect on the freedom of movement and association of many urban and suburban citizens. Much of the blame placed on judicial personnel is unjustified because it stems from a misunderstanding of the judicial role.

Other causes of the loss of authority are attributable to the explosive economic, social, and cultural change and the inability of the legal system to adapt to the problems brought about by that change. When the legal system fails to operate in a way that satisfactorily resolves the problems presented, authority and legitimacy are in question. When the status of the legal system is in doubt, the authority and legitimacy of the entire political system are weakened. The literary texts discussed in the following chapter will illustrate ways in which the legal system has failed to live up to applicable standards. Chapter 5, "The State of the American Dream," will address social, economic, and political developments that have brought additional pressure on the American legal system.

Chapter 4

# Shaking the Foundations: Problems of Legal Authority

In practice, if not in words, the American legal tradition has always acknowledged the importance of substantive results for the legitimacy and accountability of judicial action.[1]

The role of the court system in contemporary American society is paradoxical. On one hand, courts assume a central role in society. The quantity of law—legislative, decisional, and administrative—has burgeoned to the point that nearly every aspect of life is controlled by law. The threat of litigation hovers over the transactions of everyday life, public and private, and, in that sense, shapes the transactions. Law and celebrated legal cases provide a major subject for the entertainment of Americans. Cases involving controversial people and controversial actions become media events occupying center stage in the information/entertainment theater. The number of lawyers continues to grow and their creativity in designing new ways to advance their interests and those of their clients seems limitless.

At the same time, the authority and credibility of courts appear to be more and more in question. With increased access of the media to the workings of courts, the public increasingly questions and criticizes the system. Questioning and criticism are essentially healthy activities. In the process of dissecting individual tactical moves or court rulings, however, it is possible to misunderstand and undermine the nature and purpose of the system. This is especially true where critics fail to acknowledge and employ the same legal rules and standards as those which bind the system. This issue is involved in the controversy concerning cameras in the courtroom. One commentator contends: "The camera corrupts not because it lies but because it magnifies images and issues a millionfold until they are hopelessly—and often willfully—distorted. And by inviting us, sometimes virtually requiring us, to second-guess the justice system, it saps that system of its sovereignty.''[2]

In addition, a serious loss of respect for lawyers has occurred in recent years and, with that, the authority of law has been undermined.[3] The overall effectiveness of law as a source of cohesion and mediation among conflicting interests may be diminished as a result.

## OBSERVATIONS ON MEANINGS OF AUTHORITY

The term *authority* may be defined as *legitimate power*. Legitimacy depends on being derived from a system of institutionalized rules or traditions. Authority, in one sense, has a *de jure* legal meaning relating to what a person or an office is specifically permitted to do according to rules or traditions. It has a *de facto* meaning, as well, that depends upon what power a person or office is recognized by others as entitled to command. Authority, in the *de facto* sense, has a broader sweep than the technical, legal meaning.

In a democracy, *de facto* authority usually depends upon *de jure* authority, but it does not necessarily live up to its potential if full consent does not flow from those who are governed.[4] These ideas approach the meaning of authority that I wish to convey. Surely, courts, judges, and the expressions of law, both judicial or enacted, all have authority in the technical sense in our society. Their power may not be fully realized, however, unless people, communities, and institutions in society recognize this technical authority, use it, depend on it, follow and comply with it, consent to it, and respect it. The coercive function without the consensual response represents diminished *de facto* authority.

In the case of courts, legitimacy involves not only the recognized power to define the law, but also the power to enforce it. Not only litigants, but juries, witnesses, lawyers, citizens in general, and the media are directly affected by what judges do, and produce a direct response to those words and actions. The case of juries is an interesting one. While they have usually been regarded as an extension of the judge and the court, they have a large measure of autonomy in their own right because their determinations of the facts are virtually final and unappealable. Not only is the authority of the jury system at stake by virtue of what they do and how they conduct themselves, but they may directly challenge the authority of courts and judges as well. The practice of jury nullification, for example, involves repudiation of the law, courts and judges. When nullification is employed, appropriate means of applying and changing law may be bypassed in favor of methods that cannot be measured, evaluated, or controlled.

## HISTORICAL PERSPECTIVES AND TURNING POINTS

The present condition of law's authority has a complex historical background. At least two important historical periods can be identified as turning points. One is the Civil War period and the other is the Vietnam period of the 1960s and early 1970s.[5]

The first key period involved the Civil War. The observations of Professor Robert Ferguson on the diminishing force of law are pertinent:

> Americans have kept faith in law as an instrument of social order, but legal thought no longer supplies the ideological coherence it once did. The loss is a serious one in a nation that has defined itself so self-consciously through law. Long ago Tocqueville examined "the most perfect" Constitution and warned that "the government of the Union depends almost entirely upon legal fictions; the Union is an ideal nation, which exists, so to speak, only in the mind, and whose limitations and extent can only be discerned by the understanding." This conception of America insists upon the vital, continuing presence of intellect as both the primary source and the necessary tool of national definition.[6]

Ferguson points out that, around the time of the Civil War, the role of law as a unifying cultural and political force suffered a serious decline. Previously, the period from 1765 to 1840 had been a period when lawyers " 'spoke and acted with that conscious authority which is characteristic of truly creative founders.' "[7] During that period of American development, lawyers contributed their intellectual breadth, artistic insights, and political resources. The political writings of national leaders including John Adams, Thomas Jefferson, Alexander Hamilton, and James Madison drew on legal training. Likewise, the fictional writings of lawyers including Charles Brockden Brown, Washington Irving, and William Cullen Bryant reflected their legal education. After that period, lawyers relinquished their positions as generalists, humanists, and leading writers and turned away "from the earliest and most enduring aspiration of life in the New World, its vision of the future, its faith in progress. [Lawyers] had lost [their] grasp of what America was *becoming*."[8]

Against the backdrop of declining authority of courts and law after the Civil War, other developments in society contributed to a general loss of confidence in law as a means of solving society's problems. Inspired generally by the idea of evolution, the scientistic ethic became a major force beyond the realm of science, replacing the political ethic which had prevailed in both law and literature and which previously had expressed the values and concerns of the new nation. The scientistic vision, however, embodied a different approach to change. It indicated that existing forces and institutions would continually be overcome and replaced by new ones. Translated into legal terms, this suggested that Americans could not necessarily depend on courts to solve the problems presented by life.

The new scientistic perspective in life was expressed both in reality and fiction. In the social realm, if social disputes were part of the continuing fluctuation of forces, rather than interruptions of a constant scheme, courts could not successfully intervene. Previously, literature had reflected the belief that problems could be solved in courts, which were the proper arena for such matters. Now literature began to develop in which disputes and controversies were settled outside of court, either by natural forces or extralegal action on the part of individuals or groups. Legal thinking "retreated into bloodless formalism or fatalistic realism."[9]

The second key period of challenge to law's authority, the Vietnam period of the 1960s and early 1970s, was highlighted by traumatic events. As one commentator described it:

> [W]ith the 1960s came shock and frustration. It was a decade against itself; the students of affluence were marching in the streets; the nation that had never lost a war to any power was mired in a seemingly endless, unpopular, and unwinnable land war in Asia; the national consciousness was shocked by savage assassinations; and black Americans were responding to ostensible victories . . . with a paradoxical venting of outrage. It seemed as if America, so long especially blessed by the fates, had suddenly been cheated.[10]

To those events can be added the Watergate debacle which resulted in the resignation of a president and the serious undermining of faith in government and law. It can be argued, of course, that the force of law, as exercised by the Supreme Court as well as the other branches of government, responded admirably to the Watergate crisis and brought the incident to an orderly resolution. Nonetheless, it cannot be denied that major changes occurred in public attitudes toward law and authority as a result of all these occurrences. Since that time, reliance on and disrespect for law have been in constant conflict.

## PUBLIC PERCEPTION: DISSONANCE AND DISCORD

A major issue concerning the role of law in American society today is whether court decisions (jury verdicts and judge-made decisions) are considered credible and just by those who are affected by them, the public constituency, so to speak. This issue directly involves the problem of *authority*.

Every attempt to articulate the problem of authority runs into difficulties because using the terms *just* and *public constituency* involves myriad considerations and much uncertainty. The definition of the term *just* actually defies any certainty, although the combined qualities of fairness and reasonableness come close.[11] What constitutes the *public constituency* for these purposes is a complicated matter. Beyond these concerns, it is not at all clear how to ascertain and evaluate meaningfully the degree of public approval or disapproval of judicial decisions. Nonetheless, despite these problems, it is useful to identify the criteria for evaluating judicial decisions.

There is no doubt, as noted earlier, that enacted law—statutory and administrative—plays a central role in American society and that public attitudes toward legal authority are necessarily shaped significantly by legislation (e.g., by attitudes toward taxation, civil rights laws, and other legislation of broad application in society). My judicial experience, however, leads me to focus my attention on the role of courts and judicially created law.

The past decade has produced a great many highly publicized trials in which either the process or the results or both were greeted with considerable and often divisive controversy and dissatisfaction.[12] Given the media attention that can be expected to highlight, dramatize, and embellish the most controversial, celebrated cases, especially those that involve well-known personalities or bizarre crimes, public dissatisfaction and cynicism can be expected to continue. What pleases one constituency or interest group displeases another. For every perception of a criminal defendant as a powerful wrongdoer, a competing perception of the same individual as a powerless victim exists. Given the lack of consensus on such issues, the challenge remains to carry out the process of adjudication in an open, civil, sensible, principled manner in order to maintain the credibility and authority of the court system.

Given the diversity of individuals and communities in this nation, and the variety of values, standards, and moral criteria with which those constituencies will evaluate results, the process of determining the appropriate standards to use is difficult. I will propose several standards or guidelines as a starting point for discussion of the literary texts, which illustrate instances where the legal system fell short. All references to court decisions encompass a concern with the law as institution and process. With respect to each guideline, both the inherent nature of the judicial decision and the perception of that decision are important.

It is easier to point out instances of failure of the court system than it is to identify successes. It is difficult, in fact, to prescribe exactly how the system should function to avoid the perception of failure. In a real sense, the nature of the system makes failure to meet some public expectations virtually inevitable. Given the adversarial nature of the American legal system, it is possible to find someone to support even the most outrageous position in a dispute. The skills of advocates, as well as the abilities and fairness of fact finders, inevitably will vary. The rules of evidence necessarily limit what can be proven; otherwise, legal proceedings would be even more protracted than they are. The human judgments involved in interpreting the rules, in particular factual contexts, are bound to vary.

Moreover, what the applicable law is in any given situation is often open to legitimate disagreement. The burdens of proof and standards of proof transform any dispute into a matter of what can be proven rather than what the truth is. The fact that rules of general application arise from specific fact-bound controversies—later subjected to parallel reasoning and argument—regularly produces dissatisfaction with individual results. These factors and others are bound to affect public perception as to whether the result is correct and the procedure is fair.

## STANDARDS OF REVIEW: FOUR CRITERIA

While recognizing the difficulties of formulating standards that will hold true in a universal sense, I suggest that the following factors be employed in the effort to maintain the authority and credibility of court decisions. Although the standards can be used to evaluate jury decisions as well as judge-made decisions, obviously juries are not accountable in the same way that judges are. Judges must enunciate factual findings, conclusions, and the law applied. Juries are obligated to follow the legal instructions given by judges but, unless interrogatories are used, they need not specify the fact-findings nor the reasoning process. As a general rule, only the result is announced. Juries, therefore, as I previously mentioned, can engage in jury nullification, applying their own rules or general sense of fairness. While judges are accountable in jury cases for their trial rulings, jury instructions, and posttrial motion decisions, they are not accountable for jury fact-finding or the verdict. They may be held responsible for declining to set aside a verdict, however, when a proper challenge is made.

### Procedural Fairness

*Judicial decisions must protect the established rights (established by constitutions, statutes, or judicial decisions) of all individuals affected by a particular decision without discrimination or disparity of treatment.* Compliance with this principle is a necessary ingredient in preserving order and harmony in society.

### Realistic Results

*The results of judicial decisions must be realistic and coincide generally with common sense and reason.* Excessive formalism or reliance on legal fictions not adequately grounded in common understanding will result in misunderstanding and criticism. The application of legal rules, such as burdens of proof, standards of proof, presumptions, and admissibility of evidence should make sense to nonlawyers in the context of the affairs of life. When those concepts—or resulting decisions—become too attenuated with reference to ordinary understanding and experience, a serious problem with authority is likely to occur. Moreover, a problem with authority will also exist if the judicial system is incapable of rendering effective and timely decisions. Popular expectations cannot dictate how a court system operates, of course, but those expectations should be taken into account in planning for the overall operation of the court system.

### Reflect Fundamental Values and Public Morality

*Judicial decisions should not be based on a specific value system of higher morality, or respond to the public mood of the moment, or purport to dictate a governing morality.* On the other hand, judicial decisions must transcend private codes which embody narrow, exclusionary value systems, such as racial codes or codes of honor. Judicial decisions, however, will be most authoritative if they are essentially in harmony with prevailing standards and values. This is a difficult point because judges must take care not to apply their own values. Inherent in the process of judging, however, is the inevitability of making value choices. The point, perhaps, is to identify fundamental values in the course of reasoned, principled, honest, and articulated decisions.[13] Judges, of course, must also protect minority interests and preserve an environment where multiple value systems providing *core values* of morality and ethics can coexist. Besides preserving and adhering to secondary values inherent in legal texts (constitutional, statutory, and common law), the judicial system should function to resolve disputes, mediate among conflicting interests, and provide consistency and order. Judicial decisions should not be subject to political manipulation by judicial or legal officials.

### Civility in Conflict Resolution

*Adjudication should minimize conflict and confrontation.* Because American society is extremely confrontational and adversarial, law as the ordering force should serve as a model of peaceful, civil, orderly resolution of disputes. Accomplishing this goal may necessitate greater incorporation of mediation, negotiation, and other problem-solving disciplines into the existing adversarial system.[14] Litigation should not become an end in itself, generating new sources of conflict and dispute and extending litigation unreasonably. Moreover, excessive reliance on the judicial system for conflict resolution, rather than using alternative resolution methods, tends to expand the amount of litigation unnecessarily. An overused and overtaxed court system may be unable to meet the legitimate needs of those who seek judicial intervention for determination of rights or resolution of conflict. Judicial decisions must meet reasonable standards of timeliness, predictability, accessibility, and accuracy.

## EVALUATING RESULTS

Given the nature of the adversarial process, and taking into account the competing interests that are involved in every case, virtually every decision will be met with disparate responses. The test of the validity or legitimacy of a court decision, therefore, cannot be whether it is greeted with unanimous public approval. Every case involves many variables: a specific fact situation, a particular—sometimes idiosyncratic—trier of fact and decisionmaker, varying levels of competence in representation, the specific historical context, and the constraints of particular legal standards involving burdens and standards of proof.

When judicial decisions are evaluated by members of the public, including journalists, experts, or lay citizens, the evaluators never function with the same information and constraints as the decisionmaker, whether judge or jury. The evaluators will have either too few or too many facts. Rarely will an evaluator actually digest all the facts presented to the decisionmaker, even where the entire trial is available for viewing. Even if the evaluator were able to digest all the facts, the evaluator, lacking the constraints of judge or jury, likely will know additional information and opinions contained in media reports not properly available to the trier. The evaluator, moreover, is not bound by the legal standards or burdens of proof and is free to use intuition or emotion in making judgments. Just as individual litigants have particular interests that they wish to vindicate, so evaluators have their own interests at stake. Those interests may not necessarily be capable of logical or rational justification, or even articulation.

While the fairness of judicial procedures can be evaluated by applying textual standards and common sense, results of litigation cannot be judged as easily because results are the product of a peculiar configuration of facts and legal principles. Despite these impediments to evaluation, Americans constantly and regularly judge and evaluate court decisions. In a democracy, every citizen believes he or she is capable of judging guilt or innocence as well as anyone else, including judges and, certainly, as well as juries. Individual citizens examine decisions and determine legitimacy by their own standards of right and wrong. Common sense would dictate that individual results of court decisions should be judged collectively rather than singly to see if patterns of discrimination, prejudice, unfairness, or failure to meet ordinary standards of realism, common sense, and popular wisdom exist. As a whole, the system could be considered to be inadequate if, collectively, decisions are out of line or proportion. Individual case results, however, will exhibit great variations. Highly publicized, *celebrity* cases do not provide a sound basis for evaluation—or revision—of a court system or its rules.

A major consequence of judicial decisions in our society is to provide a social bond and to be a collaborative and civil means of resolving disputes. Law, taking into account the rules, policies, and procedures underlying and involved in the court decisions, provides this function by prescribing and proscribing, promising and threatening. Judicial decisions carry out these imperatives. The difference between promise and reality is the expectation factor, which plays a vital role in our society. Legitimacy and authority of law depend, in part, upon the size of the gap between expectation and result.

The practical difficulties outlined above should not be a deterrent to evaluating the judicial system. One must, however, realize the complexity and ambiguity involved. Based on the guidelines for evaluating the authority of court decisions, the following questions will serve to guide the analysis of literary texts, which illustrate situations where the system has failed to measure up.

## CROSS-EXAMINING THE TEXTS

1. Is the procedure fair? Does it protect the rights of all individuals involved in the case without discrimination or prejudice? Does the procedure comply with due process and equal protection requirements?

2. Is the result realistic? Does it meet ordinary standards of common sense and wisdom? Does it take into account the existing social and economic circumstances of the participants and society in general? Is it based on the facts presented in the case? Are those facts complete? Is the result excessively formalistic or based on legal fictions?

3. Does the decision comport with prevailing public values as well as protect other value systems? Does it transcend private codes which serve limited interests in society, even if, in some cases, they coincide with the majoritarian interests? Does the decision enhance or detract from the social, economic, and environmental climate of society?

4. Is the procedure civilized and orderly? Does it reduce conflict and confrontation and bring the controversy to an end? On the other hand, does it foster excessive or debilitating litigation?

With that background, examination of two novels written in the realistic or naturalistic tradition will illustrate some classic instances of how judicial decisions can fail. They are James Fenimore Cooper's last novel, *The Ways of the Hour*,[15] and Theodore Dreiser's *An American Tragedy*.[16] Following that discussion, examples from recent literature will illustrate how courts are perceived to fail in the contemporary context. Those works include *Libra*, *Trombone*, *them*, *Clockers*, and another of Russell Banks's novels, *The Sweet Hereafter*.[17] By judging the ways in which the legal system fails and, thereby, evaluating its effectiveness, we will be able to identify corrective measures that will remedy the problems.

## *THE WAYS OF THE HOUR*: REASONABLE DOUBT—ABOUT THE JURY

*The Ways of the Hour* is based on the criminal trial of a woman named Mary Bodine.[18] In writing the novel, Cooper was strongly influenced by his concern about a provision in the New York Constitution of 1846 which specified that, henceforth, all judges, formerly appointed by the governor, were to be elected by the people. Cooper believed that the people were better served by appointed judges who would not depend for their office on the next election.

Cooper thought that in an aristocracy, popular juries serve to restrain the abuses of special privilege. In the case of a democracy, however, he believed that the administration of criminal justice should be given to popular juries but only as restrained by an appointed judiciary. He feared that jurors would usurp the decision-making power, and elected judges would become too timid to insist on following precedent.[19] With the rotation of judges added to that predicament, ''the whole machinery of justice is left very much at the mercy of an outside public opinion'' (*WOTH*, 287). Jurors, whom he suspected of following public opinion, ''are fast becoming judges'' (*WOTH*, 18). Cooper felt that juries, while admirable in aristocracies, were unsuited to democracies. He noted that in trials in which railroad companies were pitted against people dwelling along their lines, jury prejudice was strong against the companies, making justice for them hopeless. Similarly, juries were unreasonably prejudiced in favor of local debtors when sued by distant creditors.

Cooper uses *The Ways of the Hour* to illustrate how juries make law and distort justice at the same time. He discusses various legal issues at some length. For example, the novel begins with a discussion between two characters about the federal constitution, the relationship of the state constitution to the federal, and the amount of criminal activity in the region.

*The Ways of the Hour* features the trial of an innocent woman called Mary Monson for first-degree murder based on a highly circumstantial case. After two skeletons, both with fractured skulls, are discovered in the ruins of a house after it burned, a young woman who lived there, a stranger in town who is perceived as eccentric, is charged with murder and arson. The young woman, portrayed as wealthy and aristocratic, attempts to conceal her identity. She is ably represented by a lawyer, John Dunscomb, who is skeptical about her innocence although his good friend, Dr. McBrain, is convinced of it. The discussion between the two men ranges over many topics of current interest. They discuss, for example, the abuses by the press: "[I]t is fearful to reflect that a system, of which the whole merit depends on its power to extract facts, and to do justice on their warranty, should be completely overshadowed by another contrivance which, when stripped of its pretension, and regarded in its real colours, is nothing more than one of the ten thousand schemes to make money that surround us, with a little higher pretension than common to virtue" (*WOTH*, 82).

Awaiting trial after the coroner's inquest and indictment by the grand jury, the young woman is confined in jail under very poor conditions, worse than those for convicted prisoners. Dunscomb's nephew suggests a theory. The skeletons had been thought to be those of an elderly man and woman who owned the house where Mary was residing. He posits that, instead, they were of the old woman and the German woman who worked for them; and the murderer was the old woman's husband, who was known to be ill-tempered and alcoholic.

Mary, who reveals that she was traveling extensively in Europe and as far as Jerusalem prior to coming to Biberry, a small village in lower New York State, has trust in the fairness of the judicial system. She is unaware, however, that her aristocratic nature and manner will do her harm in her jury trial. Dunscomb, however, recognizes that a case is in jeopardy when an aristocrat is involved. Dunscomb, in fact, worries that an impartial jury cannot be impaneled in the village, given the present state of public opinion and the public thirst for knowledge about a murder charge.

The charges are to be tried separately and Mary will stand trial initially on the accusation of murdering Peter Goodwin. The murder charge pertaining to his wife, and the arson charge, will follow. The trial revolves primarily around her possession of a particular gold coin, which some witnesses of questionable veracity and accuracy claim they saw in the possession of the deceased woman. Mary's defense consists of an attack on the weakness of the circumstantial case against her, plus the offering of Dr. McBrain's testimony that both skeletons are of females, thus totally discounting the prosecution's theory that the murder victims are husband and wife.

Mary is convicted and sentenced on one count of murder—that of Peter Goodwin, the husband. Before sentencing, Mary delivers an articulate, reasoned plea that the jury verdict was erroneous. She points out the absence of any evidence that the deaths resulted from murder, as opposed to being accidentally caused by fire. The judge, beginning to doubt her sanity because of her flushed appearance and the strange nature of some of her statements, sentences her to death by hanging. At that moment, a woman approaches the bar and produces the living but "drivelling creature" (*WOTH*, 462) named Peter Goodwin, the alleged victim.

Despite her exoneration by the supposed victim's appearance in the courtroom, Mary is required to stand trial on the remaining murder charge. In her second trial, she secures an acquittal, but only because she takes over the cross-examination of a crucial witness who gave damaging testimony at the first trial about the allegedly stolen gold coin. The witness admits that she took the gold coins belonging to the deceased. Ultimately, the facts come to light—that the fire was accidental and that the skull fractures were caused by a plough which fell from the second floor as the garret was consumed by fire.

Mary is discharged. Cooper, however, presents a scenario in which justice can result only outside the formal mechanisms of law and the court system. The situation in Cooper's novel is a precursor of the modern fictional view of law as incompetent. The wife of the sheriff remarks, "It's altogether the most foolish trial we have ever had in Dukes, though they tell me foolish trials are getting to be only too common" (*WOTH*, 477).

Mary Monson is an outsider in the provincial town where the murder takes place. The jurors clearly are motivated by a popular prejudice against the wealthy and cultivated—both of which she represents. The jurors are incapable of recognizing the demagoguery that takes place. The lawyers portrayed in the novel belong to two different categories common to Cooper's writing.[20] The defense lawyer, Dunscomb, is an aging, wealthy Christian gentleman, well-trained in the common law. The district attorney, Timms, is portrayed as a clever lawyer who is seeking to fulfill his own political ambitions. While he has risen professionally above his class origins, he resents the gentry that he tries to emulate. Dunscomb believes that the judiciary should be unhampered by democratic principles, while Timms recognizes that potentially profitable law is made by popular juries. The two lawyers represent the two pre–Civil War images of lawyers—educated gentleman and unscrupulous manipulator. The district attorney, rough as he is, is riding the wave of the future because he understands popular prejudice and is unfettered by ethical scruples. Dunscomb has fallen out of touch with the changing times.

Dunscomb's fears about the mindlessness of juries are borne out by the jury verdict. Until that time, however, it appears that justice will be done. The district attorney, after making prejudicial remarks about Mary's aristocratic nature, delivers a summation that is fairly restrained and neutral. The judge's charge is fair—even favorable to the accused—and emphasizes the weakness of the circumstantial case against her. After the charge, the general opinion favors the likelihood of acquittal. The jury's verdict of guilty comes as a shock in light of the factual and legal context; the judge sentences Mary to death.

The reasons for the jury's utter disregard of facts and law are not made entirely clear. Cooper, however, seems to be making the point that elected judges, such as Mary's judge, cannot command the respect of the popular jury; they follow popular opinion rather than lead it. Mary is exonerated ultimately not because of the integrity of the judicial system, but because her supposed victim appears suddenly in the courtroom. In her second trial Mary is acquitted because she takes over the cross-examination of the crucial witness herself.

Dunscomb's response to the failure of the system is to suggest repressive measures. He believes that the populace should not be entrusted with making, executing, or interpreting the law. Moreover, he supports curtailing liberty of the press: "As respects proceedings in the courts, there never will be any true liberty in the country, until the newspapers are bound hand and foot" (*WOTH*, 140). In the preface to the novel, Cooper remarks that, despite the many injustices of jury trials, the problem is to develop an alternative (WOTH, vi).

*The Ways of the Hour* portrays the failure of the law in several respects, according to the questions posed earlier. By operating irrationally, based on prejudice against Mary, the jury denies her a fair trial. By the same measure, the verdict finds her guilty of murder when she is, in fact, innocent of any crimes. The jury's loyalty is to its own private code which is based on a kind of class discrimination, this time against the interests of the privileged class. As a consequence of the jury's miscarriage of justice, Mary is sentenced to death, the ultimate force authorized by law. In the second trial, while she is acquitted, that does not occur through the legitimacy of law and legal procedures, but by her own actions. The authority of law is fully undermined in the novel.

## *AN AMERICAN TRAGEDY*: AMBIGUOUS INTENT

Theodore Dreiser directly expressed his purpose in writing his naturalistic novel, *An American Tragedy*:

> I had long brooded upon the story, for it seemed to me not only to include every phase of our national life—politics, society, religion, business, sex—but it was a story so common to every boy reared in the smaller towns of America. It seemed so truly a story of what life does to the individual—and how impotent the individual is against such forces. My purpose was not to moralize—God forbid—but to give, if possible, a background and a psychology of reality which would somehow explain, if not condone, how such murders happen—and they have happened with surprising frequency in America as long as I can remember.[21]

*An American Tragedy* is based on an actual case involving the murder of a female factory worker by Chester Gillette, the man who had made her pregnant.[22] Gillette was convicted of murder in the first degree. The facts of the murder in the novel can be succinctly stated. Clyde Griffiths is the son of itinerant preachers living in desperate conditions of poverty. Clyde is restless and a dreamer and resents his parents' religious work in the mission house and on city streets. Clyde broods about the freedom his sister has obtained by running away to elope. While working as a bellhop in a large Kansas City hotel, Clyde's horizons expand and his hopes rise. He is overcome with enthusiasm for material things and an extravagant lifestyle. At this point, however, he can only view the magic of a glamorous world from the outside.

Good fortune visits Clyde in the person of his uncle, Samuel Griffiths, a wealthy factory owner in upstate New York. Samuel is pleased by his nephew's vision of him as the hero of an American success story. Samuel offers Clyde a job in the factory along with a chance to work his way up in the family business. Clyde accepts the offer. Clyde becomes attracted to a new factory worker, Roberta Alden. He seduces her and they begin an affair. Clyde is portrayed as being in the grip of a mechanistic universe and is unable to resist the physical attraction.

Later, Clyde becomes involved with Sondra Finchley, an aristocratic local woman whom he met through his business connections. He decides to reject Roberta. He envisions his fortunes rising even higher as he begins to be accepted into Sondra's social world. Clyde's plans are thrown awry, however, when Roberta reveals that she is pregnant. When she demands that Clyde marry her, he decides that she should abort the pregnancy. That plan being unsuccessful, he fantasizes about her death. Plotting to cause an *accidental drowning*, he brings Roberta to a remote lake resort.

Roberta's death appears as an inevitable consequence of the events that Clyde orchestrates. In a rented boat on the lake, Clyde is paralyzed by doubt and confusion. Unable to carry out his plan, Clyde strikes out angrily with his camera at Roberta when she attempts to dispel his visible torment. At that moment, he did not intend to murder her: "not even then with any intention to do other than free himself of her—her touch—her pleading—consoling sympathy—her presence forever—God!" (*AT*, 492). After the blow, Clyde rises to apologize. The boat capsizes and Roberta calls for help to save her from drowning. Clyde hears a "voice at his ear" (*AT*, 493) and is torn with conflict between saving her and allowing to take its course what appears to be the accidental death that he had hoped for and planned. Although the capsizing of the boat is unintended, Clyde's conscious decision not to save Roberta results in her death. Clyde is a tormented, doubt-ridden actor who is caught on the precipice where accident and intention are in an extreme state of tension.

Clyde is apprehended after his flight from the scene of Roberta's death. After a trial resulting in his conviction for murder, he is sentenced to death and electrocuted. The process leading from capture to execution, however, reveals a great deal about Dreiser's views of law. Dreiser's narrative of Clyde's life before Roberta's death raises questions about the effectiveness of legal definitions in accurately judging human actions. Dreiser, himself, stated that Clyde's trial was intended to show how "the snap judgments of juries are inadequate in those knife-edge cases . . . where there is a subtler distinction to be made than the one between black and white."[23]

Dreiser created a homicide so ambiguous that the "very terms of law seem no longer adequate."[24] Even Clarence Darrow, who wrote his own novel about a murder[25] and gave many speeches on the subject of criminal justice, concluded that "on the basis of the novel, it would be impossible to determine Clyde's guilt."[26] It is difficult to render a truly accurate decision as to Clyde's moral or legal guilt because of the sheer complexity of the evidence and the criminal law classification scheme that is incongruent with reality.[27] Nonetheless, because Clyde's actions, as established at trial, can be made to fit into the existing categories of criminal conduct, he is found guilty.

The story in the novel closely resembles the actual case which gave Dreiser his basic material. Dreiser, however, made several significant changes in order to create more uncertainty about the murderer's culpability. The victim in the real case had more revealing wounds than Roberta. Moreover, the murderer apparently used a tennis racquet, which was found with strings broken. Gillette testified at trial that the victim, Grace Brown, committed suicide by jumping into the lake. "[A]fter some ineffectual efforts to rescue her,"[28] and without seeking help, he went about his own affairs for two days without informing anyone. The Court of Appeals, in affirming the conviction, stated:

> We are mindful at every step that this is a case of circumstantial evidence, and that the only eye-witness denies that death was the result of crime. But in obedience to the most exacting requirements of that manner of proof, the counsel for the People . . . has investigated and presented evidence of a great number of circumstances for the purpose of truly solving the question of the defendant's guilt or innocence. . . . [W]e are compelled to say that not only is the verdict not opposed to the weight of evidence and to the proper inferences to be drawn from it, but that it is abundantly justified thereby.[29]

In addition to the crucial problem of making reality fit into arbitrary patterns of criminal conduct, the legal system that convicts Clyde is shown to be inept, corrupt, and hypocritical.[30] The men who participate in Clyde's trial barely even try to uncover the truth. Clyde's attorneys are convinced of his guilt and decide to fabricate a story for his testimony. They also try unsuccessfully to find and destroy incriminating evidence. They have undertaken Clyde's defense because of their political opposition to the district attorney, who prosecutes the case to further his own political ambitions. The prosecution suppresses and fabricates evidence in the effort to obtain the conviction, which is crucial for political reasons. The district attorney ignores ambiguous evidence in building his case against Clyde. He is prejudiced against Clyde, whom he perceives as a rich idler. He even secures a special term of court so the trial can be held prior to the election in which he is a candidate for a judgeship. The trial is pervaded by legal fictions at best, and, at worst, by lies and deception which no court official or participant in the system, including Clyde, undertakes to counter.

The twelve jurors selected were "with but one exception, all married. And with but one exception, all religious, if not moral, and all convinced of Clyde's guilt before ever they sat down, but still because of their almost unanimous conception of themselves as fair and open-minded men, and because they were so interested to sit as jurors in this exciting case, convinced that they could pass fairly and impartially on the facts presented to them" (*AT*, 638–639). To the surprise of no one, the jury convicts Clyde of first-degree murder, a charge which, given the judge's specific instruction, was not the appropriate charge. The judge correctly charged the jury that Clyde's intent to murder, but not his motive, is legally pertinent and that his failure to rescue Roberta cannot be first-degree murder. The jury, however, ignores the judge's instructions. The jury turns the defense argument about mental and moral cowardice against him and convicts Clyde because he is a coward.[31] Clyde never accepts responsibility for his actions. He believes he is unfairly convicted and punished. He dies without repenting because it would affect his self-image as a victim destroyed by society.

Dreiser implies that the adversarial system fails by obscuring truth in the search for victory, the main occupation of the participants. The trial is a virtual sideshow where spectators entertain themselves. The lawyers play to the crowd of spectators as well as to the judge and to the jury, which represents the community. Both prosecution and defense present the case emotionally in an effort to influence the jury. Dreiser condemns the practice of turning a trial into a "local theatrical" for the benefit of reporters who "try cases in public print, thereby assuring that the open courtroom will be filled with bias."[32]

The court system portrayed in *An American Tragedy* fails in several important respects. As in *The Ways of the Hour*, the guarantee of fair and impartial process is not fulfilled. Clyde is as much the victim of prejudice as Mary Monson. He is presumed guilty at the start by the triers of fact and the entire trial is geared toward that end. The trial is a product of lies and distortion with no real effort to ascertain the truth. Worse yet, the district attorney is motivated by his own ambitions to secure the conviction at virtually any cost. As in the Monson case, the jury's utter disregard of legal instructions, in favor of its own prejudices, is inexcusable.

A second aspect of failure actually involves both the fairness and correctness standards. The entire criminal process lacks fairness and integrity because it operates based on arbitrary fictions that classify human behavior in legal terms that carry with them the coercive power of the state. A legal system, admittedly, includes categories of criminal conduct that likely will not take into account all the subtleties of human behavior. When those classifications fail to account for important variations in human behavior or to reconcile reality with the reconstructed reality of the courtroom, however, the system has failed. The law that guides court decisions must be sufficiently fine-tuned to take into account ambiguities, at least those of major proportions. To the time of his death, Clyde is obsessed with the question of his moral and legal guilt. The jury and court officials do not even honestly reach the issue of legal guilt, having been diverted from that fundamental question by the enterprise of fabricating stories that, while not true, at least meet the arbitrary and artificial classifications of law.

While these failures are the principal ones, the pervasive influence of the social class code is also evident. Because the jury and the district attorney are moved by their prejudice against Clyde, whom they perceive as representing a social class foreign to them, the law fails to transcend that code. Ironically, Clyde's uncle and Sondra's family conspire to distort the trial, in order to protect their reputations. Additionally, by functioning with deception and manipulation, the legal system fails to inform the people in society of the social and economic conditions that can produce or, at least, allow this type of crime to occur.

Although *An American Tragedy* portrays a legal system that is oblivious to the effects of the realities of the world, the appellate decision in the *Gillette* case is well-grounded in the realities of the factual situation. The court gives close attention to the facts and seems concerned with the truth-seeking function of the jury. Rather than focusing on the weaknesses in proof, the Court of Appeals views the evidence as a whole and finds the verdict "abundantly justified."[33] The evidentiary claims are easily dismissed and a prosecutorial misconduct claim is summarily disposed of by the court. In concluding, the court commented on the verdict:

> [W]e think that it was based on the substantial features and essential character of the case which was fairly established against him, and that so long as the conduct of an accused is to be tested in such an investigation as this, by the intentions and purposes which ordinarily prompt human acts, and by the consequences which ordinarily follow them, no other result reasonably could have been expected in this case than that which has overtaken the defendant.[34]

## AUTHORITY IN CONTEMPORARY CONTEXT

*The Ways of the Hour* and *An American Tragedy* illustrate dramatically some of the ways in which court decisions fail to comply with the spirit of the law and, in the process, fall short of meeting reasonable public expectations of fairness and common sense. Some of the literary works discussed earlier, including *The Pioneers*, "That Evening Sun," "Percy Grimm," and *The Virginian*, provide additional examples of the system's failure. Of the contemporary novels, *Libra, Clockers, them*, and *Trombone* present striking fictional instances of the system's failure that are highly relevant to the real world. In *Libra*, the historical fact is that the assassin, Oswald, was entrusted to the Dallas criminal justice system. That trust was betrayed with extraordinary drama when Jack Ruby shot and killed Oswald in an incident that revealed the ineffectiveness of the system. The fact that

Oswald never got to trial, making it impossible for guilt to be determined in an orderly manner, has had a lasting impact on the American psyche.

In *Clockers*, the criminal justice system is presented as both ineffective and corrupt.[35] The drug trade goes on unimpeded by prosecution or conviction. The war on drugs is mocked and degraded. Both sides in this street war are conspiratorial participants in the exploitation of the addicts. Whatever justice there is occurs outside the courts and outside formal law enforcement. The main punishment to be feared is that delivered by criminals, not the justice system. Strike, for example, however sympathetic a character, fears most of all being released from police custody to face his malevolent boss, Rodney. In the end, he is assisted in escaping from street punishment and official punishment by a police officer. The world of the streets presented in *Clockers* is probably not far off the mark as a description of the urban drug trade.

In *Trombone*, of all the people who commit crimes, only Dean is prosecuted. The organized crime boss remains untouched and Ray is allowed to depart for new territory. Law appears to be essentially ineffective at dealing with criminal activity. So, too, in *them*, virtually all the criminal activity occurs without official disapproval. As noted, Howard Wendall, a policeman, commits one of the many crimes that involve the Wendall family members.

All of the literary works discussed to this point have involved criminal law. Most literature that deals with law, in fact, tends to focus on crimes rather than civil wrongs. One exception is a current work by Russell Banks entitled *The Sweet Hereafter*.[36] The story involves a school bus crash that kills fourteen children and the legal aftermath of the tragedy. On a winter morning in a small town in upper New York State, a school bus veers off the road, crashes through a guardrail, and plunges through the ice in a water-filled sandpit. In short order, the town attracts a plethora of plaintiffs' tort lawyers seeking to sign up clients. The goal of the lawyers, once they have enlisted clients, is to target the affluent or *deep-pocket* defendants.

The story of the incident is told by four characters, who present their versions of the crucial facts in narrative style. All of them struggle, not only with the relevant facts, but with their own personal backgrounds and values. The first narrator or witness is the bus driver, Dolores Driscoll, an established member of the community. She explains what happened in a manner that exonerates herself. Her version is acceptable to the lawyers because their focus is on defendants who have greater resources. The lawyers who are pursuing clients also engage in lawsuits against each other arising out of claims of improper solicitation. The town is enmeshed in the legal web.

The next narrator is Billy Ansel, the father of twins killed in the accident. Billy was a witness to the accident since, according to his custom, he was following the bus at the time of the accident. A veteran of Vietnam, his life has been filled with random violence and inexplicable death, like that of the accident. He resents the lawyers and refuses to join the lawsuit. He does not believe that litigation or money will quell his pain. He rues the fact that "there'll be all kinds of appeals, and I'll be tangled up in this mess for the next five years. . . . This thing is never going to go away'' (*TSH* 194). He is, however, a crucial witness for the lawyers and claimants.

The third narrator is the key lawyer, Mitchell Stephens, who represents the popular image of an aggressive personal injury lawyer. He feels fully alive only when pursuing a major cause of action. He believes that misfortunes or accidents do not exist, only injustices that demand a remedy in court. He believes in his role as protector of the wronged, but is ready to manipulate the facts and the people to accomplish his personal goals. Although a caricature of the modern trial lawyer, he represents both the best and worst qualities of those who function in our adversarial system.

The final narrator is Nichole Burnell, a victim of the accident who survived but is confined to a wheelchair. She is torn with conflict between her personal need for justice and the public desire for justice by means of the lawsuit. She has and will continue to suffer real injury as a result of the accident. Her greater need, however, is to exact revenge against her father (based on her personal agenda) by thwarting the lawsuit which he is intent on joining. In the end, she lies about the cause of the accident, placing the full blame on the driver for speeding, and undermines the basis for recovery against *deep-pocket* defendants. The lawyers and the law that they represent are thwarted. The townspeople return to their normal lives of civility but not before executing symbolic revenge against Dolores, the driver, who is now forced to bear the full weight of blame.

One of the major questions that emerges from the story is whether law is the appropriate vehicle for determining responsibility in the case of a civil wrong or whether the community should bypass the legal avenue in favor of seeking resolution without adversarial conflict and monetary damages. For the various reasons outlined, the legal method is rejected and the townspeople find ways of accomplishing resolution without legal intervention. There is a powerful suggestion that law and lawyers inflame conflict and separate people rather than assist them in dealing with their needs. The prevailing morality of the community leads the citizens to accept the result produced by Nichole's action. The townspeople, except Billy, had been eager to pursue the monetary damage route advocated by the lawyers. Fair or not, the book presents an indictment of lawyers and the role of law. One message clearly is that truth and justice are to be found outside the court system.

The unfavorable view of law and lawyers presented in *The Sweet Hereafter* is based, in part, on misunderstanding the role of law and on false expectations of what can be accomplished in court. Despite several legal inconsistencies and questionable assumptions as to law and procedure, the novel presents some highly relevant ethical and moral issues. To the extent that lawyers or judges promote or fail to correct misunderstandings or false expectations, the indictment is fair. In order to maximize the authority of court decisions, judges should take into account the guidelines suggested at the outset in addition to applying the law faithfully.

## SETTING THE RECORD STRAIGHT

Beyond the guidelines discussed above, there is much that judges can do—by way of education and communication—in order to enhance the authority of the court system, even given the inherent limitations of the judicial role. One of the key problems is the public misconception about the roles of judges and courts. Many people believe inaccurately that courts can solve problems of crime and violence in society or problems related to family breakdown. Problems of this sort are complex, far-reaching, and virtually insoluble, even for the policy-making branches of government. Exaggerated expectations lead people to blame courts and judges for failing to solve such problems.

A related problem is the misunderstanding of the judicial role in applying existing law. This topic is a popular one in American jurisprudence. Judge Learned Hand, for example, wrote extensively about the qualities of judges and judging, and the extent to which judges are free to decide.[37] Professor John Hart Ely illuminated the topic in propounding his representation-reinforcing theory of judicial review.[38] Judges are bound to follow the law embodied in constitutions, statutes, and decisions of higher courts. Evidence rules restrict what can be proven. Statutes and cases dictate what must be proven in order to establish a cause of action or criminal charge. Constitutional provisions, as interpreted by appellate courts, require judges to exclude criminal evidence and confessions even when such evidence appears to be probative.

Education and communication by judges can be increased beyond their present levels in order to inform the public about the role of judges and limitations upon courts. Lawyers can be called upon to inform clients accurately of what can be expected of courts in particular circumstances. Judges should explain decisions thoroughly so that the public will understand why courts operate the way they do.

Problems exist, as well, that are the responsibility of judges to correct and ameliorate. Court dockets and court personnel can be more effectively managed. Delays can be reduced; competence can be demanded of all court personnel. Judges can make courts more accommodating, understandable, and adaptable to the needs of litigants. Methods of resolving disputes, other than adversarial methods, need to be more widely employed. Law schools can assist greatly in this respect by producing lawyers who are trained in nonadversarial methods of problem-solving and dispute resolution, including mediation, negotiation, and arbitration. Legislative enactments that affect the operation of courts need to be identified at early stages. Even while recognizing that the present challenges to the authority of courts are part of a larger cultural phenomenon that challenges institutions of all types, judges and other court officials can work at communicating more effectively to the public the purpose, functions, and limitations of the court system in order to ensure that public expectations, at least, are grounded in reality.

Chapter 5

# The State of the American Dream: Optimism, Progress, and the Word of Law

> Our problem as a society is that we have fostered disconnectedness; we have created a false separateness between social research and policy-making, thinking and politics, ideas and power. . . . [R]ead Cicero's *Republic*, where the state is a harmonious orchestra, blending like musical tones the various classes, a concord aided by an idea of justice; read these, and whatever you think of them, you will not find a vision of a state where ideas and power can be distinct, where the power of ideas could ever be unconnected to a forceful public good.[1]

> America is continuously struggling for its soul.[2]

An optimistic belief in progress has been a central idea or attitude throughout the course of American history. That idea or attitude has traditionally been counterbalanced and tested by another attitude—skepticism and pessimism about the realities of political, economic, and social conditions. It is fair to say that the two competing currents of thought and attitude have been, and remain, in conflict in the American psyche.

American optimism and belief in progress have their roots in the period of the European Enlightenment. Although the term Age of Reason is sometimes used interchangeably with Enlightenment, some historians confine Enlightenment to the eighteenth century, when the ideas and attitudes of rationalism had spread from a small group of intellectuals to a wider group of educated citizens. A wide variety of ideas developed during this period through the writings and debates of philosophers and philosophes, including Voltaire, Rousseau, Locke, and Hobbes. Among the important themes were the social contract theory and the idea of natural rights in political philosophy. Reason, nature, and the idea of progress were the central ''idea clusters'' of the Enlightenment.[3] It is important to note that the Enlightenment ideas, including, for example, the debates about the role of society—whether humans are corrupted by society or whether society provides the means for our moral nature to flourish—are not distinctively American debates.

The Enlightenment spread from the Continent to America where Thomas Jefferson and Benjamin Franklin came to be the embodiment of American Enlightenment ideas. Jefferson, in particular, became the "social philosopher of American democracy."[4] He believed that in order to exercise democratic self-rule wisely, people had to improve themselves. On an optimistic note, Jefferson wrote, for example: "When I contemplate the immense advance in science and discoveries in the arts which have been made within the period of my life, I look forward with confidence to equal advances by the present generation, and have no doubt they will consequently be as much wiser than we have been as we than our fathers were, and they than the burners of witches.[5] The idea of progress is so much a part of American thinking that we easily forget how recently the idea came into being.

Competing attitudes of pessimism, cynicism, and disillusionment have also existed alongside traditional American optimism and belief in progress. In early literature, it is easy to see such strains, for example, in the writings of Hawthorne, Melville, and Poe. The negative outlook has often gone hand in hand with distrust of the legal system as the means of achieving justice. The tension between the attitudes of optimism, on one hand, and pessimism, on the other, has been especially visible at certain periods; for example, after the Civil War, around the time of the Depression, and in the 1960s, with the Kennedy assassination and the Vietnam War.

As noted, disillusionment concerning the high expectations of progress and prosperity existed during the latter half of the nineteenth century. Two writers of that period, Frank Norris and Stephen Crane, employing realistic and naturalistic images in their literary works, brought these messages home clearly and vividly. Both authors wrote "American tragedies." In *Maggie, A Girl of the Streets*,[6] Crane related his own knowledge of the forces that drive people to ruin in urban life. In *The Octopus*,[7] Norris explored the vast economic forces of America that can absorb and destroy individual lives.

Several decades later, John Dos Passos, Nathanael West, and F. Scott Fitzgerald produced works that portrayed the disillusionment that continued well into the twentieth century. Dos Passos wrote *The Big Money*,[8] West wrote *The Day of the Locust*,[9] and Fitzgerald wrote *The Great Gatsby*.[10] Still later, in the second half of the twentieth century, current strains of cynicism and disillusionment were portrayed or suggested in a plethora of literary works including *Libra*, *Clockers*, *them*, and *Trombone*.

Distrust of the legal system is related to disillusionment with the fundamental values and goals of American society. When faith in those values and goals diminishes, skepticism concerning the institutions and processes responsible for effectuating them naturally follows. The resulting disillusionment that exists—which touches on the problem of legal authority—represents a continuing current in American culture. The following discussion focuses on literary works that raise questions about traditional American ideas of progress and optimism about human nature.

## ENLIGHTENMENT LEGACY

Before going on to examine the literary works, it is useful to take a closer look at several ideas growing out of the Enlightenment that are central to American life. As one scholar characterized it, American culture is associated with a two-part equation—*progress* and *primitivism*—that depends, for its application, on a sense of optimism. The optimism is based, in part, on a view of history that embodies rejection of ties with the past, acceptance of the present, and hope for the future, and, in part, on confidence in the value of human civilization and fundamental goodness.[11]

The first part of the equation is the idea of *progress*. The second is the belief in the basic virtue of human nature, sometimes referred to as *primitivism*, which is essentially a moral outlook. The assumption of both beliefs has been criticized as internally inconsistent—a paradox. ''How can we believe that 'natural' man is essentially good, that his 'nature' tends to actions that are virtuous and valuable, and at the same time be convinced that increasingly complex social organizations and developments of techniques for manipulating nature are also good?''[12] That fundamental question found its answer in the definitions of *nature* and *natural*. The nature of human beings is to be social. In moving from isolation and clannishness to more advanced forms of social interaction, humans used their natural inclinations and potential. Progress and primitivism were, therefore, linked in the American consciousness.

## THE AMERICAN IDEA

Ralph Waldo Emerson, who is said to have termed the above cluster of beliefs the *American idea*, was referring to the catalyst that would make sense of the whole range of impressions of America. The related term'' 'American Adam' . . . was . . . a metaphor for a belief in the goodness of man, which then makes the progress of nations possible.''[13] The future of democratic government was seen to depend on a form of belief in the essential goodness of human beings who could be trusted to create and preserve a society that could continually be improved. ''The possibilities of the future based upon an assumption of the goodness of man and nature . . . is the 'idea' of America: the way in which Americans themselves, and the rest of the Western world, have made sense of the American experience.''[14]

Consistent with the American idea, courts ''pursued an instrumentalist view of the law. Judges expressly took responsibility for reshaping American laws to fit new social needs.''[15] That role required courts to admit that ''their rulings embodied resolutions based on the facts and policies; they did not claim that rules of decision determined the outcome.''[16] Law and morality were seen as coextensive; courts could deal with both standards. Accompanying this view was the belief that law embodied a moral consensus. The case of *Swift v. Tyson*,[17] for example, determined that a uniform rule of decision, found in federal common law, was desirable for both political and commercial reasons. Joseph Story believed that Christianity was an ingredient in the common law. The common law, in his view, involved morality and custom. According to Story: ''[T]he common law consists of positive rules and remedies, of general usages and custom, and of elementary principles . . . which cannot now be distinctly traced back to any statutory enactment, but which rest for their authority upon the common recognition, consent and use of the State itself.''[18]

While this American idea prevailed throughout most of the nineteenth century, it was severely tested by the American experience of the Civil War and beyond in the twentieth century, and has been called into question regularly by major writers thereafter. For some, scientism filled the intellectual void. Scientism enabled judges to ''avoid discussing questions of policy and expediency, questions which, in essence, were viewed as legislative.''[19] For others, the Civil War demonstrated the supremacy of politics over law.

The cultural movements known as realism and naturalism which flowed naturally from scientism shook the foundations of both the literary and the legal worlds during the nineteenth and twentieth centuries. The idea that natural forces and events could disrupt and control human social systems, laws, and order challenged the basic assumptions that underlay earlier confidence in human systems of law and order. The scientific theory expanded into ''literature and law and economics and politics alike.''[20] The idea of the immutability of law ''as a self-sufficient organism, prepared to solve the most novel problem by means of deductive logic''[21] gave way to the school of legal realism, of which Oliver Wendell Holmes was a principal spokesman. Holmes distrusted ''the simple acceptance of the old and the tried; without more, he distrusts as well the construction of any elaborate theory, for he believes that in time, it too must topple . . . working hypotheses are needed . . . 'as all life is an experiment.' ''[22] The fictional literature of that period reflected the same scientific forces.

## CITING THE AMERICAN IDEA

The American idea embodying the dual ideas of progress and optimism about human nature persists in American legal culture as well as social culture. Much of the work of the Supreme Court during the tenure of Chief Justice John Marshall reflects this outlook. Marshall's doctrines ''*made* constitutional law.''[23] Marshall was probably the greatest of the nineteenth-century judges who ''built and molded doctrine—scaffolding (as they saw it) to support the architecture of human affairs.''[24] References to various aspects of the American idea in U.S. Supreme Court decisions in the last half of the twentieth century are numerous. The dissenting opinion in *Barsky v. Board of Regents of University of State of New York*[25] referred to the opportunity to work—self-sufficiency—as ''the most precious liberty that man possesses.''[26] The dissent even quoted Emerson's view of the American idea as stated in his essay on politics: ''A man has a right to be employed, to be trusted, to be loved.''[27] The dissenter went on to state his personal version of the American idea:

> It does many men little good to stay alive and free and propertied, if they cannot work. To work means to eat. It also means to live. For many it would be better to work in jail, than to sit idle on the curb. The great values of freedom are in the opportunities afforded man to press to new horizons, to pit his strength against the forces of nature, to match skills with his fellow man.[28]

Another aspect of the American idea—the dream of justice—was expounded in *Warth v. Seldin.*[29] In that case [a zoning case involving rights to construct low- and moderate-income housing in the city of Rochester], the dissenting opinion stated that ''cases such as this one reflect festering sores in our society; and the American Dream teaches that if one reaches high enough and persists there is a forum where justice is dispensed.''[30] Finally, home ownership as part of the *American dream* was noted in *Nordlinger v. Hahn,*[31] a case involving a taxpayer challenge to a California property tax law limiting increases in assessed value to 2 percent except in cases of improvement or change in ownership. The equal protection argument was that the law harmed younger and poorer California families in their efforts to acquire property.

While many variations of the American idea persist in American legal, social, political, and literary culture, the possibility of achieving aspects of the American idea—what I would call *pursuing the American dream*—has been seriously challenged by economic, social, political, and legal developments and changes occurring in the twentieth century. If the idea has value as a guiding force in the next century, the achievable goals embodied in the idea must be adapted to accommodate the present realities of American life. If the idea continues in a mythical form, the pursuit may be more frustrating than inspiring. The present realities include the manner in which citizens participate in the political, economic, and social dimensions of society, and an assessment of the economic opportunities that exist in our technological society. Many of the same material goals that have existed throughout American history continue to endure but the ability to achieve them varies greatly throughout society. The following literary texts provide examples of conflict and disagreement concerning the American idea in society.

## *THE OCTOPUS*: RAILROADING CORRUPTION

*The Octopus* and *The Pit* were the first two parts of Norris's projected trilogy, an epic narrative of American business. He envisioned this trilogy as a supplement to the "great national event" of the conquest of the West.[32] *The Octopus* was planned to tell the story of the struggle between the ranchers and the Southern Pacific Railroad. *The Pit* dealt with the financial struggle for control of the wheat market. Norris projected that the final part of the trilogy, *The Wolf*, would tell the story of the worldwide export of American wheat. Norris, however, died at the age of thirty-two before writing the final segment.

A major theme of *The Octopus* is the ability of a large economic organization to corrupt and destroy the lives of human beings within its grip. In the power struggle involving the interests of the railroad and the farmers, the farmers have brought an action against the railroad to lower the rates for carrying grain. They learn that the decision of the court has gone against them on the basis that the lower rates set by the commissioners would make it difficult to operate the railroad at a profit. The judge, therefore, restores the higher rates. The farmers accuse the judge of being corrupt and conspiring with the railroad and the Railroad Commission. The law is worse than incompetent; it is corrupted by the railroad interests. The farmers are faced with economic disaster. The railroad is presented as a huge bureaucracy with innumerable regulations and immense power—an octopus with tentacles reaching into all the power centers of government.

Into the midst of the struggle arrives Presley, an Easterner and a poet who is returning to California from Europe with the idea of writing an epic poem. Presley is visiting the ranch of Derrick, the leader of the struggle against the railroad. Much of the story is told from Presley's point of view. He gradually realizes the proportions of the events that are occurring, studies history and economics in order to enhance his understanding, and eventually takes action by throwing a bomb.

Violence, which the law is powerless to prevent, erupts on numerous occasions. When the farmers and railroad men confront each other, the farmers misinterpret what is happening and open fire. As a result of attempting to thwart the power of the railroad, many deaths occur, with the farmers bearing by far the worst of the destruction. Because the farmers have disobeyed the marshal's orders, the railroad men who shot and killed some of them bear no legal consequences. Early in the story, one of the farmers, Dyke, who has been double-crossed by the railroad, lashes out and robs a train, killing a guard in the process. He is convicted of murder and sentenced to life imprisonment. The novel is replete with instances of the savage nature of men overcoming their civilized selves. Violence is seen as the inevitable result of competing forces engaged in a power struggle. The fact that violence and corruption destroy even good people seems to be a natural phenomenon.

The course of events changes Presley from a romantic poet into an anarchist.

In the process, he is torn between a romantic view of the West and a naturalistic view of the country. He is driven by the injustice of the railroad's encroachment on natural values into a sense of social responsibility and, eventually, action. He longs to kill Behrman, an agent of the railroad. He muses: "Oh, to sink his fingers deep into the white, fat throat of the man . . . to pay him back for the long years of extortion and oppression, to square accounts for bribed jurors, bought judges, corrupted legislatures, to have justice for the trick of the ranchers' railroad commission" (*O*, 382).

The law is corrupt and exercised solely in favor of the railroad: " 'If there's a law in this land—' 'If there is, it is in Shelgrim's [head of the railroad] pocket. Who owns the courts in California? Ain't it Shelgrim?' " (*O*, 195–196). Even Lyman Derrick, a lawyer and son of the leader of the League of Farmers, cooperates with the railroad in destroying his father in order to enlist the power of the railroad in his political ambitions.

In the end, the railroad wins the struggle and takes control of the farmers' valley. The leader of the farmers' struggle suffers devastating losses at the hands of natural forces. The injustice of the defeat and destruction at the hand of the natural forces is disproportionate to any of the farmers' actions. Human law plays no significant role; all actions and consequences are outside the law. Despite the destruction that occurs in the course of the novel, Norris somehow delivers an optimistic message. Vanamee, portrayed as a mystic or "born poet" as opposed to Presley, a "made poet," urges an optimistic view on him—a view that seems oddly out of place with many of the events of the story. Vanamee tells Presley: "Evil is short-lived. Never judge of the whole round of life by the mere segment you can see. The whole is, in the end, perfect" (*O*, 448).

Despite the victory of the railroad in swallowing up the ranches, several events occurring near the end of the novel seem to bear out the optimistic view of Vanamee. Behrman, a thoroughly evil character without redeeming qualities, motivated solely by a desire for wealth and power, trips and falls into the hold of the ship, *Swanhilda*, and is "drowned" in his own wheat. The event is a pure accident, an act of destruction by the natural forces of the universe. While Behrman is not the principal agent of the railroad, Norris seems to be suggesting that the natural forces of the environment carry the universe toward good, rather than toward evil or mere nothingness. At the end of the novel, Presley boards the *Swanhilda*, which is carrying a load of wheat for starving people in India, suggesting again that some good may come from the suffering. Although the novel as a whole contains elements of both optimism and pessimism, Norris concludes the book with a positive statement:

> *But the WHEAT remained* . . . that mighty world force, that nourisher of nations. . . . Falseness dies; injustice and oppression in the end of everything fade and vanish away. Greed, cruelty, selfishness, and inhumanity are short-lived; the individual suffers but the race goes on. . . . The larger view always and through all shams, all wickedness, discovers the truth that will, in the end, prevail, and all things surely, inevitably, resistlessly work together for good. (*O*, 458)

Whether the optimistic or pessimistic view prevails, it is clear that the events portrayed in *The Octopus* occur outside the reach of human law. The American idea of progress is seriously questioned in this text, even if some concept of universal progress emerges from the events.

## *MAGGIE, A GIRL OF THE STREETS*: ILLUSION AND DELUSION

Stephen Crane, also writing with a naturalistic viewpoint, portrayed his disillusionment with the American idea in a story with an urban setting. Crane's inscription on copies of *Maggie* that he presented to several friends reads:

> It is inevitable that you will be greatly shocked by this book but continue please with all possible courage to the end. For it tries to show that environment is a tremendous thing in the world and frequently shapes lives regardless. If one proves that theory one makes room in Heaven for all sorts of souls (notably an occasional street girl) who are not confidently expected to be there by many excellent people.[33]

Crane's inscription suggests a theory that one's environment is part of one's fate. Maggie is what she is because her world is the way it is. The events in the novel do tend to support that interpretation. The novel, however, contains suggestions that other factors are involved as well in determining Maggie's fate. These other factors include Maggie's failure to perceive and interpret accurately the people and events occurring around her and her consequent failure to make correct personal judgments about her own course in her world. Whether the force of the environment alone determines the human consequences in the story or whether inevitable human weaknesses contribute, the end result is a world without hope or optimism—a world where the American idea of progress and goodness does not exist.

A brief summary of *Maggie*, a book which Crane wrote at the age of twenty-two (just seven years before his death) and published at his own expense when he could not find a publisher, will provide the necessary background. At the beginning of the narrative, Maggie and her brother, Jimmie, are children living in the slums of New York City with their alcoholic and abusive parents. In the opening scene, which describes an ironic event that suggests a major theme of the story, Jimmie is engaged in an apparently chivalric endeavor: "A very little boy stood upon a heap of gravel for the honor of Rum Alley. He was throwing stones at howling urchins from Devil's Row, who were circling madly about the heap and pelting him" (*MGS*, 127).

Jimmie, unable to hold his own against the rival gang, is losing the fight when an older boy, Pete, later Maggie's seducer who is responsible for her *ruin* in the eyes of the wretched community, happens along and disperses the Devil's Row boys. The punishment that next befalls Jimmie is characteristic of the violence within his family. First his father, then his mother, kick and beat Jimmie to punish him for fighting. The entire incident reveals the operation of the honor code of the streets. Pride and respect in the eyes of the community (even the community of urchins) demands violence. In Jimmie's case, the other gang broke one of the rules by piling on when he was engaged in a fight with one boy. He was still bound, however, to fight to the end against the whole group. The irony of honor and pride being bound up in the defense of a heap of gravel is striking, but that kind of self-delusion is seen repeatedly in the course of events.

After Jimmie's father breaks up the fight, Jimmie and his father approach the dreary building where they live. Maggie appears: ''A small ragged girl dragged a red, bawling infant along the crowded ways'' (*MGS*, 130). The life of the family is pervaded by violence and turmoil. Both parents are filled with alcohol most of the time and filled with anger and hatred all of the time. The children live in terror. A neighbor's question to Jimmie cuts to the essence of the family's life: '' 'Eh, child, what is it dis time? Is yer fader beatin' yer mudder, or yer mudder beatin' yer fader?' '' (*MGS*, 134).

Maggie, despite the abusive and gloomy environment, ''blossomed in a mud puddle'' (*MGS*, 141). She grows to have compassion, fine sensibilities, and is hard-working. She meets Pete, who has become a bartender, by occupation, and a high-living man in this part of town. Maggie is attracted to Pete, whose fine clothes and style impress her. She misjudges him completely, however, and perceives him as the ideal man and her hero. She is seduced by Pete, who has no honorable intentions; ultimately, Pete abandons Maggie.

Maggie has moved out of her wretched home, in the meantime, and is condemned by her mother and brother for her scandalous affair with Pete. Ironically, they perceive her as a fallen woman and curse her. Their harsh words persuade her to leave home. After she has left, her mother declares: ''May she be cursed for ever!'' (*MGS*, 159). Maggie's mother never considered her a pearl (as Hester, in *The Scarlet Letter*, saw her child, Pearl), but she cannot understand how her daughter could fall so low. The mother, of course, has no sense of her own sorry situation.

After Pete abandons Maggie for another woman, Maggie attempts to return home but finds herself unjustly condemned in the eyes of the entire slum community as well as those of her family. Despite their degrading lives, rank with alcoholism, crime, violence, and child abuse, the community judges her guilty of violating a code of honor that imposes special standards of conduct on young women. Perhaps, however, as the only flower growing in their ''mud puddle,'' she is the natural object of revenge for their unhappy lives. Rejected by her family, she seeks out Pete who, in an ironic twist, repudiates her because her reputation is ruined and he is fearful that his reputation will be stained.

Maggie resorts to life on the streets where, apparently, she is successful for a while, but finally falls from grace even there and throws herself into the river. Her death is greeted without compassion or grief, but only with false mourning.

As a final insult, her mother sheds a few tears, but only after finishing her meal and coffee, and pronounces that she will forgive Maggie for her sins.

As for faith in the law as the organizing force of social order, Maggie is outside the protection of the law, as much as Nancy in ''That Evening Sun.'' Not only does the law fail to protect her, the representatives of the law, in fact, are accomplices in the criminality and violence. Maggie's mother, like so many other patrons of arraignment courts, is a well-known figure greeted by court officials with familiarity if not warmth. She banters with her acquaintances among the police justices. She has been arrested repeatedly for drunkenness and takes to excusing her conduct by a story of her daughter's disgrace. One justice finally says: ''Mary, the records of this and other courts show that you are the mother of forty-two daughters who have been ruined. The case is unparalleled in the annals of this court'' (*MGS*, 170).

The law in Maggie's world basically allows the code of the streets to prevail and govern, intervening only when necessary to preserve the society outside the slum community or to maintain minimal order. Neither law nor morality are vital forces. The roots of violence are close to the surface in the urban world of *Maggie*. Violence is acceptable in the slum culture. The people of the slum have little motivation to behave differently. Just as violence is seen as a necessary component in the code of the streets in urban American in the 1990s, so violence was seen as an essential and inescapable element in Maggie's world.

The themes that emerge from a close reading of *Maggie*—environmental determinism or fatalism, illusion and delusion, violence, and distrust of law as a source of justice as well as order—are common themes that run through much of American literature. The aspects of self-delusion that govern Maggie's interaction with her environment, leading to her self-destruction, consist of false perceptions of the facts, erroneous interpretation of the meaning of the facts, and inability to make sound judgments about her own behavior. Similar self-delusion is present in the behavior of virtually all the characters in the novel.

The themes of environmental determinism, illusion/delusion, violence, and distrust of law are further illustrated in *The Big Money, The Day of the Locust*, and *The Great Gatsby*. Analysis of these works reveals more about the fading of the American dream.

## *THE BIG MONEY*: SUBORDINATION AND DISILLUSIONMENT

Dos Passos, a writer of the 1920s and 1930s and a contemporary of Fitzgerald and Hemingway, was deeply interested in politics. He moved through various stages of political ideology, from early idealism to identification with the downtrodden, hostility to the economic and political establishment and association with communism and, finally, conservatism. His monumental trilogy *U.S.A.* carried out his purpose of presenting in fiction the social history of his lifetime. In doing so, he proved how the idealism of the eighteenth and nineteenth centuries of Emerson, Whitman, and Jefferson gave root to the idealism of the twentieth century.

Early in his career, as a student at Harvard, he expressed his apocalyptic vision: ''Until Widener is blown up, and [Harvard President] A. Lawrence Lowell assassinated and the Business School destroyed and its site sowed with salt—no good will come out of Cambridge.''[34] That apocalyptic vision resonates with the thinking of Nathanael West, as expressed in *The Day of the Locust*, in which Tod Hackett is in the process of painting on canvas his apocalyptic vision of Los Angeles when a human explosion occurs in the streets. That explosion, itself, brings to mind the Los Angeles riots of 1992 surrounding the acquittal of police officers in the Rodney King case. The failure of the jury's decision to satisfy portions of the citizenry fueled the riots. Although both *The Big Money* and *The Day of the Locust* were written more than fifty years ago, both are remarkably relevant to events of the 1990s.

The *U.S.A.* trilogy employs a wide variety of narrative styles drawn from journalism, including news headlines produced via a NEWSREEL technique (providing social and political background), a ''camera eye'' which provides subjective comment,[35] and numerous case histories. The series traces the lives of many characters who appear and reappear through the course of history from the beginning of the twentieth century to the Great Depression. At the midpoint of the trilogy are the First World War and subsequent peace negotiations.

Two historical characters who have important roles in the story are Sacco and Vanzetti, the two anarchists who were accused of murdering a paymaster in Bridgewater County, Massachusetts.[36] Dos Passos was greatly troubled by their convictions. Controversy, in fact, continues to the present concerning the circumstances of their trial. The trial has cultural as well as legal significance for American society and stands as a reminder that the judicial system is highly vulnerable to public sentiment, a fact which is continually brought home to modern Americans. In that sense, the case has a continuing relevance for American society.

The final portion of *The Big Money* deals with the failed efforts of many factions of the political left to free Sacco and Vanzetti and culminates with the beating of a fictional character, Mary French, an alienated and idealistic woman who has become radicalized by the historical events. NEWSREEL LXVI informs the reader: ''HOLMES DENIES STAY . . . CHICAGO BARS MEETINGS . . . *For justice thunders condemnation* . . . WASHINGTON KEEPS EYE ON RADICALS . . . *Arise rejected of the earth* . . . SACCO AND VANZETTI MUST DIE . . . *I feel better that you will not come to the death house so that you could not see the horrible picture of three living in agony waiting to be electrocuted*'' (*BM*, 460–461).

Dos Passos presents his own opinion about the corruption of the judicial system, hopelessness of the cause of the reformers, and despair and resignation at the fact that ''we are two nations'' (*BM*, 462). He creates a bleak portrait of defeat and abandonment of the American dream. He perceives that the law, as the instrument of the rich and powerful, has failed in its role of fairness and justice. Dos Passos presents the immigrants and, presumably, the poor and downtrodden who make up one of the "two nations" (*BM*, 462), as faithful to the "clean words our fathers spoke" (*BM*, 462) and the rich and powerful who control the branches of government, as the "strangers who have turned our language inside out" and corrupted the words that constitute the governing texts. In his view, the law is in the hands of those who exploit the power it bestows for their own purposes—they sit "with their feet on the tables under the dome" (*BM*, 462).

The viability of the American dream was questioned by Dos Passos as he portrayed the prevailing historical climate in *The Big Money*. He saw violence committed by the state against the true inheritors of the "clean words" of the founders. He perceived that hypocrisy and delusion on the part of the rich and powerful were evident. They pretended to represent the American idea and the American dream but they were, in his view, illegitimate representatives, just as Percy Grimm was the illegitimate agent of the law in Faulkner's story. Dos Passos's message was that when law is subordinated to power or wealth, it can become a political device of those who control it.

## *THE DAY OF THE LOCUST*: APOCALYPSE NOW

Nathanael West's portrait of America is every bit as discouraging as that of Dos Passos. Nearly everyone in this novel is severely afflicted by disillusionment and apathy. There are silent people waiting for a disaster, such as an airplane crash, to shake them out of their dreary lives. Homer Simpson, an acquaintance of the protagonist, Tod Hackett, sits motionless in his home, his own consciousness too paralyzed even to create a wish, much less a desire.

Even Tod, a young artist graduated from the Yale School of Fine Arts, and the sanest person in the story, spends much of his time dreaming. On one occasion, he dreams about the invasion of California by the "pick of America's madmen" (*DL*, 118). Tod decides that "the milk from which it had been skimmed was just as rich in violence . . . There would be civil war" (*DL*, 118). An explosion of violence does occur at the end of the novel, while a massive crowd is waiting for a glimpse at celebrities who are scheduled to appear. The complete scope of Tod's vision, however, appears in the huge, apocalyptic painting which Tod is creating. Even as he is being swallowed up by the monstrous mob which lurches out of control, Tod's imagination is working on his painting.

The crowd, composed mostly of middle-class people, grows to huge proportions and is beyond the control of the police. The people, once a crowd, become a mob on a rampage. Individual people lose their restraint along with their identity in the anonymity of the multitude. In such a setting, personal restraint gives way to violence unconstrained by individual conscience, as Robert Penn Warren portrayed so well in *Night Rider*. West describes the development of the mob scene:

> New groups, whole families, kept arriving. He could see a change come over them as soon as they had become part of the crowd. Until they reached the line, they looked diffident, almost furtive, but the moment they had become part of it, they turned arrogant and pugnacious. . . . They were savage and bitter, especially the middle-aged and the old, and had been made so by boredom and disappointment.
>
> All their lives they had slaved at some kind of dull, heavy labor . . . saving their pennies and dreaming of the leisure that would be theirs when they had enough. . . . Where else should they go but California, the land of sunshine and oranges?
>
> Once there, they discover that sunshine isn't enough. . . . Nothing happens. (*DL*, 177–178)

West goes on to describe their jaded lives:

> Their boredom becomes more and more terrible. . . . Every day of their lives they read the newspapers and went to the movies. Both fed them on lynchings, murder, sex crimes, explosions, wrecks, love nests, fires, miracles, revolutions, wars. . . . The sun is a joke. Oranges can't titillate their jaded palates. Nothing can ever be violent enough to make taut their slack minds and bodies. They have been cheated and betrayed. (*DL*, 178)

The narrator, Tod, is enveloped in the escalating violence of the crowd. Even though he is injured, he focuses on his apocalyptic painting. Earlier, he had envisioned showing Los Angeles on fire. Now, he saw the painting: ''Across the top . . . he had drawn the burning city. . . . [T]he mob [came] carrying baseball bats and torches. . . . No longer bored, they sang and danced joyously in the red light of the flames'' (*DL*, 184).

The roots of the violence that erupts can be found in the apathy and disillusionment of the people, who have realized that their dreams could not be fulfilled. Far from the utter destitution and misery of the people in Maggie's slum world, these people are victims of their own inability to translate their wishes into goals or their dreams into achievable desire.

They are trapped in the same type of self-delusion as Crane's characters. Having established illusory wish-goals for themselves—goals that they falsely believe will produce fulfillment and happiness—they no longer can perceive the world around them accurately nor can they interpret the factual realities wisely. They, therefore, cannot set realistic goals for their personal courses in life. Lost in their boredom, misery and bitterness, they await external happenings to relieve their purposeless existence. They crave ''explosions''—dramatic catastrophes that may bring momentary relief from the numbness that conceals the dull pain of their existence. Whether deterministic—because it represents an inescapable truth about humankind—or self-induced—because it is within their power to control—their world is bleak and devoid of the hope of progress traditionally inherent in the American idea and in the promise of America's founding texts. Neither law nor morality serves as a sufficient ordering force for their world.

Once again, as in *The Octopus* and *Maggie*, the representatives of the law are portrayed as accomplices in the scheme that renders the people powerless and hopeless. In *The Day of the Locust*, the police are false and deceptive, as they drag people off from the threatening crowd only to beat them privately. No external meaning exists for the realities. Perhaps this is what Tod intuitively understands as he begins to scream in concert with the screaming siren, as he loses contact with the real world and the illusory world created by his paintings.

## *THE GREAT GATSBY*: LOST DREAMS

At the end of ''Winter Dreams,'' a short story that Fitzgerald regarded as a trial run for *Gatsby*, Dexter Green faces the loss of a dream when he learns unhappy news about the girl he once loved:

> Even the grief he could have borne was left behind in the country of illusion, of youth, of the richness of life, where his winter dreams had flourished.
>
> ''Long ago,'' he said, ''long ago there was something in me but now that thing is gone. Now that thing is gone, that thing is gone. I cannot cry. I cannot care. That thing will come back no more.''[37]

Several years later, Fitzgerald repeated that thought in describing *Gatsby*: ''the loss of those illusions that give such color to the world that you don't care whether things are true or false so long as they partake of the magical glory.''[38]

The story of Gatsby, a story about destroyed illusions and lost dreams, is narrated by Nick Carraway, a young Yale graduate and bond salesman, who gradually moves into the rich, idle, self-indulgent Long Island world of Gatsby and Daisy, the object of Gatsby's ''winter dreams.'' The novel contains a thoroughly American story of progress and success, compromise and corruption, disillusionment and destruction. While Gatsby has managed to translate his wishes into desires, and desires into realities, he has done so by deception, self-delusion, and corruption. The reality cannot satisfy the dream, and destruction results, leaving a residue of ashes in place of the green freshness that once was America.

James Gatz, a poor boy from the Middle West, is driven to realize his dream of success and wealth. By the time of America's entry into World War I, Gatz had become Jay Gatsby, a lieutenant stationed in Kentucky, with a girlfriend from Louisville, Daisy Fay, who was to embody all his dreams. After he was sent to France, however, she married the handsome, athletic, and rich Tom Buchanan. After the war, Tom and Daisy are living in Long Island, leading a reckless and idle life, with Tom seeking excitement in adultery.

Gatsby, who is still obsessed with Daisy and has become rich from his underworld-connected activities, takes a house near the Buchanans, and begins giving extravagant parties for the denizens of the Jazz Age. His goal is to recapture Daisy and rescue her from her miserable life, thus realizing his dreams.

Nick Carraway brings Daisy and Gatsby together, and Gatsby nearly succeeds in convincing Daisy that she never loved Tom. In the showdown scene involving Gatsby, Daisy, and Tom, Gatsby insists that Daisy publicly repudiate her love for her husband. Daisy breaks down at that point and Tom regains control. In desperation, she cries out, " 'Oh, you want too much!' . . . 'I love you now—isn't that enough? I can't help what's past.' She begins to sob helplessly. 'I did love him once—but I loved you too' " (*GG*, 133). Tom then exposes the illegal source of Gatsby's wealth and wins Daisy back.

That same day, Daisy, driving Gatsby's car, accidentally strikes and kills Tom's current mistress, the wife of a garage owner. Ironically, the fabulous automobile, which was one of Gatsby's symbols of wealth and success, contributed to his destruction. Tom convinces the garage man, who wrongly suspects that Gatsby was his wife's lover, that Gatsby had killed the woman. The garage man shoots and kills Gatsby, who is waiting for word from Daisy, and then kills himself. Tom and Daisy, immune in "their money or their vast carelessness" (*GG*, 180), disappear and "let other people clean up the mess they had made" (*GG*, 181).

Gatsby, in many ways, embodies the American dream of prosperity and material success. His life has been devoted to fulfilling his romantic dream of wealth and power. In order to sustain that dream and his progress toward it, he maintained an almost adolescent self-delusion about his relationship to the world. James Gatz "invented just the sort of Jay Gatsby that a seventeen-year-old boy would be likely to invent, and to this conception he was faithful to the end" (*GG*, 99). Initially, he cut himself off from his past as youthful America, inspired by thinkers like Emerson, cut itself off from the European past. In believing that his dreams would last forever, he was convinced that he could recapture the past with Daisy, given enough wealth and power. In that sense, his vision resembles one version of the American dream—the delusion that youth and beauty can be recaptured perpetually if only one can make enough money.

As a romantic dreamer who undertakes to realize his dreams in the most expedient way, he symbolizes the American experience. He ignores the fact that he corrupted his dream by selecting materialism as the means and, then, by amassing his fortune through illegal methods. Gatsby has even condoned the use of the violence that pervades the unsavory world of Meyer Wolfsheim, the racketeer-gambler who is Gatsby's business associate. Ironically, Gatsby dies by violence which results from a series of mistaken assumptions. Gatsby feels free to rewrite his own history as he chooses. In the end, however, the illusory nature of his existence is revealed by the fact that the only people who attend his funeral, besides Nick, are four or five servants, the postman from West Egg, and Gatsby's father, Mr. Gatz, bearing the name that Gatsby had left behind. Gatsby is bound by the past but cannot recapture and relive his dreams of the past. His life was an illusion fabricated from false values.

Tom and Daisy, despite their wealth, live out their "American dream" in delusion. They both disparage Gatsby's ill-gotten wealth. They indulge, however, in their own extravagant lifestyle. Tom has neither ideals nor integrity; he is fully self-indulgent and incapable of taking responsibility for any of the deaths that occurred. He remains in a moral wasteland without remorse or responsibility. Daisy is morally bankrupt, having been demeaned by her husband's infidelity, but dependent upon him for maintenance of the splendid lifestyle to which she is accustomed. Money, however, brings her neither love nor fulfillment.

With the exception of Nick Carraway, the major characters lack insight into their lives. Blinded by their illusions, they neither perceive nor interpret reality accurately. Consequently, their lives are as aimless and purposeless as the inhabitants of West's California wasteland. Nick, however, is a sophisticated observer of human nature. He is capable of perceiving astutely, interpreting correctly when he chooses, and of drawing moral conclusions from the events and behavior. After the series of events bring a close to Gatsby's life, Nick has acquired a sense of moral responsibility and no longer wishes to remain in the morally vacuous world. He returns to the Midwest. He rejects the utter selfishness and corruption of the world of Gatsby and the Buchanans. He does, however, respect Gatsby's pursuit of a dream, even a corrupt one, as superior to a life of total self-indulgence: "Gatsby believed in the green light, the orgiastic future that year by year recedes before us. It eluded us then, but that's no matter—tomorrow we will run faster, stretch out our arms farther. . . . And one fine morning—So we beat on, boats against the current, borne back ceaselessly into the past" (*GG*, 182).

Law clearly does not provide the framework of order and justice in the world of Gatsby and Buchanan. Gatsby operates outside the law. His ascendancy and his downfall occur as a result of forces outside the law. The garage man, not the law's representatives, exacts punishment (albeit mistakenly) for his wife's death, and then imposes the ultimate punishment on himself. Neither Tom nor Daisy is ever held legally—or morally—responsible for the deaths. Inequality prevails in Gatsby's world, where the America portrayed is divided into two classes (recalling Dos Passos's words)—those who partake of Gatsby's world and those who remain on the outside.

On one occasion, Gatsby is stopped by a policeman, apparently for speeding, but, when Gatsby waves a white card from his wallet before the policeman's eyes, the policeman merely responds: " 'Right you are,' agreed the policeman, tipping his cap. 'Know you next time, Mr. Gatsby. Excuse *me*!' " (*GG*, 68). When Nick asks about the white card, Gatsby informs him that he did the commissioner a favor once and receives a Christmas card every year. The representative of the law is the accomplice of the racketeer. The code of social class and wealth controls all, even the law. Nick's closing thoughts evince a sense of determinism, if not hopelessness. We cannot change our past, nor can we recapture it. We are bound by our past and cannot escape its limitations. Our past shapes our identity.

In his final days on Long Island, before leaving for the Midwest, Nick continues to hear, in his imagination, the sounds of Gatsby's parties coming from his home. One night, he hears, as well, "a material car there, and saw its lights stop at his front steps. But I didn't investigate. Probably it was some final guest who had been away at the ends of the earth and didn't know that the party was over" (*GG*, 181). A dream that is based on unrealistic visions of material success is not viable. New visions are needed to replace outworn dreams, faulty perceptions, and unsound interpretations. The new courses to be designed need to take into account present economic realities.

## THE DREAM IN LATE-TWENTIETH-CENTURY LITERATURE

### *Libra*: Corruption at the Core

The assassination of John F. Kennedy sent shock waves through American society. The event and its aftermath represented not only the utter failure of government security to prevent the fatal attack and failure to bring the assassin to trial, but also, in the eyes of many, failure of government to discover or disclose the full breadth of the underlying conspiracy. Speculation continues to this day concerning whether one or more federal agencies were somehow involved in a plot, whether organized crime or revolutionary organizations were involved, and whether Ruby was acting alone or in concert with others. It is safe to say that the material with which *Libra* is concerned goes to the heart of the American ideas of progress and optimism about the moral goodness of humans and the authority of the legal system. The events in Dallas and their consequences reverberate to this day. They were, no doubt, amplified in effect by the other political assassinations that followed.

### *them*: No Escape

For the Wendall family, American life is suffocating rather than liberating. The promises of opportunity and freedom are meaningless to them; they are involved in a struggle to survive the violence and disillusionment that oppress them. The circumstances of life permit no escape, save into mental illness. Oates's portrayal of American society in this novel is bleak and unpromising. Little hope of progress exists and little faith in human goodness is suggested. Like *Libra*, this novel deals with life in the 1960s, a period when forces of pessimism and disillusionment gathered strength.

### *Clockers*: Street Survival

Price's novel of the urban drug world presents a sordid view of life on America's city streets as we approach the millennium. Hopelessness and violence prevail; death from AIDS stalks the drug addicts. The forces of the "war on drugs" are easily bought off with the rich profits of the drug merchants. Escape is virtually hopeless and, when it does seem possible, it happens outside the law. The only version of the American dream that exists is a purely material one—temporary material wealth through drug selling. The cynical view of drug selling characterizes it as no more than economic survival.

### *Trombone*: Profiteering in Crime

The view of late-twentieth-century American society presented by this novel is nearly as disheartening. Criminal activity is justified in terms of economic survival and the law is basically ineffective in combating the forces of corruption. A few hopeful notes exist, however. Ray is portrayed as essentially good and his criminal conduct is rationalized away in terms of expediency. He is allowed to escape unscathed by the criminal law, while his father is caught. He prevents violence from occurring on one occasion and helps Iris to escape her sordid life. Although Ray and Iris head for new territory, that does not seem sufficient to create optimism for the future or belief in societal or individual progress.

The literature selected for discussion presents differing views of problems in American life at various times in our history. The situations portrayed represent circumstances which give rise to disillusionment with the promises of the American dream. Recognizing that these situations call for the exercise of personal responsibility as well as societal responsibility, the novels do lead us to focus attention on vulnerable points in our societal fabric. The drug problem, violence, corrupt or ineffective law enforcement, lack of economic opportunity, inappropriate manipulation of economic or political power by corrupt individuals or organizations—all these situations bear close examination and correction. They all involve the legal system as well as the other branches of government.

## JUDICIAL VIEWPOINTS

It is not difficult to find a wide assortment of judicial decisions that illustrate the fading of American dreams of progress and, in addition, changes in public attitudes signaling adaptation of the traditional dream to present realities. In the former category of fading dreams are decisions in the areas of foreclosure and bankruptcy. Since the onset of the most recent economic recession, the judicial system has witnessed a noticeable increase in numbers of both types of actions.[39]

Other subjects of litigation that involve expectations of various groups about the American dream include the Haitian refugee cases,[40] the continued litigation on enforced school desegregation,[41] and the Savings and Loan scandal of the 1980s.[42] These situations involve traditional American ideas and claimed abuses of power by individuals, affecting the dreams of others. The resulting disillusionment directly affects the vitality of the American dream.

In the latter category of adaptations to present realities are decisions dealing with environmental issues and SEC (Securities and Exchange Commission) and private actions concerning insider trading violations. The amount of litigation during the 1990s in both categories may be evidence of modification of the traditional dream to encompass legal and political action involving goals and values reflecting societal values as well as individual values.[43]

*Basic Inc. v. Levinson*[44] concerned private enforcement of the Securities and Exchange Commission's Rule 10b-5 prohibiting, in connection with the purchase or sale of any security, the making of any untrue statement of a material fact or the omission of a material fact that would render statements made not misleading. The action was brought by former shareholders of Basic against the corporation and some of its directors. The decision traces the development of this area of law in the decades of the 1970s and 1980s The development of this field of litigation represents the increasing attention to the matter of protecting the investing public from abuses of individual insiders.[45]

*Nordlinger v. Hahn*[46] provides a final example of litigation that illustrates the impact of judicial decisions on features of the traditional American dream in view of modified economic circumstances. In this case, which was discussed earlier in this chapter, the challenged constitutional amendment embodied an acquisition value system of taxation whereby property would be reassessed up to current appraised value upon new construction or change in ownership. The Supreme Court upheld the acquisition-value assessment scheme against an equal protection challenge.

The discussion of legal and literary texts makes evident that the traditional American dream, arising from American ideas of progress and optimism, has lost some of its promise for some citizens because of changing economic and social circumstances in society. Some of that diminishing effect has come about involuntarily but some has occurred through direct action by government in order to respond to broadening societal goals. The latter changes may be beneficial to society as a whole because they represent an effort to shape the force of economic and social change. To the extent that the traditional dream embodies material values that cannot be widely fulfilled in our complex contemporary society, the question remains whether the loss of that aspect of the dream may be offset by positive developments in other areas of American life, including greater access to opportunities for social and political participation by more individuals.

It is important to note that the existence of high expectations about the promise of American life or about desirable opportunities does not necessitate that those expectations or opportunities should be either legislated into existence or judicially decreed as constitutional rights. Neither does it mean that all material aspirations of individuals must be realized as a matter of law. The constitutional principles that create the hope of freedom provide a protective framework for all individuals but do not guarantee material affluence or even economic equality.[47] When unrealistic material goals are allowed to have an unwarranted influence on our public policy, a danger exists that we will fall into the trap of converting citizenship into merely another variation of consumerism.

The process of revitalizing the institutions of our society in order to shape the process of change involves recommitting ourselves to the fundamental principles that define us as Americans. To carry out this revitalization, we must view our governing texts, not only as statements of principle and tradition, but as instruments that have impact on people. It is essential, as well, to understand the impact of law on individuals and also to be sure that all individuals have the opportunity to participate in the process of recommitment. In so doing, the ability to understand the impact of our written texts on individuals will be enhanced.

Our society, moreover, involves interdependence and interaction among individuals. Identifying and recognizing this interdependence is vital in order to prevent the type of moral blindness that occasionally has afflicted us at times in our history. If revitalization is to occur in an orderly, peaceful way, we must retain the capacity of self-examination and self-improvement.

Representation in societal matters, therefore, is an integral part of the process of revitalization. Representation has a variety of meanings. In one sense, it means the way someone is portrayed to others. A related meaning is concerned with the effect of definitions. The portrayal of the images of people and their behavior has an important bearing on actual behavior. Cause and effect in representation and behavior, in fact, are often confused or inverted. For example, a victim of violence may be rendered passive and subdued by the violence. That may result in the victim being seen—represented—as somehow naturally deserving of or having complicity in the violence—a dangerously false portrayal. The effect of violence becomes self-justifying and, ironically, generates more violence as it retards the development of its victims. This pattern can be seen in the case of victims of family violence, slavery, poverty, and drug abuse, among other conditions. Inclusion and participation in the political decision-making process is another aspect of representation and a key to societal harmony and stability.[48]

It is preferable for the process of revitalization to take place by means of political dialogue and action rather than as rights-based confrontation in the judicial arena. In the political sphere, all interested parties can participate and resolutions that take into account the full range of positions can be negotiated. The judicial branch is not an appropriate forum for what is essentially political decision making. The judicial process should operate on a principled, rather than political, basis. I suggest in the next chapter, however, that, consistent with a principled approach, adjudicative decision making can serve the vital function of mediating among competing and conflicting interests.

Part III

# The Judicial Role in Cultural Revitalization

Chapter 6

# Taking Responsibility: Societal Change and Judicial Decision Making

> [L]aws and institutions must go hand in hand with the progress of the human mind. As that becomes more developed, more enlightened, as new discoveries are made, new truths disclosed, and manners and opinions change with the change of circumstances, institutions must advance also, and keep pace with the times.[1]

Legal, economic, and social changes are usually assessed in terms of their impact on society as a whole. This is especially true now that important developments are rapidly transmitted throughout society, at least in headline or sound-bite form, by the sprawling information and entertainment networks. The real impact of change, however, is experienced on the individual level. The choices and decisions that people make with respect to their lives often occur in response to broad social, economic, and legal changes and developments. Within the personal dimension, the impact of language is felt, changes in perception occur, fears reveal themselves, and acts of personal courage surface. The most far-reaching legal and social developments ultimately come into focus by observing the ways individuals act and interact with others. In that dimension, the forces of societal change are shaped when people begin to think and act differently concerning other people, institutions, events, or ideas—and concerning themselves. There, the process of cultural regeneration begins as individuals and communities respond to change.

Individual action and interaction occurring in the process of attempting to secure control of life in the face of change are often evaluated in a psychological or sociological context. Viewing those actions in a legal context brings to bear other highly relevant factors. Individual coping with and shaping of change occurs within a context that is created by law, especially in American society where law pervades all aspects of life. Law is a major component of societal change and a major factor in the individual response to change.

After sketching briefly the phenomenon of legal, economic, and societal change in America, I will focus on Mark Twain's *Huckleberry Finn*, John Steinbeck's *The Grapes of Wrath*,[2] Wendell Berry's *A Place on Earth*,[3] and Russell Banks's *The Sweet Hereafter*, all of which serve as examples of individual responses to change. Finally, Saul Bellow's *Herzog*[4] will be analyzed for its suggestions concerning an effective judicial response to societal change and conflict.

These novels illustrate the way individuals respond to change—economic, social, and legal—and how they internalize the process of shaping change. The process of individual adaptation to social and economic developments and the pursuit of individual ideas of the American dream have certain characteristic elements and images. Literary works reveal the tension between the possibility of achieving the American dream and the obstacles that stand in the way. Four of the five novels cited above deal with events occurring in earlier historical periods. Only Banks's novel was written in this decade about a contemporary situation. The older novels have great value, however, in our inquiry. To a large extent, the nature of human action and interaction is timeless. What those four novels reveal about human patterns of coping and adapting, albeit with respect to past historical events, is meaningful as we consider contemporary situations.

Following up on the ideas gleaned from *Herzog*, the discussion will continue with an analysis of opinions in six recent U.S. Supreme Court cases. These opinions offer guidelines and values that will prove useful in the work of restoring cohesion and vitality to American society. The opinions highlight the elements of appropriate judicial response to change in order to reestablish a sense of direction in our national life.

## CIRCUMSTANTIAL AND LEGAL CHANGE

American society, from its inception, has undergone constant change in virtually all facets of its existence—geography, demography, economics, law, politics, technology, employment, industrialization, and social structure. The continuation of change, perhaps rather dramatic change, is inevitable. In fact, the idea of change as desirable and even necessary has been an integral part of American political culture. Although it is not possible to predict specifically the forms of future change, it is possible to identify some likely patterns.

One approach to this subject suggests that change generally takes two forms, circumstantial and legal. By *circumstantial change*, I refer to societal change that has occurred by reason of technology, demography, environmental conditions, international affairs, or other causes not directly determined or brought about by governmental action taking the form of law. *Legal change* refers to change that has occurred by governmental action through law in an effort to initiate change (or renewal of commitments to essential principles) or to respond to the existing and often changing social or economic conditions.

Both circumstantial and legal change occur regularly in America, usually in concert. In fact, the sweeping social, technological, demographic, and economic changes that have occurred, particularly in the latter part of the nineteenth and twentieth centuries, have necessitated significant legal changes in order to accommodate circumstantial change. In addition, much of the legal change has occurred because of fluctuating political ideas about the inappropriateness or unfairness of existing cultural and social conditions. While the basic political structure has remained reasonably constant, significant legal changes have occurred within that political structure.

In terms of circumstantial change, the twentieth century has produced unprecedented social transformations which have altered significantly the economic and social character of the country. In the course of the century, the nation transformed from a nation of farmers to a nation in which the economy was dominated by large industries relying on blue collar labor, and then on to a sophisticated, technology-based society dominated by highly trained, white collar employees. The society that once was completely controlled by the white male segment of the population has gradually changed into a society where political and economic authority is increasingly shared by women, nonwhites and members of minority ethnic groups. While these groups have not realized their full potential in terms of political, economic, and social strength, they have made significant strides during the course of this century.

It is indisputable, however, that the decades of the 1980s and the 1990s have witnessed political change—and accompanying legal change—that has altered the goals and direction of American society. The emergence of distinctly conservative thinking on the part of the electorate has already brought about significant changes in state and federal legislation. In the course of restoring more traditional American values, the approach to national issues has changed; even the definition of what constitutes national issues has changed in the process. Taking into account this shift in popular political thinking, the stories—legal and literary—of past decades are valuable, not only in helping us to see how individuals react to various aspects of change, but in evaluating and illuminating the present situation and problems.

## SOCIAL CONSEQUENCES: DISUNITING

Problems have resulted from the circumstantial changes of the latter part of this century. For example, the gap between rich and poor appears to be widening. It is common knowledge that cities have been largely abandoned by the middle class, leaving vast economic and social problems for the remaining poor populations. The peace and security of citizens in cities and suburbs alike are threatened by what seems to be uncontrollable crime and violence. The court system is barely able to manage the burgeoning volume of criminal, civil, and family cases in an efficient and fair manner. Serious erosion of the authority of governmental institutions and widespread disillusionment with the political process has resulted.[5] Continuing racial tension, poverty, problems of the homeless, failure of social welfare programs, and the perceived absence of a shared value system are some of the accompanying features.

These developments have also contributed to negative cultural developments in American society. The cultural condition that has resulted has been described in various ways by commentators. Robert Hughes, for example has called it the *Culture of Complaint* in his book by that name.[6] Arthur M. Schlesinger, Jr., has described it as *The Disuniting of America* in his book with that title.[7] Various features of this cultural condition have also been described as fragmentation, separation, cultural fraying, abuse excuses,[8] disillusionment with the political process, and excessive rights-based litigation.[9] It may well be that this cultural phenomenon, whatever it is called, is a predictable and natural outgrowth of our system of government, our technology, and our cultural qualities, together with several major historical events—the Vietnam conflict and the ending of the Cold War, among others. Regardless of the causes, the malady seems to have metastasized significantly.

It is reasonable to question whether the institutions and processes of government have transformed sufficiently to keep pace with circumstantial change and whether they are able to deal effectively with the problems presented by the centrifugal forces at work in the culture.

## POLITICAL AND LEGAL OBSTACLES: SUFFOCATING THE SYSTEM

One of the difficulties in managing the fast pace of change is the political reality that our democratic form of government involves frequent elections (leading to virtually continuous political campaigning) and, therefore, frequent reorganization of our governmental institutions and processes. The political change produced by elections is not necessarily related to the underlying circumstantial change, whether social, technological, demographic, or economic. Political change, more often than not, seems to be directed by the need to consolidate political power rather than by social or economic policy. Even when political change has an independent economic or social purpose, political energy is often focused on maintaining the status quo by ignoring the circumstantial change that needs to be addressed.

Another difficulty with political response to circumstantial change has been pointed out by James O. Freedman in his description of the stages of existence of administrative agencies—the governmental organizations that are commonly created to deal with social and economic changes. Freedman's illuminating description of those stages is worth noting because it is relevant to any discussion of the effectiveness of government bureaucracies:

[A]dministrative agencies can be described as passing through several stages of existence. . . . They are usually born amid high hopes that government, at last, has taken effective action in creating a new mechanism to carry out the nation's goals in an area requiring dedicated attention. Fired by the public support that brought them into being, they act with enthusiasm, vigor, and adaptive flexibility. But these same agencies come to adolescence surrounded by charges that they have . . . become complacent and tired. The problems within the agencies' jurisdiction often prove more intractable than their creators anticipated, the task of continually confronting resistant social phenomena becomes increasingly frustrating . . . and the intensity of the public support that they enjoyed initially begins to wane as new problems engage the nation's attention. Agencies then enter upon maturity, a period in which their processes become institutionally routinized and greater emphasis seems to be placed upon conformity to bureaucratic norms than upon innovative achievements. And finally—in one of the few reliable laws of governmental behavior—administrative agencies hardly ever die.[10]

Freedman's observation applies to a broad range of governmental activity. In recent years, legislative bodies have increasingly delegated their political decision-making responsibilities to administrative agencies that are beyond the reach of the political process. Their officials cannot be voted out of office. An important recent example of such delegation is the congressional creation of the United States Sentencing Commission as an independent body of the judicial branch with power to promulgate binding sentencing guidelines for the federal courts. That delegation of authority over judicial matters was held constitutional in *Mistretta v. United States* and remains a source of continuing controversy.[11] Justice Scalia's vigorous dissent in that case, on the basis that there is "no place within our constitutional system for an agency created by Congress to exercise no governmental power other than the making of laws,"[12] deserves close attention.

Examples of the ways in which government bureaucracies and the laws that define and empower them operate to frustrate and humiliate citizens in defiance of common sense are rampant. Philip K. Howard, in his recent book *The Death of Common Sense: How Law Is Suffocating America*,[13] states, for example:

We seem to have achieved the worst of both worlds: a system of regulation that goes too far while it also does too little. This paradox is explained by the absence of the one indispensable ingredient of any successful human endeavor: use of judgment. In the decades since World War II, we have constructed a system of regulatory law that basically outlaws common sense. Modern law, in an effort to be "self-executing," has shut out our humanity.[14]

As examples, Howard mentions the provisions of OSHA, the Occupational Safety and Health Administration Act of 1970, and RCRA, the Resource Conservation and Recovery Act, both of which have required enormous expense and record-keeping, often securing only spotty compliance with minimal benefit to society.

## EXERCISING CONTROL OVER CHANGE THROUGH LAW

A vital question in considering the future of American society is whether the American people will exercise control to direct and shape circumstantial change. Another concerns how much direction and shaping should occur consistent with the basic principles of our democracy. If we ignore our responsibilities or if we simply resist the forces of social and economic change, change will occur without the benefit of societal control and direction.

Virtually all the unresolved social, political, and economic problems caused by and arising from circumstantial change in America during the past century have had a legal dimension, and have presented themselves as legal problems. Whether or not that is desirable, or inevitable, are other issues. American democracy, especially during the latter half of this century, has operated with a strong orientation toward court adjudication of societal problems. While a case-by-case adjudication of the problems framed in the form of lawsuits has been accomplished, many of the cultural and social problems presented in that format remain unresolved, awaiting more comprehensive and far-reaching resolution in the political process.

## CONQUERING CHANGE: FICTIONAL VIEWS

Both *Huckleberry Finn* and *The Grapes of Wrath* are concerned with the process of response to and shaping of social, economic, and legal change. Each novel features movement from one place to another, both literally and figuratively. In each narrative, in fact, there is a specific *literary vehicle* used to portray that movement or process. In *Huckleberry Finn*, the vehicle consists of rafting on a river; in *The Grapes of Wrath*, trucking on a highway. In both novels, in the course of response to change, a certain ideal society comes into being—a temporary utopian environment that cannot be maintained once the movement ceases and the return to *reality*—conventional society and routine life—occurs. At that point, other priorities take over and, generally, the sense of community created during the movement or process of change succumbs to individual concerns and increased insularity. Each story contains tension between the optimistic belief in progress and fulfillment and, typically, the confrontation of unanticipated obstacles that prevent or, at least, impede and delay fulfillment of the American dream. Both stories illustrate the way individuals can respond constructively to societal events and change, even under adverse circumstances. *A Place on Earth* and *The Sweet Hereafter* deal with many of the same issues. Although the role of community is a vital element, the importance of geographical place assumes a major role as well. In *The Sweet Hereafter*, lawyers and the law together are a dominant force in the change that the community must confront.

## *HUCKLEBERRY FINN*: ADVENTURES ON THE RAFT

Mark Twain's *Huckleberry Finn* was published in 1885. Twain placed the story, however, some forty to fifty years earlier in the era of slavery. Between the time in which the plot was set and the time of writing and publication, the Civil War was fought. Although the slaves had theoretically been freed, in actuality, the social and economic status of the former slaves remained substantially the same. In other words, the law had changed but the social attitudes and economic realities had not.

The novel is the personal story of Huck Finn, the son of Pap, who was the town drunkard. Although Huck has been living with the Widow Douglas and her sister, Miss Watson, he resists their efforts to civilize him. After his father learns that he has come into some money (which, actually, is safely in the hands of Judge Thatcher), he kidnaps Huck and holds him prisoner in a small shack across the river. Huck decides to escape to avoid the terrible beatings that his father inflicts. He devises a plan by which he will hide on Jackson's Island, but will leave clues to suggest that he has been murdered.

Huck carries out his plan and, while hiding out on the island, he meets Jim, Miss Watson's runaway slave. When they learn that Jim is being sought for the murder of Huck, the two escape by floating down the Mississippi River on a raft. The remaining portion of the novel recounts the adventures of Huck and Jim as they attempt to escape to the free states in the North and to avoid the various disasters that they encounter in their travels. In the end, they meet up with Tom Sawyer, who devises several fantastic and unrealistic plans in order to free the captured Jim. After an episode in which Tom is shot in the leg, they discover that Miss Watson had freed Jim before she died. The novel concludes as Huck decides to abandon civilized society and head out into new territory.

The novel operates at three levels.[15] The first level is Huck Finn's personal story. The second level is the story of the interaction of traditional law, invoked or represented by Pap and Judge Thatcher, and private codes, represented by the racial and slave code as well as Tom Sawyer's code of private *law*. Huck's own code is also involved. On the third level, the novel is a story of legal authority and social change—how changes in systems and rules of law are transformed into social change.

Huck and Jim leave their previous world behind and enter a new *society* on the river in which the legal institutions and rules they left behind have no meaning. Huck, in fact, *dies* by his own fictitious hand and is reborn in the new world of the raft. Huck and Jim become equals and Huck's perception of Jim changes. Jim becomes a person instead of property in Huck's eyes. Before their mutual journey, Jim even regards himself as an object of property: "I owns myself, en I's wuth eight hund'd dollars. I wisht I had de money, I wouldn' want no mo" (*HF*, 54).

The transformation in Huck's perception of Jim occurs at two turning points in the story. The first turning point follows one of Huck's pranks on Jim. Huck had been separated from Jim and the raft. When Huck finally returns to the raft, Jim is asleep. Huck then pretends that Jim has been asleep the whole time and that Huck's disappearance was only a dream. Jim is fooled for a time but, when he realizes that Huck has been making fun of him, he rebukes Huck. For the first time, Huck understands Jim's devotion to him and that Jim experiences human feelings. Huck, with difficulty, brings himself to offer an apology:

> It made me feel so mean I could almost kissed *his* foot to get him to take it back. It was fifteen minutes before I could work myself up to go and humble myself . . . but I done it, and I warn't ever sorry for it afterward, neither. I didn't do him no more mean tricks, and I wouldn't done that one if I'd 'a' knowed it would make him feel that way. (*HF*, 90)

The second turning point occurs after Huck has decided to turn Jim in. When he is put to the test, he has a change of heart and lies to the slave hunters to protect Jim.

The process of change, as it is translated into action in *Huckleberry Finn*, involves an interaction of language, meaning (old and new), and human perception (and cognition). *Huckleberry Finn* suggests that law—and the social structure defined by law—"does not change in an unflinchingly linear way, nor does it change easily. . . . [Change occurs] by fits and starts, zigzags from new to old, temporarily fails, and reverts to the old order in the process."[16] When changes in human perception about ideas or people synchronize with the change in legal language, new meanings take hold and social change is possible. These changes in perception occur when Huck and Jim are on the river—the landscape of social change where the realities and restrictions of everyday society do not hold them back.

The degree of change that becomes permanent once Huck and Jim leave the river and return to society, however, is limited because of the difficulty in reconciling the disparity between Jim's position in society and Huck's position. Huck operates at the margin of his society—partly by reason of his social status, partly by choice. Although he is on the lowest level of white society, he is within the "textual community" of the society.[17] He is literate and appears to be an insider.

Huck does not fully understand, however, the texts of this society; he is a literalist and cannot comprehend the implied meanings of the texts and stories of society. He accepts the community's controlling texts and stories and is accepted by society. He is able to manipulate the various moral and legal principles as he maneuvers his way around the obstacles that cross his path. Huck's actions are judged according to society's standards, often conflicting, and he judges himself to be bad according to those standards. He does not question the authority or legitimacy of those texts. He is morally blind to the inherent evils of slavery and does not question the texts of society that authorize it. He is free to leave society when he chooses. In the end, Huck is accepted back in society but chooses to depart for the frontier: "But I reckon I got to light out for the territory ahead of the rest, because Aunt Sally she's going to adopt me and sivilize me, and I can't stand it. I been there before" (*HF*, 283).

Jim, on the other hand, does not have that range of possibilities available. Because he is not literate, he is unable to understand many of the textual stories of society. Because of his racial, economic, political, and social position in society—a slave—he cannot maneuver, as Huck can, through the corridors of society. As an *object*, his position is fixed. He is judged by society's laws and moral texts but he cannot manipulate those texts as Huck can. Twain, in fact, did not choose to tell the story from Jim's point of view. Jim expresses his wish to reunite his family and, while we can imagine his feelings about that, we do not learn them directly.[18]

Huck demonstrates personal courage but lacks moral vision in the fullest sense. He faces a moral dilemma: rebellion or conformity. He can choose to rebel against the laws and customs of society by befriending and assisting Jim or he can conform to the law and society's moral standards. He does begin to see Jim as a person and takes risks to save him from recapture, but does so, at least in part, out of his commitment to his own private code of honor by which he has pledged to help Jim. We do not know from the story whether one of the reasons for his rejection of society and decision to head west (as Leatherstocking did) is Huck's moral vision.

Huck rejects the possibility that Aunt Sally is going to civilize him; he does not want to be part of the society. In this story, personal interaction between Huck and Jim has, indeed, managed to bring about some changes in the attitudes and perceptions of both. On the raft—afloat on the river, a symbol of change—Jim became, for Huck, a person rather than property. Jim's continued exclusion from the society, however, is a severe limitation on the extent of change. Not until Jim can fully express himself and make his own choices in society can legal change fully materialize.

Significant legal change occurred in society from the time of the *Dred Scott* decision in 1856[19] to the Emancipation Proclamation in 1863 and the adoption of the Fourteenth Amendment in 1868. Human nature, however, does not necessarily change until individual changes in perception occur. Changes in legal language can always follow changes of heart, but changes in legal language cannot, alone, produce changes in heart.[20] When society wishes to bring about change, of course, language is a vital starting point because language can initiate the process of changing the way people think. Family violence and societal violence are major themes in *Huckleberry Finn*. In family violence law, "[w]ords of legislatures and judges forbid and punish family abuse. Words of historians, novelists, . . . [and] social workers . . . depict and decry domestic violence. . . . But are there words to describe family violence that do not make it seem routine and familiar?"[21] Family violence is an ongoing societal problem; it accounts for a significant volume of cases in our criminal justice system today.

The lessons of *Huckleberry Finn*, clearly have broad applications within the context of American society.

## *THE GRAPES OF WRATH*: RUIN AND REBIRTH

John Steinbeck's novel of social awareness demonstrates how human capacities expand and how people attempting to survive under desperate conditions form communities and develop law. The novel was written to illustrate the desperate plight of the farm families, known as "Okies," as they migrated to California from Oklahoma to escape economic ruin when their land turned into a wasteland because of drought and dust storms in the era of the Great Depression. Throughout the southern midwestern states, farmers were no longer able to make a living because of adverse weather, pressure from land banks, and machine farming. They either sold out or were forced out of the farms on which they had been tenants. Steinbeck describes how individuals adapt, create their own codes of conduct, and form new communities in response to the social and economic changes which are thrust upon them.

The narrative portion of the novel focuses on one family—the Joads—who are struggling to survive by migrating to California, pursuing the promise of a new life. Along with the Joad family narrative, Steinbeck interposes chapters in the novel to explain more fully the general historical and social context in which the narrative takes place. The novel, like *Huckleberry Finn*, draws on imagery to illustrate the process of change. In this case, rather than a river, the symbol of the process of change is a road on which the Joads travel by truck. A similar pattern of tension or confrontation between the hope for fulfillment of their dreams and the realization of the obstacles standing in the way is present.

As the novel begins, Tom Joad is hitchhiking to his parents' farm in Oklahoma. He has just been paroled from the Oklahoma state prison after serving four years of his seven-year sentence for killing a man. Tom expresses no regret for the homicide and, at this stage in his life, is interested only in his own comfort and welfare. On the road, he meets Jim Casy, an itinerant preacher who has decided to give up his preaching and just live with the people. Casy has developed an Emersonian view of the world, believing that his soul is only a small part of a larger soul.

Casy accompanies Tom to the family farm which they find deserted. They discover that the family is staying with relatives and making preparations for the move to California in hope of finding productive land. The narrative recounts the ordeal of the family's migration by truck, including the deaths of the two grandparent Joads. When they reach California, they are unable to find work. Instead, they encounter an economic situation where the migrant workers are oppressed by the landowners.

The Joad family moves on, searching for work. They arrive at a large farm in another district. Labor agitators are attempting to keep the migrants from taking the work because of the unfairly low wages that are being offered. They discover that Jim Casy is involved in organizing a strike against the orchard owners who are threatening to cut wages in half. When deputies find and kill Casy, Tom reacts angrily and kills one of the men with an axe handle. Although Tom commits murder as an act of revenge rather than self-defense, he experiences a new awareness and a rebirth. Once he separates from his family and leaves his personal concerns behind, Tom devotes himself to the economic causes of the migrants.

In the course of their journey, despite—or perhaps because of their hardships—the migrants expand their personal concerns into social concerns and, in the process, learn to form new communities. As in *Huckleberry Finn*, a utopian society exists along the way. At the outset of their journey to California in search of the symbolic "grapes of hope," they are understandably focused on their own survival. Ma Joad is the bulwark of the family and her determination and hopefulness maintains the family during their search. She holds the family together and prevents her husband, who is less courageous, from losing his will. She represents both the power of individual will and the moving force of community action.

In a chapter describing the westward migration, Steinbeck explains the daily process of building new communities. At the end of each day of travel, the cars of the migrants pulled into makeshift campgrounds. As many as twenty families might gather in a particular spot with a spring. In the course of the evening, they would become one family with shared losses and hopes.

The families gradually learned to build communities that lasted for one night and, in the morning, were disassembled. During that short time, leaders emerged, rules of law were acknowledged and *adopted*, and codes of conduct came into being. They learned the rights that were essential for human dignity, such as the right of privacy in the tent, the right to keep the past private, the right to accept or decline help, the right of expression, and the rights of the needy and sick to have help.

The families also learned what conduct to outlaw: "the right to intrude upon privacy, the right to be noisy while the camp slept, the right of seduction or rape, the right of adultery and theft and murder. These rights were crushed, because the little worlds could not exist for even a night with such rights alive" (*GW*, 214). The rules became more sophisticated as they traveled on:

> [R]ules became laws, although no one told the families. It is unlawful to foul near the camp; it is unlawful in any way to foul the drinking water; it is unlawful to eat good rich food near one who is hungry, unless he is asked to share.
>
> And with the laws, the punishments—and there were only two—a quick and murderous fight or ostracism; and ostracism was the worst. For if one broke the laws his name and face went with him, and he had no place in any world, no matter where created. (*GW*, 214)

Steinbeck is in accord with the social and political philosophy of several writers in the American tradition, including Whitman, Emerson, and Jefferson, as he expresses his views on the social plight of the Okies. Like Whitman, he expresses love for all humanity and for manual labor. Like Jefferson, he professes a preference for agrarian life where people live close to the land. Like Emerson, he speaks of the oversoul as well as the idea of self-reliance. The central idea is the realization of human interdependence. All people are part of a greater whole that transcends their present reality. As they search for solutions to their economic and social misfortunes, they are transformed from exclusive self-concern to a recognition of the need for community. The competing needs for individuality and community become the focus of the events, with the importance of community interdependence emerging as their salvation.

*Huckleberry Finn* and *The Grapes of Wrath* demonstrate the ways in which social, economic, and legal change is felt and responded to by individuals. Language and text have to be translated into human action and interaction before response to change actually occurs. The processes can happen sequentially or in concert. The way we think and talk about ideas is important, but the way we express that thinking in action is crucial. Both are necessary but often one precedes the other. As social and economic change occurs—as it does constantly in American society—a continuing process of reapplying our fundamental texts, containing our principles and values, to make sense and order out of that change is necessary. This is one of the functions of law. In this sense, law should not be a rigid force that kills the spirit of change or attempts to prevent or thwart the inevitable, but, rather, the process of applying fundamental principles to changed circumstances. The interaction of the past with the present, and the connection of our experience with our societal texts are crucial factors in directing future change.

Running through the cultural history of America is the tension between individualism and society. That historical tension produces serious concerns today. The fear of fragmentation, a powerful motivation for the adoption of the federal constitution, has materialized significantly in recent years. American society, for a variety of reasons, has fallen prey to chronic complaint and blaming, ethnocentric separatism, and division. The influential information/entertainment media have contributed to that condition, and some forces within the legal profession have fostered it as well.

## *A PLACE ON EARTH*: ENTERING THE FUTURE

The setting for this novel is the hill country of northern Kentucky during the final six months of the Second World War. The peaceful lives of the inhabitants of the small agricultural community in which the story takes place have been affected by the events of the war principally because of the young men who have been called away. The story revolves around Mat Feltner, his wife, and his pregnant daughter-in-law. Their lives have been particularly disrupted by news that Mat's son, Virgil, has been reported missing in action. The principal focus of the narrative is on the process of change in Mat as he gradually comes to grips with the uncertain status of his son. In more general terms, the process of the war's impact on the whole community is illustrated.

Although no more definite word is received about Virgil, gradually, through courage and determination, the characters accept the reality that he is dead. Each of the main characters first separates from, then rejoins, the family and the community. Mat demonstrates personal courage, in the face of pain, in accepting the death and in facing the realization that he must now confront the values and goals of his own life. Both the community of people and the physical place bring comfort to Mat. The powerful forces of society, acting through law, have swept over his life with traumatic change. Neither he nor his community has any sense of control over the events occurring outside their place in America. After receiving word of the atomic bomb being dropped on Hiroshima, Mat grapples with the idea:

> He has felt his mind borne, like a man in a little boat, on the crest of history, in a violence of pure effect, as though the event of the war, having long ago outdistanced its cause, now escapes comprehension too, and speeds on. It has seemed to him that the years of violence have at last arrived at what, without his knowing it, they had been headed for, not by any human reason or motive or wish but by the logic of violence itself. And all the events of the war are at once altered by their result—though he can't yet tell how or how much. (*APOE*, 443–444)

One of Mat's major discoveries is the role of the present in preparing for the future. He ruminates:

> I realize that I've never looked at a tree or a piece of ground, or any natural thing, without understanding that it's involved in an endless preparation—for the future, for continuance and renewal. But to see myself and other men in that way—until a few months ago I'd never had to do that, except in the limited sense of wanting to provide for Virgil. But now that Virgil is gone from the future I see that what my life leads toward is the future itself. It's a part of my condition. (*APOE*, 525)

The sense of continuity that links past, present, and future, and connects all the individuals within the community, bears consideration. Both time and place, in those senses, are factors in defining what we are and where we are heading, as individuals and, together, as a society. As we confront societal change on a large scale, those points which underlie the idea of personal responsibility should be borne in mind.

## *THE SWEET HEREAFTER*: RESTORING PEACE AFTER THE LAWYERS

*The Sweet Hereafter* also portrays a community that is deeply affected by the death of its children. In this story, however, the tragic event occurs within the community. The accident that brings about the deaths plainly produces change. Beyond that, however, outside forces of society descend upon the community, producing change in another sense. Law, lawyers, and the realities of judicial process besiege the townspeople. What those legal forces represent, in essence, is the contemporary way of resolving the disputes and problems that flow from what is essentially a legal transgression. People who once lived harmoniously, we are led to believe, are cast into adversarial combat with one another. They are in the process of relinquishing their authority to resolve the disputes to lawyers and courts.

The course of the litigation is altered, of course, when one of the children, for purely personal reasons, thwarts the process. The community beats away the forces of legal change and returns to the normal state of civility. The only exception is that the bus driver is now unfairly forced to assume the full burden of responsibility for the incident. The tension between the individual and society as a whole is brought into focus in this story. Here, law and lawyers are the fragmenting force, separating individuals and bringing the community into disarray. Only by rejecting the legal solution is harmony restored in the community. The citizens reject the changed ways brought in from the outside and return to their original state of civility.

## *HERZOG*: HUMAN AMBIGUITY

By means of his own journey through conflict and change, Bellow's protagonist, Moses Herzog, achieves a fundamental insight into the appropriate way to live amidst the contemporary chaos. Herzog's quest to find justice, to discover his humanity, and to preserve his individuality in the face of the chaotic world symbolizes the predicament of many Americans attempting to cope with contemporary society. Herzog expands on the problem as he ponders:

> what it means to be . . . [human]. In a city. In a century. In transition. In a mass. Transformed by science. Under organized power. Subject to tremendous controls. In a condition caused by mechanization. After the late failure of radical hopes. In a society that was no community and devalued the person. Owing to the multiplied power of numbers which made the self negligible. . . . Which permitted savagery and barbarism in its own great cities. (*H*, 201)

*Herzog* takes place within a time span of five days, although much of Herzog's life is compressed into those days by means of memory flashbacks. Herzog loses, then finds, himself during that time span. The crucial incidents that occur are deeply rooted in law, just as much of modern American life is permeated and controlled by legal problems and legal decisions. Herzog's quest is a shared quest—the quest of American society and of the individuals who compose it. The lessons he learns as he searches for answers bear upon the quest of individuals within American society to develop appropriate ways of ordering and focusing society, consistent with fundamental principles and present realities. While it is clear that law is merely one element in the equation, it is a vital element. Law cannot provide all the answers or remedies for the problems in American society. However, a legal system that allows for maximizing human potential while providing the framework for personal security is an essential ingredient in a healthy and vigorous society. Herzog's story is a starting point for an analysis of the necessary ingredients of that society.

Herzog is an unemployed college professor. He is divorced and alienated from his children and his siblings. He suffers through a hostile relationship with his former wife, Madeleine. He has been betrayed by his best friend, Gersbach, who is living with Madeleine. Herzog is an intellectual who is uncertain of his own values and goals and has lost his sense of meaning in life. His attempts to create order in his life through intellectual thought fail him, yet he is bonded to that way of living. His scholarly pursuits have led him to believe that he was the source of *law*, responsible for guiding humanity with his intellectual thought. Herzog sees the present stage of civilization as a time of continuing self-awareness in the development of human civilization, rather than as a time of decline.[22]

The crisis in the novel occurs when Herzog goes to the municipal court to meet his lawyer, Simkin, to discuss the custody arrangement for his daughter, June, who currently lives with Madeleine. While waiting for Simkin, he watches four legal proceedings. The shattering experience that results from his observations of the court proceedings leads him to decide impulsively to fly to Chicago where Madeleine and Gersbach are living with June. Armed with an old pistol and two bullets from his father's home, he conceives a plan to kill Madeleine and Gersbach based on his fears that they are neglecting his daughter. He ultimately abandons his hastily conceived plan. He spends two days in Chicago and, after taking June to the aquarium, he is involved in a minor traffic accident and arrested for possession of the handgun without a permit. After his brother obtains his release from jail on bond, and following a bitter confrontation with Madeleine at the police station, he returns to Ludeyville with a new outlook, the change in heart that he had been seeking.

This short outline of events provides the necessary background for a closer look at the change in heart that begins with Herzog's experience at the courthouse. Herzog enters the court building and, with time to pass while he waits for his lawyer, he enters a courtroom, nodding at the magistrate, who takes no notice of him. The first proceeding, which involves a robbery case, does not move Herzog. The second proceeding raises his interest level. Herzog is surprised when the magistrate handling the case displays a human reaction to the situation. After calling for a plea by the accused, he stops the proceedings to warn the lawyer to advise his client that a guilty plea will jeopardize his opportunities to pursue his medical career. Herzog had taken the judge to be a political hack. Herzog hears a third case, involving an attempted robbery. He feels ill and leaves the courtroom.

At this point, Herzog has become impatient waiting for his lawyer at the courthouse. He telephones Simkin's office and is told that Simkin is somewhere in the courthouse. Herzog begins to search for him. Entering a criminal courtroom, he finds a jury trial about to begin. He quickly becomes engrossed in the proceedings and forgets about his lawyer. In this proceeding, a young woman and the man with whom she had been living in a slum hotel are accused of murdering her three-year-old son. The child had been fathered by a married man who had lived with her for several months and then had deserted her. Both defendants, easily recognizable by their demeanor and clothing, appeared unmoved by the testimony about them.

The mother was a neglected child herself and is unattractive, sullen, and clumsy. She had a fourth-grade education and an IQ of 94. According to her lawyer, she had been diagnosed as having a brain lesion capable of altering her behavior radically. A poor, crippled creature, she had been sexually abused as a child and virtually abandoned by her family. After giving birth to the child, instead of giving it for adoption, she moved in with the other defendant at a miserable hotel with which Herzog was familiar.

Herzog sits forward, mouth dry, straining to hear the testimony, engrossed in the sordid story related by the medical examiner who is now on the stand. He testifies to the evidence of violent death. The child's body contained numerous bruises, broken ribs, lung and liver damage, and brain injury. Throughout the testimony, Herzog is struck by the stark contrast between the unthinkable brutality and violence of the subject matter and the restraint and calmness of all the participants in the trial—judge, jury, lawyers, and both accused. As Herzog listens to the next witness describe the mother's neglect, he realizes that he cannot comprehend the cruelty involved.

The witness is the hotel clerk, a repulsive creature. He testifies that the child cried a lot and, when he investigated, he found that the boy was kept shut in a closet for discipline. On the day of the death, there was a lot of noise. When the clerk heard something falling, he went upstairs to investigate. When he opened the door to the apartment he saw the mother hurl the child against the wall. The other defendant was lying on the bed smoking. The clerk, frightened at the woman's aspect—she was red-faced and screaming—left and called the police who found the child dead.

The defense lawyer waives cross-examination; the witness stands. At that moment, Herzog flees the courtroom, fearing that he will be sick. He stumbles into the corridor, bumping into a woman with a cane who silently identifies him as a fool. He is overcome with horror and despair at the courtroom drama. He tries to generate some feeling for the dead child but can only experience his own human feelings. He can neither cry nor pray. He wonders what is left in America to pray for. Are justice and mercy possible?

Herzog has looked into the void of the "wastelanders," those who are bound by their apocalyptic vision of human life. He has this experience in the "citadel of justice, a courtroom."[23] His sickness is "existential nausea. . . . In the reality of this negation, intellect, justice, and compassion are merely empty words. . . . Herzog experiences here the dark night of his soul.''[24] He is convinced that intellectual justification and affirmation are impossible. This realization leads the way to his abandonment of an intellectual approach to life's problems in favor of an emotional approach.

Later, after his decision not to use violence to avenge himself against Madeleine and Gersbach, Herzog begins the process of restoring his mental health and becoming human in a new and more complete sense than before. He had reached the depths of the human condition when he saw the courtroom portrayal of the hideous evil of which human beings are capable. That evil appeared all the more overwhelming by the dispassionate, unemotional trivialization of the evil at the hands of the legal system. To Herzog it was as though the evil not only existed but was ignored or dismissed with little notice by the human beings entrusted with confronting it.

Herzog realizes that he need not be bound to rely on intellectual reasoning alone: ''Did I really believe that I would die when thinking stopped?'' (*H*, 265). A further step toward mental and emotional health—the full entrance into humanity—occurs when he recognizes that brotherhood and love make a person human. Humans do not live for self alone but for interaction with other humans as well. Other people are not mere distractions from freedom of self but the means of defining oneself.

Herzog has only to undergo one final experience with the law—not as observer but as participant this time—before his spiritual growth is complete. After an outing with June at a Chicago park, he is involved in a minor automobile accident. When the old pistol is discovered in the car, he is arrested for possession of a pistol without a permit. He wonders if this is the reality he has been searching for, down in the ranks of ordinary life. As he sits in a jail cell waiting for his brother to bail him out, he concludes that this is not the sought-after reality. ''This . . . was not the sphere of *his* sins. He was merely passing through. Out in the streets, in American society, that was where he did his time'' (*H*, 303).

His experience as the object of law's force brings him to recognize how deeply the law penetrates his and everyone's life. He realizes the disparity between reality and the law's perception and treatment of reality. He observes: ''Clumsy, inexact machinery of civil peace. . . . The dream of man's heart . . . is that life may complete itself in significant pattern'' (*H*, 303). Released on bail, and free of the bondage of law's machinery, Herzog has a chance to pursue the final stages of his emancipation. One facet of his growth is the acceptance of ambiguity as a sign of health. He also believes that he is spared one of the afflictions of intellectuals—that is the tendency to hate and reject the very civilization that makes their lives possible.

In the process of enlightenment through which Herzog comes to grips with the personal chaos of his life, thereby restoring order, several additional points emerge. Herzog becomes convinced that the present stage of civilization represents not decline but, rather, a period of heightened self-awareness as society continues to develop. Faced with the dilemma of deciding what it means to be human in the mechanized world of today which lacks the traditional certainties, standards, and limits that previously guided humanity, he discovers some answers for himself—in emotion, personal caring, love, and brotherhood.[25]

Herzog also discovers two key elements of the ability to cope with the contemporary world. Those elements are a realistic view of human events and the acceptance of personal responsibility for himself. In arriving at this view, he rejects two alternative outlooks on life, both of which are fatally flawed. One outlook, which he calls "crisis ethics," (*H*, 317), always sees the present situation as a crisis. This idea, which has dominated much of contemporary times, justifies ignoring individual responsibility for our actions and our lives.[26]

The other outlook, "potato love" (*H*, 66), appears different but actually has similar qualities. This idea involves a worldview that only through an inspired state can humans bring order to the chaos. This view, which Herzog calls a low-grade, universal sentimentalism, suggests the existence of an ideal imaginary situation that appears to be the only reality. Both rejected outlooks share the misconception that the world can be changed by a grand gesture.[27] They spring from the desire to avoid personal responsibility for one's own life.

Herzog comes to believe that both extreme outlooks actually coincide and represent a similar attitude toward human life and history. He believes that those who promote the views are driven essentially by their need to fulfill their private desires. For them, life is simple; they operate with a worldview that is limited by their own narrow vision. Herzog arrives, instead, at a view that sees the world as it is, rather than as an illusion created by his own wishes. He decides to adopt the philosophy of those who refuse to:

> shy away from the complexity and uniqueness of every situation by opting for a single clear-cut solution, but on the contrary try to face and understand and control, knowing that their work will take a long time, that it will require patience above all things, and that it will constantly be undermined by extremists. They accept man as he is, try to keep close to the ins and outs of his thoughts and feelings. They accept a personal responsibility for history.[28]

Herzog determines not to impose his own pattern on reality, not to reject ambiguity, and not to slot people into pigeonholes in his mind. He recognizes that human life is far more complex than any of the models designed to explain it. In studying his new awareness, we can identify two factors essential to the kind of judicial decision making that can cope with the problems of contemporary society: realistic assessment of human problems unconstrained by limitations of the evaluator's own worldview, and placing a high value on the concept of personal responsibility—for one's actions and role in society.

## HOW COURTS FAIL

Herzog has made a number of discoveries that illuminate some of the ways in which courts can fail: failing to assess and understand human behavior on a realistic basis; failing to recognize the complexity and ambiguity of human events; failing to require individuals to take responsibility for their own actions; failing to protect human values and to promote societal responsibility; failing to appreciate the full human consequences of violence; and failing to create a sense of coherence among the conflicting interests involved. When courts function mechanistically, without being directed by a realistic assessment and understanding of human behavior and without reinforcing the goals of individual responsibility and societal well-being, they are incapable of serving either truth or justice.

## HOW COURTS SUCCEED: JUDICIAL GUIDELINES

Applying the ideas found in *Herzog* to judicial decision making and building on the ingredients of *authoritative* systems discussed earlier, judicial decisions should be grounded in *sound judicial principles* and on a *commonsense* appreciation of individual and societal behavior. They should take into account *human consequences* and *practical realities* in addition to other interests and values. They must be concerned with *societal well-being and security* as well as *individual autonomy*. Moreover, decisions should promote the idea of *personal responsibility* and should serve as *mediating influences* among the conflicting interests involved.

Attention to these guidelines (which I will expand on in the next chapter) is essential in order to secure not only the authority of the judicial system but its institutional integrity as well. These guidelines are not designed to be applied according to any formula or routine, but, of necessity, must involve a balancing and weighing process appropriate for the individual case to be adjudicated. A purely intellectualized system of law that is out of touch with human realities, for example, lacks fundamental authority and credibility. A system of law that does not take into account the ambiguities of life—and the details of the particular factual situation—will not be effective in producing order and harmony in society. Appropriate attention to the guidelines can enable judges to assist in shaping and directing the forces of societal change, all the while recognizing that law can provide only a partial answer to society's problems.

## SELECTED SUPREME COURT OPINIONS

Several recent U.S. Supreme Court opinions reflect close attention to one or more of these guidelines or elements. Recognizing that most judicial decisions are received with mixed approval and disapproval, it is vitally important that the underlying jurisprudence be sound and sensible. I have chosen six opinions for analysis based on their inclusion of these elements. *Arizona v. Evans*[29] and *Wilson v. Arkansas*[30] are Fourth Amendment cases and *Payne v. Tennessee*[31] is a death penalty case. *Withrow v. Williams*[32] is a habeas corpus case. *Board of Education of Kiryas Joel Village School District v. Grumet*[33] is a First Amendment case and *United States v. Lopez*[34] is a Commerce Clause case.

## *ARIZONA V. EVANS*: JUSTICE O'CONNOR'S COMMON SENSE

The concurring opinion by Justice O'Connor in *Arizona v. Evans* embodies all the elements outlined above. In this case, Evans was arrested by Phoenix police during a routine traffic stop when a patrol car's computer indicated that there was an outstanding misdemeanor warrant for his arrest. After a search of his car revealed a bag of marijuana, he was charged with possession. Evans moved to suppress the marijuana as the fruit of an unlawful arrest since the warrant had been quashed prior to his arrest. The trial court granted the motion but the Court of Appeals reversed on the ground that the exclusionary rule's purpose would not be served by excluding evidence obtained because of an error by employees not directly associated with the arresting officers or their police department. The employees had neglected to delete the warrant from the computer files. The Arizona Supreme Court reversed and rejected the distinction between clerical errors committed by law enforcement personnel and clerical mistakes made by court employees.

Chief Justice Rehnquist, writing for the Court, held that the exclusionary rule does not require suppression of evidence seized in violation of the Fourth Amendment where the erroneous information resulted from clerical errors of court employees. The Fourth Amendment does not expressly preclude the use of evidence obtained in violation of its commands, and exclusion is appropriate only where the rule's remedial effects are thought most effectively served. Justice Rehnquist used as an analogy the reasoning in *United States v. Leon*[35] in which the Court determined that there was no sound reason to apply the rule to deter misconduct on the part of judicial officers.

In Justice O'Connor's concurring opinion, joined by justices Souter and Breyer, she reaffirmed the principle that "the exclusionary rule imposes significant costs on society's law enforcement interests and thus should apply only where its deterrence purposes are 'most efficaciously served.' "[36] She went on, in addition, to raise a complex issue underlying the specific issue in the case. Justice O'Connor observed that "[w]hile the police were innocent of the court employee's mistake, they may or may not have acted reasonably in their reliance *on the record-keeping system itself.*"[37]

Noting the advent of powerful, computerized record-keeping systems, she warned that the police may not rely blindly on this technology. "With the benefits of more efficient law enforcement mechanisms comes the burden of corresponding constitutional responsibilities."[38] Justice O'Connor's concurring opinion identifies realistically the complexities underlying the specific case and acknowledges the realistic concerns involved. It further suggests the need for mediation among the competing interests represented in the situation. Moreover, it specifically addresses the concerns about individual autonomy and societal values and firmly addresses the idea of individual responsibility. The value of protecting individual autonomy is acknowledged but overall societal values are not cast aside in the process. Justice O'Connor based her analysis on sound constitutional principles. She applies these principles with a commonsense approach to the realities of modern life. The opinion is a model of sound jurisprudence, balancing principle and practical realism and expressing appropriate concern for the full range of values deserving recognition in our society.

## *PAYNE V. TENNESSEE*: JUSTICES REHNQUIST AND SOUTER FACE REALITY

Sound judicial decision making is illustrated by the majority and a concurring opinion in *Payne v. Tennessee*.[39] That decision overruled decisions in *Booth v. Maryland* [40] and *South Carolina v. Gathers* [41] concerning the admissibility of evidence and argument relating to the victim and the impact of the victim's death on the victim's family at capital sentencing hearings. Justice Rehnquist, writing for the Court, held that the Eighth Amendment erects no *per se* bar prohibiting a capital sentencing jury from considering victim impact evidence or precluding a prosecutor from arguing such evidence at the hearing.

A concurring opinion by Justice Souter explored more of the subtleties of the relationship concerning *Booth, Gathers*, and the case at hand. Justice Souter explained his reasons for believing that those cases were wrongly decided. In addition to basing his position on the constitutional analysis, he addressed the reasons why *Booth* and *Gathers* set an "unworkable standard of constitutional relevance that threatens, on its own terms, to produce such arbitrary consequences and uncertainty of application as virtually to guarantee a result far diminished from the case's promise of appropriately individualized sentencing for capital defendants." [42] The problem, in his view, was that *Booth* and *Gathers* would require the exclusion of important contextual evidence at the guilt phase as well as the sentencing phase, thus seriously reducing the comprehensibility of most trials for jurors. Examining carefully the importance of the doctrine of *stare decisis*, Justice Souter concluded that *Booth* and *Gathers* must be partially overruled.

The opinions of both Justice Rehnquist and Justice Souter reflect the process of applying sound principle in a commonsense manner and are obviously deeply concerned with the human values involved. Moreover, the opinions deal effectively with the dual concerns of individual autonomy and societal welfare and security. They are concerned, in addition, with the process of mediating among the conflicting interests of the defendant, the victims' families, and society. Underlying both opinions is the issue of the responsibility of the criminal defendant for taking the life of the victim and producing the impact on the family. Justice Souter's concurrence is notable for the extent to which it addresses the realities of the jury system and the effect of the evidence at issue on individual jurors. Moreover, he makes an effort to deal directly with the principle of *stare decisis* and attempts to uncover reasons why the Court should exercise its authority to overrule existing precedent in this instance. The special concern with addressing fully the *stare decisis* issue represents an exercise in judicial responsibility necessary to maintain the authority and legitimacy of the Court.

## *WITHROW V. WILLIAMS*: JUSTICE O'CONNOR—TRUTH AND SOCIETY SHOULD PREVAIL

On the civil side, *Withrow v. Williams* arose from a petition for a writ of habeas corpus brought by a Michigan state inmate in the federal district court. The district court granted the petition which raised a claim based on *Miranda v. Arizona*.[43] The issue on appeal was whether the rule in *Stone v. Powell*,[44] which limits federal habeas review when a state has given a full and fair chance to litigate a Fourth Amendment claim, should bar habeas review of Williams's claim. Justice Souter, writing for the Court, held that *Stone*'s restriction on the exercise of federal habeas jurisdiction does not extend to this claim that the petitioner's conviction rests on statements obtained in violation of *Miranda* standards. Souter distinguished the *Miranda* situation because it safeguards a fundamental trial right.

Justice O'Connor, disagreeing on that issue, filed a powerfully reasoned opinion beginning with the words:

> Today the Court permits the federal courts to overturn on habeas the conviction of a double-murderer, not on the basis of an inexorable constitutional or statutory command, but because it believes the result desirable from the standpoint of equity and judicial administration. Because the principles that inform our habeas jurisprudence—finality, federalism, and fairness—counsel decisively against the result the Court reaches, I respectfully dissent from this holding.[45]

In her opinion, Justice O'Connor discussed in depth the relationship between state and federal courts, the history of the exclusionary rule, the reasons for and scope of *Miranda*, and the costs to society resulting from the enforcement of the exclusionary rule. O'Connor concluded that there is little marginal benefit to enforcing the exclusionary rule on habeas because it "comes too late to produce a noticeable deterrent effect."[46] She further concluded that, under these circumstances, "the rule divert[s attention] from the ultimate question of guilt, squanders scarce federal judicial resources, intrudes on the interest in finality, creates friction between the state and federal systems of justice, and upsets the constitutional balance upon which the doctrine of federalism is founded."[47]

Giving close attention to the role of truth-seeking in the judicial process,

Justice O'Connor stated that, on collateral review, the costs to society are too high to allow damage to the truth-seeking function, considering fairness, federalism, and finality. Justice O'Connor weighed heavily the fact that *Miranda*'s application on habeas review may preclude the "just application of law altogether" because the order excluding the statement may be issued long after trial, "when a new trial may be a practical impossibility."[48] Determining that most of the *Miranda* claims raised on habeas review frequently involve "purely technical *Miranda* questions that contain not even a hint of police overreaching,"[49] she asserted that "Any rule that so demonstrably renders truth and society 'the loser,' . . . bear[s] a heavy burden of justification, and must be carefully limited to the circumstances in which it will pay its way by deterring official lawlessness."[50]

The opinion is a comprehensive analysis of the functions of habeas review and the *Miranda* safeguards in the context of the guiding principles of fairness, finality, and federalism. Justice O'Connor addressed her concern for individual responsibility as well as the responsibility of state and federal courts. Her reasoning is grounded in the human realities involved in the application of *Miranda* and takes into account the historical background of the *Miranda* rule plus the state-federal relationship. The opinion, grounded solidly in a commonsense reading of the Constitution, explores all aspects of individual and societal rights and values and attempts to mediate on a principled basis among those conflicting rights and values.

## *BOARD OF EDUCATION OF KIRYAS JOEL VILLAGE SCHOOL DISTRICT V. GRUMET*: JUSTICE O'CONNOR AND THE REALITIES OF THE ESTABLISHMENT CLAUSE

Another opinion by Justice O'Connor that pays close attention to the judicial guidelines is her concurring opinion in *Board of Education of Kiryas Joel Village School District v. Grumet*,[51] a First Amendment Establishment Clause case. The case involved the constitutionality of a statute creating a special school district, following village lines, for a religious enclave incorporated as a village for the purpose of excluding all but practitioners of its strict form of religion. Justice Souter, for the Court, concluded that the statute crossed "the line from permissible accommodation to impermissible establishment"[52] by bringing about an impermissible "fusion" of governmental and religious functions. He indicated that the legislature delegated civic authority on the basis of religious belief rather than on neutral principles.

Justice O'Connor, concurring in the result, addressed some crucial issues in her separate opinion. She framed the issue: "The question at the heart of this case is: What may the government do, consistently with the Establishment Clause, to accommodate people's religious beliefs?"[53] She began by discussing the historical context of the present case—the realities of the situation—consisting of previous accommodation problems involving the same religious group.

She concluded that accommodation had occurred and "[w]hat makes accommodation permissible, even praiseworthy, is not that the government is making life easier for some particular religious group as such. Rather, it is that the government is accommodating a deeply held belief."[54]

Justice O'Connor joined the Court's opinion, however, because she thought that "this law, rather than being a general accommodation, singles out a particular religious group for favorable treatment."[55] Under these circumstances, she believed that it is "dangerous to validate what appears to me a clear religious preference."[56] What makes the concurring opinion noteworthy, however, is that she went on to address the issue of the extent to which the Establishment Clause does not require "hostility to religion, religious ideas, religious people, or religious schools. . . . It is the Court's insistence on disfavoring religion in *Aguilar* that led New York to favor it here. The Court should, in a proper case, be prepared to reconsider *Aguilar*, in order to bring our Establishment Clause jurisprudence back to what I think is the proper track—government impartiality, not animosity, towards religion."[57]

Justice O'Connor went on to express her approval that Justice Souter did not focus on a single Establishment Clause, explaining:

> It is always appealing to look for a single test, a Grand Unified Theory that would resolve all the cases that may arise under a particular clause. There is, after all only one Establishment Clause, one Free Speech Clause, one Fourth Amendment, one Equal Protection Clause. . . . But the same constitutional principle may operate very differently in different contexts . . . and setting forth a unitary test for a broad set of cases may sometimes do more harm than good.[58]

Recognizing the complexities of Establishment Clause jurisprudence, she concluded that a single test was inappropriate. This opinion, therefore, serves the principles guiding this analysis. Justice O'Connor's opinion gives appropriate attention to legal principles and also takes into account the realities of the problem. Her opinion identifies, with a commonsense approach, the complexities of the situation and weighs carefully individual rights and societal well-being. In addition, it acknowledges the human values underlying Establishment Clause jurisprudence and mediates among all the conflicting values involved. Justice O'Connor's reasoning is broad-based and fully grounded in the realities of the situation in addition to the individual and societal values at stake.

## *WILSON V. ARKANSAS*: THE KNOCK AND ANNOUNCE PRINCIPLE IN FACTUAL CONTEXT

In this case, a unanimous Court decided that the common law knock-and-announce principle forms a part of the Fourth Amendment reasonableness inquiry but that the reasonableness determination itself is properly made by the trial courts. The petitioner, Sharlene Wilson, was charged with various state narcotics offenses. She filed a motion to suppress evidence seized from her home during the execution of a search warrant, claiming that the search was invalid because, among other reasons, the police officers had failed to "knock and announce" before entering her home. Her convictions were affirmed by the Arkansas Supreme Court which rejected her argument that the Fourth Amendment requires police officers to knock and announce prior to entering a residence.

Justice Thomas analyzed the history of the common law knock-and-announce principle, concluding that the rule is "embedded in Anglo-American law."[59] The Court went on to hold that, although the common law knock-and-announce principle is now required to be part of the reasonableness inquiry, the outcome will depend on the particular circumstances involved in any given case: "This is not to say, of course, that every entry must be preceded by an announcement. The Fourth Amendment's flexible requirement of reasonableness should not be read to mandate a rigid rule of announcement that ignores countervailing law enforcement interests."[60] The presumption in favor of announcement would yield under a variety of circumstances including the threat of physical harm to police, the fact that police are pursuing a recently escaped arrestee, and where police have reason to believe that evidence would likely be destroyed if advance notice were given. The Court remanded the case to the trial court for a reasonableness determination.

The opinion is significant for its balanced analysis of principle and practical realism and for taking into account individual rights and societal interests. The opinion mediates among all of those interests and produces a principled solution that allows room for future practical application under specific factual circumstances.

## *UNITED STATES V. LOPEZ*: A LESSON IN FEDERALISM

The respondent, Alfonzo Lopez, a twelfth-grade student, arrived at his high school in San Antonio, Texas, carrying a concealed .38 caliber handgun with five bullets. Confronted by school authorities, he admitted that he was carrying the weapon. He was later arrested and charged under Texas law with firearm possession on school premises and indicted for violation of the Gun-Free School Zones Act of 1990 that Congress had enacted pursuant to its authority under the Commerce Clause of the federal constitution.

After the state charges were dismissed, the respondent moved in the district court to dismiss his indictment on the grounds that the federal statute was unconstitutional. That motion having been denied, Lopez was convicted in a bench trial and appealed the conviction to the Fifth Circuit Court of Appeals, which reversed his conviction, holding that the federal statute exceeds the power of Congress under the Commerce Clause. Chief Justice Rehnquist, writing for the Court in this five-to-four decision, affirmed, holding that if the government's theory of the effect of crime on education and economic activity were accepted,

Congress would have virtually no limit to its power to regulate not only education, but also family law, child custody, criminal law, and all areas of state sovereignty.

Justices Kennedy, O'Connor, and Thomas concurred in separate opinions and four justices dissented. Although Justice Rehnquist's opinion contains a recitation of relevant precedent concerning the Commerce Clause, Justice Kennedy's opinion is a noteworthy example of principled analysis, grounded in realism and common sense, of the relationship of the federal government to the states. Kennedy begins by cautioning that: "The history of the judicial struggle to interpret the Commerce Clause during the transition from the economic system the Founders knew to the single, national market still emergent in our own era counsels great restraint before the Court determines that the Clause is insufficient to support an exercise of the national power."[61]

Following a survey of relevant precedent, Justice Kennedy discusses in concrete terms the important features and implications of the subject of federal and state balance: "This framework has been sufficiently flexible over the past two centuries to allow for enormous changes in the nature of government. The Federal Government undertakes activities today that would have been unimaginable to the Framers. . . . [T]he powers conferred upon the Federal Government by the Constitution were phrased in language broad enough to allow for the expansion of the Federal Government's role."[62]

The opinion then turns to the role of the Court in the design of government:

> Of the various structural elements in the Constitution, separation of powers, checks and balances, judicial review, and federalism, only concerning the last does there seem to be much uncertainty respecting the existence, and the content, of standards that allow the judiciary to play a significant role in maintaining the design contemplated by the Framers. Although the resolution of specific cases has proved difficult, we have derived from the Constitution workable standards to assist in preserving separation of powers and checks and balances.[63]

After reminding the political branches of government of their sworn obligation to preserve and protect the Constitution and the federal-state balance of power, in the first instance, Justice Kennedy goes on to render a practical and realistic analysis of the implications of the federal government attempting to regulate a matter of educational concern. To allow that to occur would foreclose "the States from experimenting and exercising their own judgment in an area to which States lay claim by right of history and expertise."[64]

Justice Kennedy's concurrence is remarkable for its comprehensive and sensible analysis of the relevant principles that apply to the case, along with its realistic evaluation and weighing of the factors involved, including individual values, societal interests, and responsibilities of each branch of government. The opinion concludes by effectively mediating among all the conflicting interests involved and resolving the situation in a way that preserves the important principles for future application. In doing so, Justice Kennedy draws clear distinctions between the political decision-making processes of the executive and legislative branches and the principled methods of the judicial branch that are required by the Constitution. The opinion is a lesson in political science and jurisprudence, achieved with a realistic and mediating approach.

## WHEN CORE CONSTITUTIONAL PRINCIPLES CONFRONT CHANGE

This discussion began with the subject of change, one of the dominant forces in American life since the inception of the nation. The focus in the literary stories was on the personal impact of change and the ways in which individuals attempt to control the changing forces in their lives. Although I have concentrated on *Herzog* for insights that apply to judicial matters, all the stories discussed in this chapter are concerned with the critical elements. In each story, the characters confront the complex difficulties and brutal realities presented in their lives. Each story involves a disruption of the social, economic, legal, or political system, or all of them. Although the protagonists react differently, they ultimately take into account societal values as well as their own individual priorities. The protagonists conclude by taking personal responsibility for their own present and future lives. In the process, they consider the conflicting interests that involve them in order to create or recreate a sense of order and harmony in their lives and their relationship to society. The stories teach that not only judges and other public officials, but all citizens must take personal responsibility for their own lives and for their contributions to society.

The American experience has been deeply affected and shaped by change of all types, including economic, social, and technological. The core principles guiding the republic through the centuries, however, have remained essentially constant. These principles, embodied in the federal and state constitutions and other basic texts, provide a moral and ethical, as well as legal and political, foundation for our individual and collective private and public lives. Rhetoric that deals with the subject of changing our institutions and procedures is a familiar feature of political campaigns. Americans quite properly tend to dismiss much of that rhetoric as insubstantial. Americans are aware, however, that circumstances do occur that legitimately require us to consider modifying, adapting, or recommitting our institutions and procedures in order to cope with change, whether social, economic, or technological.

Without question, there are limitations inherent in the democratic form of government that directly affect the way our society can be mobilized to prepare for and shape the changing circumstances that must be addressed. Consistent with our democratic principles, however, there is much that can be done by all branches of government to ensure that our institutions and procedures are adequate to meet new challenges. The executive and legislative branches must employ direct political decision making for such action. Some institutional and procedural change in the judicial branch must be accomplished by means of political methods. In addition, the guidelines introduced in this chapter can assist judicial decision making to deal with changing circumstances presented in the form of controversies and issues requiring resolution.

## SUPREME COURT REAFFIRMATION

In language that brings to mind the river and the road as literary vehicles portraying change as traversing past, present, and future, the U.S. Supreme Court recently discussed its commitment to our core constitutional principles in the following words:

> Our Constitution is a covenant running from the first generation of Americans to us and then to future generations. It is a coherent succession. Each generation must learn anew that the Constitution's written terms embody ideas and aspirations that must survive more ages than one. We accept our responsibility not to retreat from interpreting the full meaning of the covenant in light of all of our precedents. We invoke it once again to define the freedom guaranteed by the Constitution's own promise, the promise of liberty.[65]

The judicial branch, because of its leading role in shaping the values and goals of American culture, is faced with the task of addressing effectively the changing circumstances of society. At the same time, judicial decisionmakers must preserve and protect the core principles of our democracy. I have suggested some criteria that may be used by courts and judges in order to serve both goals. As revealed in the discussion of the literary texts, these criteria are derived not only from law but from a broad range of cultural sources.

# Chapter 7

# Synthesis: Justice in Our Time

> What this country needs is a good five-cent synthesis.[1]

> [T]he predicament of modern man: how to retain one's precious individuality in these terrible times, how to be human in the face of the powers and forces that threaten to annihilate the self.[2]

The time has arrived to assemble the results of this inquiry into American law, literature, and culture. The central role of law in our society from the earliest times is beyond dispute. Alexis de Tocqueville was one of the first observers to identify and articulate American reliance on law, just as he identified so many other features of American culture. Another influential commentator, Thomas Paine, proclaimed in 1776: "In America, the law is king."[3] In American society, virtually all social, economic, and political issues eventually become legal issues. One fundamental problem, in fact, is that these issues are too often dealt with principally in the legal process—in the form of rights adjudication—rather than in the political process where they could be examined and debated more fully and, at least potentially, could be resolved more comprehensively and effectively.

Stories are a central part of our culture, and literary works have traditionally played a vital role in expressing, explaining, and illustrating the important social, legal, economic, and political issues that concern the American people. Literary works, which have drawn heavily upon legal ideas and events, have helped to shape the public discussion of issues and to stimulate thinking about solutions. Because law has played a vital role in the development of American society, legal stories are also part of the cultural core. Both legal and literary stories, therefore, are relevant and integral components of American culture.

It may be that legal and literary stories are more closely linked than ever before. The boundaries that separate real from fictional, factual from figurative, and informational from entertaining have become more and more blurred because of the way the media tell stories. The media embellish courtroom stories, sometimes to the point of fictionalizing them, even as they are unfolding. An example of this phenomenon is the common practice of producing television movies about celebrity or sensational criminal cases during—or even before—the actual trials. As the media have gained greater access to the sources of legal stories—both inside and outside the courtroom, the media often shape the course and outcome of these stories.

I have addressed some of the underlying legal forces and relationships in American society. These forces have cultural as well as legal identities. As so many of the writings of all types—legal, political, and literary—have shown, the relationship between the individual and society is fundamental. In contrast to other cultures where individualism does not have the same elevated and protected status, the inherent tension between individualistic and societal values has produced an enormous number of legal decisions, a vast quantity of political discourse, and an outpouring of literature. The tension is ongoing—and perhaps unresolvable—ever to be debated and litigated as new and more complex situations arise. Some forms of individualism play constructive roles while others threaten the stability of our social structure.

In recent years, an increasing amount of cultural fragmentation can be observed in American society. This phenomenon causes American society to divide into separatist cultural groups or communities which demand special recognition and rights for their members. Some separatist interest groups, which typically are formed along racial, ethnic, or gender lines, resist the idea of integration into society as a whole, preferring instead to promote a fragmentation of American society. In attempting to justify their actions, they reinterpret and distort American multiculturalism to mean the *inability* of diverse elements in society to unite into a cohesive whole, as opposed to the proven *ability* of Americans to coexist in a common culture with mutual respect. Each of these separatist groups has its own exclusive code which rejects attempts at integration and resists the pursuit of mutually agreeable solutions. The impact of this fragmentation, in concert with other factors, has brought about changes in the composition of traditional groups and communities in our society. Recent political surveys suggest, for example, that a realignment of political interest groups has produced clusters of viewpoints rather than traditional party alignment.[4]

With respect to each component of the overall social structure—individual, community, and society—I have tried to illustrate how the forces of change play out in the actions of individuals. It is fair to say that legal decisions generally involve the interrelationship of these components and that legal decisions generally reflect underlying social problems. These observations are especially significant in addressing the problems of American society because of our preference for legal resolution of social problems.

Three of the major problems that afflict American society—violence, loss of institutional authority, and failure of the traditional dream of progress—have both cultural and legal dimensions. They have become significant legal problems because Americans have relied on the legal system to an extraordinary extent, and because Americans have developed unrealistic expectations of what the legal system can and should do about major social problems. The chronic problem of societal violence, criminal and situational, is a classic example. Although the judicial system is neither designed nor equipped to bear responsibility for protecting society from crime and criminals, the popular perception is that the judicial system is responsible and has failed in that respect.

The consequences of violence typically materialize in court in the form of criminal prosecutions. Courts must adjudicate guilt on a case-by-case basis and impose sentence after conviction. Criminal courts, however, are the *emergency rooms* of social pathology. They can deal with individual outbreaks of our societal ills but are not equipped to produce comprehensive solutions. Effective handling of crime and violence by the judicial system may well deter some crime and violence, but courts are not the most appropriate place for a remedial approach. Reduction of crime and violence in our society depends upon concerted action by the executive and legislative branches of government, acting in concert with judges, lawyers, and individual citizens, with all participants taking responsibility for their roles.

Loss of authority and the decline of the American dream of progress are cultural problems by nature. As with the violence problem, however, they are seen primarily as legal problems. Both conditions are closely related and involve at their essence the degree of confidence and trust in government on the part of the people. The degree of confidence defines the extent to which the authority of government and, specifically, of courts are acknowledged and respected. Toqueville astutely observed: "The inhabitant of the United States . . . is restless and defiant in his outlook toward the authority of society and appeals to its power only when he cannot do without it."[5] This condition is accentuated when the structure of society is weak and ineffective.

The skepticism and disillusionment concerning American government that became pronounced during the 1960s, especially during the Vietnam period, has had a continuing impact on the nation. That condition has contributed to the social fragmentation and disrespect for authority that exists today. The political outlooks of groups that questioned the authority of government in general, and law in particular during the 1960s tended to stand for *liberal*, antiwar viewpoints. When the fabric of society becomes weakened, a wide variety of dissident groups exploit that vulnerability. Those who question the authority of law today represent a much broader spectrum of political ideologies.

Before turning to positive steps that can help to restore the authority of law, three negative cultural conditions or attitudes that are harmful to American society bear close attention. These conditions doubtlessly arise from a complex combination of social, economic, legal, and political factors. They are closely related to typical concerns of Americans—concerns about losing control, falling apart or winding down as a society, and abandoning core historical principles.[6] The very nature of our democratic society tends to create a certain amount of systemic instability and uncertainty that ensures the continued existence of these concerns. In a society not committed to democratic principles, these concerns would command little attention. They are relevant and unresolved (perhaps unresolvable) in our society, however, because the nature of democratic society does not lend itself to permanent resolution with respect to the status of societal relationships and values. The nature of our democratic society involves continuous discourse about societal goals, which are frequently modified, and sometimes abandoned.

## PERCEIVED LACK OF OPPORTUNITY TO DIRECT ONE'S LIFE

The first negative condition that influences American culture is the *perceived lack of opportunity to direct one's life*—the erosion of individual opportunity. This condition, whether perceived or, in fact, real, reflects the historic concern about being controlled and is easily identifiable in issues that include racial tension, affirmative action, conflict between labor and management, lack of access to housing or educational opportunity, restrictions on exercise of property rights, economic coercion, and discriminatory employment practices. These and other related issues arise primarily from social and economic sources. In our culture, however, they usually become legal problems to be resolved by judges, juries, and lawyers, rather than by politicians. Ironically, the choice of adjudication as the method of dealing with such problems virtually ensures that the problems will arise again, producing future work for the judicial system because case-by-case adjudication resolves only the specific, fact-based dispute before the court and is not capable of producing a negotiated solution that applies to a broad range of problems.

The prevalence of this condition can also be attributed to the extensive crime and violence in our society. The causative factors of crime and violence have deep roots in our culture and, conversely, the conditions caused by crime and violence are equally pervasive. The high level of crime and violence causes many Americans to be anxious about their physical safety and produces a serious restriction of their freedom. Because crime and violence have increased markedly, the capacity of our criminal justice system is overwhelmed. Political institutions usually focus on short-term conditions and solutions, preferring to deal with the problem on a superficial level. They concentrate on enacting more criminal laws, enhancing penalties, and building prisons. Such measures, while often justified, do little to change the conditions that contribute to the *production* of violence and crime. Legislation that substantially increases the number of criminal cases to be litigated can be counterproductive, in fact, when it immobilizes the court system.

Despite the scope of the public safety problem today and the anxiety that it causes, there is not enough genuine, informed discussion in the political forum concerning the factors that may contribute to crime and violence. Although judges and other court officials acquire valuable knowledge about the causes and patterns of crime and violence, that knowledge is generally not preserved or shared with private or public agencies charged with reducing crime and violence. Consequently, that wisdom is applied only in case-by-case adjudication and is rarely available for comprehensive problem-solving approaches to the problem.

## SELF-CENTERED INDIVIDUALISM

*Self-centered individualism*, along with a corresponding erosion of cooperative, societal values, is directly related to apprehension about societal fragmentation and the perception of a lack of opportunity to direct one's life. Self-centered individualism, which has characteristics of both imperial individualism and defensive individualism, continues to increase in our society. Our culture increasingly has become weakened by an excess of excuse, blame, and assertion. These responses to problems emerge in the course of excessive rights-based litigation that has been well documented by legal scholars and others.[7] This condition may be a natural phenomenon in a society that places so much emphasis on individualism and individual rights and where the entertainment/information media superstructure plays such a prominent role in shaping the tastes, values, and material aspirations of individuals as consumers.

The excuse, blame, and assertion reflexes find nurturing and support in a society that favors adversarial litigation based on conflicting rights over political negotiation of social problems. Self-centered individualism manifests itself on a collective basis in the form of groups which demand recognition for their separate identities, often based on claims of historical victimization. Some of these groups are part of the new, distorted multiculturalism that prefers to emphasize differences rather than common values and concerns.[8] As I noted earlier, the process of fragmentation may be, in part, an extension of the process that began in the 1960s. This brand of American solipsism relies on values that tend to corrode the cooperative values that are essential to solving the vast number of problems that we face as a society.

## ABDICATION OF PERSONAL RESPONSIBILITY

Self-centered individualism—whether exhibited individually or asserted by groups of individuals promoting separatist agendas—is closely related to a third negative attitude or condition in American culture: the *abdication of personal responsibility* or accountability for oneself and for the well-being of our democratic society as a whole. The concern about winding down, illustrated by the fading of the American dream of progress and the loss of authority of the legal system is integral to this condition. The concern about winding down is self-defeating, as was evident from the course of events in Bellow's *Herzog*. An apocalyptic worldview perpetuates a failure to perceive and accept complexity and ambiguity, and discourages individuals from taking responsibility. This view detracts from the effort to seek negotiated solutions to society's problems. In this regard, balancing of concern for societal well-being along with individual autonomy is desperately needed.

The concern about falling away from past principle and promise is also directly involved. This concern emerges in the form of resistance to recognizing change and inability to accept ambiguities. It also takes the form of rigid application of core principles to present reality without recognizing how institutions and processes may have to be adapted to embrace faithfully those core principles. These conditions tend to destroy the social fabric of the nation and to produce social, political, and cultural fragmentation which, itself, reinforces the conditions and perpetuates the problems.

In general, there appears to be an increasing failure to understand or acknowledge the reasons underlying the perceived loss of opportunity to direct one's life; an enhanced promotion of the idea of self-centered individualism to the exclusion of concern for societal values; an undue emphasis on rights-based adjudication as a way of resolving social and political problems; and an abdication of individual human responsibility for oneself and for society as a whole. All these problems accelerate the ongoing social fragmentation and erosion of our civic life.

Although the foregoing negative conditions are cultural problems that affect our society as a whole, they often compel our attention in the context of legal and judicial decision making. While courts and judges must address issues that are properly raised in the context of litigation, they should address issues with broad political or social implications using the greatest degree of judicial restraint. It is wiser to deal with those issues in the political process. Because courts are properly called upon to protect rights, it is not easy, in some situations, to distinguish between appropriate judicial action to protect rights and inappropriate judicial intervention in political matters. A judge who is able both to recognize the difference and to act with integrity and restraint is worthy of great respect and admiration.

In advocating use of the political forum, I am mindful of the reservations of the American people regarding the capacity of political institutions to deal effectively with such problems. The *Times-Mirror* survey noted earlier reported considerable skepticism along these lines. The survey concluded, for example, that "[t]he American electorate is angry, self-absorbed, and politically unanchored. Thousands of interviews with American voters in July 1994 found no clear direction in the public's political thinking other than frustration with the current system, and an eager responsiveness to alternative political solutions and appeals."[9] The survey also revealed a considerable amount of inconsistent thinking about social and political issues and goals. One hopeful sign was the evidence of strong skepticism and criticism concerning the news media, particularly the television medium. In an age where the media have developed enormous power in shaping the perceptions, knowledge, and opinions of the public as well as the very events being reported, a healthy skepticism is not only desirable but essential.

It remains to be seen whether our political institutions and the people who operate them can meet the challenge of understanding and acting upon the serious problems that confront the nation or whether self-interest will prevail. Election-oriented strategies will not suffice to deal intelligently with the complex social problems that demand long-range consideration and sound decision making. Even taking into account the inconsistent expectations and aspirations of the American public, there is considerable room for improvement in the way the political system deals with the troublesome problems facing today's society. One commentator indicated that rights-based talk often overtakes political as well as judicial discourse: ''Our stark, simple rights dialect puts a damper on the processes of public justification, communication, and deliberation upon which the continuing vitality of a democratic regime depends. . . . It impedes creative long-range thinking about our most pressing social problems.''[10]

Courts have limited institutional capability of dealing with problems comprehensively:

> [T]here are serious problems in judge-led reform from the standpoint of democratic legitimacy. Reform through the courts may dampen the practice of citizenship, an individual and collective good. . . . Constitutional law is an uneasy amalgam of substantive theory and institutional constraint. In developing constitutional principles, courts must be attentive not only to the best substantive interpretation of the relevant text, but also to institutional limits on judicial capacity.[11]

There are, however, ways in which courts, judges, and lawyers can address some of the underlying problems and conditions. The examples of judicial decisions that contain the essential ingredients for coping with change that I suggested can be used as models by judges and lawyers as they function within the legal system. Recognizing the myriad factors that contribute to results in individual cases, I suggest that as institutional guidelines for judicial decision making, the factors introduced in the preceding chapter deserve consideration. These factors expand on the principles of authority referred to in Chapter 4.

- *Principle.* Judicial decision making should be principled, that is, based primarily on sound judicial principles that have evolved over time or have general application beyond individual cases, rather than being essentially political or pragmatic. The distinction between *principled* and *political* is crucial because it differentiates judicial decision making from executive and legislative decision making. The term *principled* has at least two meanings in this context. The first meaning, which is *procedural*, refers to the fundamental judicial principles including, for example, *stare decisis, res judicata*, due process, and other general principles. *Principled* in the second sense, which is *substantive*, means that each judicial decision must rest "on reasons with respect to all the issues in the case . . . that in their generality and their neutrality transcend any immediate result that is involved."[12] The idea of compulsory adherence to neutral principles will be tempered by the second factor which gives due consideration to the result. Adherence to principle, however, will serve to enhance the authority of judicial decision making by assuring procedural and substantive fairness.[13]

- *Realism.* Judicial decisions should be realistic, that is, grounded in the realities of life in American society, in all their complexity and ambiguity, and should take into account the full range of viewpoints represented in society. This factor promotes judicial authority by assuring that results will not seriously conflict with common wisdom and the standards of public morality which people aspire to uphold. Judicial decision making will, therefore, be generally in accord with the times. As noted, this factor serves to complement and temper the adherence to principle in decision making. It allows for participation and representation in the judicial system that would not otherwise be possible.[14]
- *Values.* Judicial decision making should take into account human values and concerns in addition to others, and should acknowledge the importance of overall societal values, including safety and security, in addition to concerns about individual autonomy. Moreover, judicial decisions should promote the importance of individual responsibility for oneself and for the well-being of society as a whole. This factor serves judicial authority as well.
- *Mediation.* Consistent with operating on a principled, rather than a political basis, judges, in making decisions, should attempt to mediate among the competing and conflicting interests represented in the litigation. This will maximize the institutional authority of the judicial system by producing results that take into account the various interests represented in the process. Judges, in applying the law, should attempt, wherever possible, to reconcile—rather than separate—the interests of the participants with that of society as a whole, as well as reconciling past precedent with present problems, giving due regard for future implications. The goal of civility as well as authority is served by this factor.

By employing these four institutional factors or principles, judges can enhance the authority and influence of the judicial system. The factors are not meant to be applied mechanistically or even prioritized, but to be applied sensibly, based on careful evaluation and reasoning with due regard for the particular case being adjudicated. To the extent possible, the impact of the present decision on future controversies should be anticipated where appropriate. Judges, of course, must act with appropriate restraint when dealing with questions that are essentially political and should defer in these cases to the legislative and executive branches. I am aware that, in identifying these guidelines, I am open to some familiar arguments. For example, I anticipate questions concerning my consideration of values, such as individual and societal values and personal responsibility, as well as my emphasis on realistic results and common sense.

The factors that I suggest however, are not, in conflict with established judicial policy and practice. Values inevitably will be incorporated in judicial decision making because human beings are involved in the process. It is impossible to free ourselves of value choices.[15] The best we can do is to choose wisely the values we consciously incorporate. Results must be taken into account; otherwise, we fall into the trap of elevating abstract principles and generating results that make no sense in terms of the litigants and others affected by the decisions. The application of the value factor must, of course, be balanced with the principled decision making factor.[16]

The cases highlighted in the previous chapter are prime examples of the exercise of these principles by justices of the U.S. Supreme Court. Other judges obviously are not authorized to function like Supreme Court justices. Trial judges must find facts and reach legal conclusions based on the evidence and the issues presented by the parties. Appellate judges are bound by those facts and by the law established by legislatures and prior court decisions. Judges must decide particular cases and are not entitled to base their decisions on their own political philosophy, social values, or inclinations.

Both trial and appellate judges are called upon to interpret and apply law to factual situations in cases where the correct result is not clear or predictable. In these cases, the judicial philosophy of individual judges usually is a key factor in decisions because it affects the basic perception of the problem and the solution. It is vital that the results of judicial decisions, as well as the reasoning process, should be evaluated. The results should be in accord with reason, fairness, common sense, and respect for the litigants and others who will be affected by the decision. Fidelity to reasoning and consistency alone can make for hollow and empty jurisprudence.[17]

Applying these principles would help to counter the three negative cultural conditions discussed earlier: perceived lack of opportunity to direct one's life, self-centered individualism, and abdication of responsibility. Grounding decisions on present realities and relying on human values, along with other values, would address the concern about the lack of opportunity. Emphasizing societal values would counter the increased self-centered individualism. Promoting individual responsibility would address directly the abdication of responsibility. Serving as a mediating influence would accommodate all three concerns. Decision making based on principle would ensure continuity, predictability, fairness, and the authority of the judicial system.

By employing these factors or guidelines, judges can have enormous impact on the conditions that currently afflict our society. It is vital to recognize that these guidelines are not abstract legal principles. They are cultural ideas, fully authenticated outside the law. They are soundly rooted in American history and literature. The literary texts discussed in the previous chapter are but a few illustrations of these principles in the cultural context.

Beyond these guidelines that lawyers and judges can apply and promote, I submit that the legal profession is in every respect in a strong position to address these difficult cultural problems because lawyers are not bound by the same constraints as judges. Lawyers have considerable control over the cases they present and the way in which they develop facts and frame issues. Moreover, lawyers, unlike judges, operate professionally outside as well as inside the courthouse. Their professional environment extends well beyond the courtroom, in fact, into the decision making chambers of other public institutions and into the boardrooms of the private sector. In their professional lives, lawyers traverse the private sector, the public sector and, increasingly, the third institutional sector of society, which consists of associations and organizations such as labor unions, hospitals, universities, charitable and religious societies, in addition to the broad spectrum of smaller civic and interest groups. Associations that comprise this last sector have been called a variety of names, including *social* or *intermediate* institutions.[18]

The legal profession is especially well suited—as a professional community, operating throughout all the corridors of society—to apply and promote these principles of judicial decision making. The legal profession is a community of highly trained, knowledgeable professionals with the capacity to assume leadership roles in our increasingly technological society. Lawyers, to realize their leadership potential and to meet these opportunities, however, must embody more of the qualities of the lawyer-statesmen that were once vital features of practicing law. In his book *The Lost Lawyer*, Yale Law School Dean Anthony Kronman describes the qualities of a lawyer-statesman:

> [T]he outstanding lawyer . . . is not simply an accomplished technician but a person of prudence or practical wisdom as well. . . . [E]arlier generations of American lawyers conceived their highest goal to be the attainment of a wisdom that lies beyond technique—a wisdom about human beings and their tangled affairs that anyone who wishes to provide real deliberative counsel must possess. They understood this wisdom to be a trait of character that one acquires only by becoming a person of good judgment, and not just an expert in the law.[19]

The traditional teaching in this country that the practice of law is a public calling and that lawyers have a responsibility to the public, as well as to the client and the court, is thought by many to be in jeopardy in American society today. Law schools are in a powerful position to promote the public service aspects of law practice. The idea that a commitment to advance the public good is consistent with the duty to clients and the court needs to be reemphasized. Judges, too, are in a strong position to influence the way law is practiced—by their example and their teaching.

Two European commentators on American affairs—Tocqueville in the nineteenth century and Myrdal in the mid-twentieth century—produced a body of observations about American life that are well worth keeping in mind today. Among the many astute observations of Tocqueville were his comments about the important role of law and lawyers and his conclusion about the key role played by the exercise of civic responsibility, which he believed to be at a very high level at the time. Myrdal, for his part, created the term the ''American

Creed'' to describe the cluster of ideas, institutions, and habits that he observed in the United States. He noted, for example, that Americans ''of all national origins, regions, creeds, and colors, . . . hold in common the most *explicitly expressed* system of general ideals''[20] of any Western nation. They include ideals of ''the essential dignity and equality of all human beings, of inalienable rights to freedom, justice, and opportunity.''[21]

We would do well to keep these observations in mind as America enters the next century. The principles embodied in Myrdal's ''American Creed'' cannot be sustained without the exercise by all Americans of individual responsibility for themselves and for the well-being of society. The responsibility for and the shaping of our political and judicial discourse cannot be left to the whim of interest groups and the media, both of which tend to highlight and exploit disharmony, fragmentation, controversy, criticism, and complaint. Beyond that, however, it is essential in a democratic society that the people be sufficiently well-informed to prepare them for the exercise of their civic responsibilities. Our fundamental cultural values cannot survive unless we resist the forces of fragmentation and separation as we discover our common values, strengths, and bonds, and as we engage in formulating mutually acceptable solutions for our common problems.

## Chapter 8

# Conclusion

In focusing on our differences, we often overlook the common ground we share. Despite the diversity of our cultural backgrounds, viewpoints, and interests, Americans agree in principle on a great many fundamental moral and political issues, interests, and values. Americans agree, for instance, on the *sanctity of human life*, although we may disagree on when it begins or under what circumstances it may be terminated and what should be done by society to preserve its quality. Americans agree on the importance of *personal safety and security*, despite some of our own inclinations toward violent and extralegal behavior. Although we disagree on the acceptability of particular control measures, a safe and physically secure society is a goal of all Americans. Americans agree on the importance of *freedom of expression*, although we may disagree on how to define that freedom and when it may be restricted. Americans agree, too, on the sanctity of *individual autonomy and privacy*, although we disagree on when it may be subordinated to the overall good of society. We share a common commitment to establish and maintain a healthy balance of order and liberty.

Americans agree, as well, on the need to accommodate a *pluralistic value system* and to tolerate the broad spectrum of cultural values within our borders, although we are rightfully distressed when that plurality of cultures and values detracts from our common goals and values. We agree that opportunities for greater *roles for women in society* should be protected, although we disagree on how to reconcile our changing and traditional values concerning family and marriage relationships. We agree that *opportunity*—educational, economic, social, and political—should be available fairly to all, even though we may disagree on how to provide that opportunity in specific instances. We agree that all Americans should have access to *fulfilling their basic needs*, although we may disagree on the method of providing that fulfillment or the conditions attached to it. We believe in preserving *family and community ties*, even though we often act in ways that are corrosive of those cooperative values. These few examples represent the many values on which we agree, although differing on their extent and their application.

One of our greatest difficulties is deciding how to weigh and balance our competing concerns when one of our fundamental values is cast in conflict with another. The potential for that to occur in our complex, highly diverse society is virtually limitless. In the preceding chapters, I have highlighted some of the major conflicts between individual and societal values. Individuals and groups constantly compete for limited resources in situations that bring fundamental values into conflict. The challenge of resolving these conflicts is one of the most excruciating problems that judges face because they have a limited range of choices in adversarial situations. Policy-makers in the legislative and executive branches, in contrast, have available a broad range of alternatives, including political compromise. Decision-makers in alternative dispute resolution contexts, in fact, also have a broad array of choices.

The fact that Americans may disagree on the interpretation and application of these complex values and goals should not detract from the reality of our fundamental consensus. Americans generally respect the system of secular values embodied in our state and federal constitutions that includes, at its heart, the idea of protecting the pluralistic moral and ethical beliefs held by Americans. We would do well to see ourselves as part of a continuing historical process, bonded to each other and to our past and future, engaged in a common pursuit of individual and societal well-being in accordance with well-established principles.

I have noted that our federal and state constitutions serve as aspirational or visionary documents as well as strictly *legal* or regulatory texts. Judges, lawyers, legislators, and executive branch decisionmakers, as well as individual citizens, need to have a vision of society as it was, is, and may be in the future. Can we envision, for example, that a good society would be one in which: all members have a voice and perceive their interests to be fairly represented in the decision-making and policy-making processes of government; people feel hopeful and optimistic about the future and believe that opportunity exists in important areas of life such as education and meaningful employment; and individuals believe that their persons and property are safe and secure?

Can we further imagine a society in which: family and community ties and values are protected and nurtured; cooperative social values as well as individuality and autonomy are preserved; government intervenes basically to promote opportunity for individuals to pursue their own goals and to preserve personal security but does not intrude excessively on personal privacy, autonomy and initiative? Can we envision a society where: individuals feel confident that assistance in meeting basic human needs is available without creating permanent dependency; fundamental values are protected but the attitude toward change in implementing those values is open, flexible, and far-sighted? Is our goal a society where individuals possess a mutual sense of individual accountability and responsibility and, in general, where a social compact involving opportunity and accountability exists?

The goal of achieving a society where people are committed to adopting and advancing these ideals would be well served by a judicial system, acting in concert with other private and public institutions, that strives to apply the judicial decision-making principles that I have outlined above. Law, in its full cultural context, can be a central force in the revitalization of American society. The words of Ralph Ellison's *Invisible Man* bear repeating in this context: "America is woven of many strands. . . . Life is to be lived, not controlled; and humanity is won by continuing to play in the face of certain defeat. Our fate is to become one, and yet many" (*IM*, 577). The answer to the question of how we can hold our republic together lies, in part, in the common commitment to our historic ideals of democracy and human rights. It depends also on the reaffirmation of the importance of individual responsibility—for ourselves and for the well-being of society as a whole—as we search for common solutions to the problems that affect all our lives. The ideals and lessons of our past and present give us good reason to be optimistic as we greet the future together.

# Notes

## INTRODUCTION

1. *Complete Auto Transit, Inc. v. Reis*, 451 U.S. 401, 429 (1981).

2. Learned Hand, "The Spirit of Liberty," in *The Spirit of Liberty: The Bill of Rights* (New York: The Legal Classics Library, 1989), pp. 189–90.

3. Robert A. Ferguson, *Law and Letters in American Culture* (Cambridge, Mass.: Harvard University Press, 1984), p. 201.

4. Walt Whitman, *Leaves of Grass* (quoted in Ferguson, *Law and Letters in American Culture*, p. 204, n. 14).

5. A. Bartlett Giamatti, *A Free and Ordered Space* (New York: W. W. Norton & Co., 1988), p. 102.

6. See, for example, James Boyd White, *The Legal Imagination* (Boston: Little, Brown and Company, 1973); *Heracles' Bow: Essays on the Rhetoric and Poetics of the Law* (Madison: The University of Wisconsin Press, 1985); Ferguson, *Law and Letters in American Culture*; Richard Weisberg, *Poethics and Other Strategies of Law and Literature* (New York: Columbia University Press, 1992); and Peter Brooks and Paul Gewirtz, eds., *Law's Stories: Narrative and Rhetoric in the Law* (New Haven: Yale University Press, 1996).

## CHAPTER 1

1. Alexis de Tocqueville, *Democracy in America*, ed. J. P. Mayer (New York: HarperPerennial, 1988), p. 514.

2. *Whitney v. California*, 274 U.S. 357, 375 (1927) (Brandeis, J. concurring).

3. Mary Ann Glendon, *Rights Talk: The Impoverishment of Political Discourse* (New York: Free Press, 1993), p. 3.

4. Cleanth Brooks, "Faulkner and the Community," in *On the Prejudices, Predilec-*

*tions, and Firm Beliefs of William Faulkner* (Baton Rouge: Louisiana State University Press, 1988), p. 30.

5. Glendon, *Rights Talk*, p. 14.

6. Ibid., pp. 4–7.

7. Rupert Wilkinson, *The Pursuit of American Character* (New York: Harper & Row, 1988).

8. See Elizabeth V. Mensch, "The Colonial Origins of Liberal Property Rights," 31 *Buffalo Law Review* 635 (1982).

9. See, generally, Laurence H. Tribe, *Constitutional Choices* (Cambridge, Mass.: Harvard University Press, 1985), p. 394, n. 44; John Hart Ely, *Democracy and Distrust: A Theory of Judicial Review* (Cambridge, Mass.: Harvard University Press, 1980), pp. 73–104; and Francis Fukuyama, *The End of History and The Last Man* (New York: The Free Press, 1992), p. 156.

10. See Ely, *Democracy and Distrust*, pp. 48–54.

11. Paul Edwards, *Encyclopedia of Philosophy* (New York: The Macmillan Company and The Free Press, 1967), vol. 2, p. 465.

12. Brooks Atkinson, ed., *The Complete Essays and Other Writings of Ralph Waldo Emerson* (New York: Random House, 1950), pp. 45–63, 145–169.

13. Barry R. Schaller, "Getting the Stories Right: Reflections on Narrative Voice in State Constitutional Interpretation," 26 *Connecticut Law Review* 671, 673–674 (1994).

14. See, generally, E. M. Forster, *Aspects of the Novel* (New York: Harcourt, Brace and Company, 1954); and Schaller, "Getting the Stories Right."

15. See Sam B. Girgus, *The Law of the Heart: Individualism and the Modern Self in American Literature* (Austin: University of Texas Press, 1979), pp. 5–6.

16. See, generally, Patricia Nelson Limerick, *The Legacy of Conquest: The Unbroken Past of the American West* (New York: W. W. Norton, 1987) for a historically sound perspective on the American frontier.

17. Ibid., p. 25.

18. See, for example, Jack London, *The Call of the Wild* (New York: Simon & Schuster, 1974).

19. See, for example, Ernest Hemingway, *A Farewell to Arms* (New York: Charles Scribner's Sons, 1957).

20. See, for example, Tom Robbins, *Skinny Legs and All* (New York: Bantam Books, 1990).

21. 559 P.2d 1038 (Alaska 1976).

22. 95 U.S. 714 (1877).

23. See, for example, Alice Walker, *The Color Purple* (New York: Simon & Schuster, 1982); Toni Morrison, *Beloved* (New York: Plume, 1988); and Joyce Carol Oates, *Do with me what you will* (New York: The Vanguard Press, Inc., 1973).

24. Girgus, *The Law of the Heart*, p. 8.

25. 97 N.J. 178, 478 A.2d 364 (N.J. 1984).

26. Girgus, *The Law of the Heart*, p. 14 (internal quotation marks omitted). See also 559 P.2d 1038 (Alaska 1976) illustrating aspects that are relevant to this mode of individualism.

27. 69 Ill.2d 605, 373 N. E.2d 21 (Ill. 1978).

28. See Tribe, *Constitutional Choices*, p. 219.

29. See George L. Blum, "Validity, Construction, and Effect of 'Hate Crimes' Statutes, 'Ethnic Intimidation' Statutes, or the Like," 22 ALR5th 261 (1994).

30. Joyce Carol Oates, *Foxfire* (New York: Penguin Books, 1993).
31. Russell Banks, *Rule of the Bone* (New York: HarperCollins, 1995).
32. Girgus, *The Law of the Heart*, p. 15 (internal quotation marks omitted).
33. John Steinbeck, *The Grapes of Wrath* (New York: Bantam Books, Inc., 1966).
34. Henry A. Beers, *Initial Studies in American Letters* (Meadville, Pa.: The Chautauqua-Century Press, 1895), p. 185. Professor Beers, a Professor of Literature at Yale University, was personally acquainted with many of the prominent American writers of his time.
35. 438 U.S. 912 (1978).
36. 488 U.S. 469 (1989).
37. 497 U.S. 547 (1990).
38. 509 U.S. 630 (1993).
39. 392 U.S. 409 (1968).
40. Ibid. at 413.
41. James Fenimore Cooper, *The Pioneers or The Sources of the Susquehanna* (New York: Penguin Books, 1988).
42. John P. McWilliams, Jr., ''Innocent Criminal or Criminal Innocence: The Trial in American Fiction,'' in Carl S. Smith, John P. McWilliams, Jr., and Maxwell Bloomfield, *Law and American Literature: A Collection of Essays* (New York: Alfred A. Knopf, Inc., 1983), p. 57; see also Allen D. Boyer, ''Formalism, Realism, and Naturalism: Cross-Currents in American Letters and Law,'' 23 *Connecticut Law Review* 669, 674 (1991).
43. Glendon, *Rights Talk*, p. 9.
44. Ralph Ellison, *Invisible Man* (New York: Vintage Books, 1990).
45. Charles I. Glicksberg, ''The Symbolism of Vision,'' in John M. Reilly, ed., *Twentieth Century Interpretations of Invisible Man* (Englewood Cliffs, N.J.: Prentice-Hall, Inc., 1970), p. 51.
46. See Sissela Bok, *Lying: Moral Choice in Public and Private Life* (New York: Vintage Books, 1979) for a discussion of the relative roles of truth and lying in American life and culture.
47. Mark Busby, *Ralph Ellison* (Boston: Twayne Publishers, 1991), p. 40.
48. Ibid.
49. W.E.B. Du Bois is quoted in Reilly, *Twentieth Century Interpretations of Invisible Man*, p. 5.
50. 491 U.S. 397 (1989).
51. 500 U.S. 173 (1991).
52. 505 U.S. 377 (1992).
53. 496 U.S. 310 (1990).
54. 505 U.S. 377, 380, quoting the St. Paul ordinance.
55. 500 U.S. 173, 178 (1991).
56. See *City of Houston v. Hill*, 482 U.S. 451 (1987).
57. 485 U.S. 360 (1988). For a discussion of the problems involved in *Lyng*, see Aviam Soifer, *Law and the Company We Keep* (Cambridge, Mass.: Harvard University Press, 1995).
58. 485 U.S. 360, 366 (quoting *NAACP v. Claiborne Hardware Co.*, 458 U.S. 886, 933 (1982)).
59. Ibid., p. 369 (quoting *Abood v. Detroit Board of Education*, 431 U.S. 209, 234–35 (1977)).
60. See also *O'Lone v. Estate of Shabazz*, 482 U.S. 342 (1987).

61. 463 U.S. 1032 (1983).

62. (Brennan, J. dissenting) Ibid., p. 1058 (quoting *Terry v. Ohio*, 392 U.S. 1, 25–26 (1968)).

63. 445 U.S. 573 (1980).

64. Ibid., p. 586, n. 24 (quoting *Johnson v. United States*, 333 U.S. 10, 13–14, (1948)); see also *New Jersey v. T.L.O.*, 469 U.S. 325 (1985).

65. 441 U.S. 418 (1979).

66. Ibid., p. 427.

67. See also *Gilliard v. Gilliard*, 483 U.S. 587 (1987); and *Complete Auto Transit v. Reis*, 451 U.S. 401 (1981).

68. Glendon, *Rights Talk*, p. 9.

69. See, for example, Morton J. Horwitz, ''Republicanism and Liberalism,'' and G. Edward White, ''The Studied Ambiguity of Horwitz's Legal History,'' 29 *William & Mary Law Review* 101 (1987).

70. See *Planned Parenthood of Southeastern Pennsylvania v. Casey*, 505 U.S. 833 (1992).

71. See Gregory G. Sarno, ''Homicide: Physician's Withdrawal of Life Supports from Comatose Patient,'' 47 ALR4th 18 (1986).

## CHAPTER 2

1. Constitution of the United States, Amendment I.

2. William Shakespeare, *The Tragedy of Othello*, The Moor of Venice, Act III, Scene 3, lines 155–156 (New York: Harcourt, Brace & Co., 1952), p. 1079.

3. Cleanth Brooks, ''Faulkner's Ultimate Values,'' *On the Prejudices, Predilections, and Firm Beliefs of Faulkner*, p. 20.

4. ''Racial codes,'' in this context, means beliefs, attitudes, and customs affecting and governing interpersonal conduct between African Americans and other minorities, on the one hand, and whites, on the other. Before the racial code was the slave code, which controlled the relationship between the slaves and their owners.

5. William Faulkner, ''An Odor of Verbena,'' in Malcolm Cowley, ed., *The Portable Faulkner*, rev. and exp. ed. (New York: Penguin Books, 1977).

6. William Faulkner, ''That Evening Sun,'' in Cowley, *The Portable Faulkner*.

7. See Bertram Wyatt-Brown, *Southern Honor: Ethics and Behavior in the Old South* (New York: Oxford University Press, 1982), p. 435. One meaning of the charivari, also *shivaree*, was a mock ritual, such as a tar and feathering, conducted by a mob for the purpose of shaming an individual. Hawthorne's short story, ''My Kinsman, Major Molineux,'' and Mark Twain's *Huckleberry Finn* provide good examples.

8. Tocqueville, *Democracy in America*, p. 513.

9. See Francis Fukuyama, *The End of History and The Last Man*.

10. Nathaniel Hawthorne, *The Scarlet Letter* (New York: Penguin Books, 1983).

11. Owen Wister, *The Virginian: A Horseman of the Plains* (New York: MacMillan Publishing Co., Inc., 1979).

12. Robert Penn Warren, *Night Rider* (New York: Random House, 1939).

13. Joyce Carol Oates, *them* (New York: The Vanguard Press, 1969).

14. Richard Price, *Clockers* (New York: Avon Books, 1993).

15. 47 Cal. 3d 112, 763 P.2d 852 (Cal. 1988).

16. For other examples of conflict between private codes and law, see *Prince v. Massachusetts*, 321 U.S. 158 (1944); *Wisconsin v. Yoder*, 406 U.S. 205 (1972); and *Mozert v. Hawkins County Board of Education*, 827 F.2d 1058 (6th Cir. 1987).

17. 469 U.S. 45 (1984).

18. 503 U.S. 159 (1992).

19. See also *United States v. Garner*, 574 F.2d 1141 (4th Cir. 1978).

20. Wyatt-Brown, *Southern Honor*, p. 45.

21. William Faulkner, *The Sound and the Fury* (New York: Random House, Inc., 1946).

22. Cleanth Brooks, *William Faulkner: First Encounters* (New Haven: Yale University Press, 1983), p. 30.

23. William Faulkner, *Light in August* (New York: Vintage Books, 1972).

24. The name, pronounced YOK[YOCK]-na-pa-TAW-pha, is a Chickasaw Indian word meaning ''water runs slow through flat land.'' Frederick L. Gwynn and Joseph L. Blotner, eds., *Faulkner in the University: Class Conferences at the University of Virginia 1957–1958* (Charlottesville: University Press of Virginia, 1977).

25. Ibid., p. 41.

26. William Faulkner, *The Unvanquished* (New York: Random House, 1965).

27. Brooks, *First Encounters*, p. 40.

28. William Faulkner, ''Nobel Prize Address,'' December 10, 1950, in Cowley, *The Portable Faulkner*, p. 723.

29. In a short story entitled ''My Kinsman, Major Molineux,'' Hawthorne clarified the role of traditional systems of honor and shame in human affairs and revealed one means by which a community overcame its anxiety and preserved community solidarity through assertion of its core values. Wyatt-Brown, *Southern Honor*. See ''The May-Pole of Merry Mount,'' another of Hawthorne's short stories.

30. Wyatt-Brown, *Southern Honor*, p. 14.

31. Richard Slotkin, *Gunfighter Nation: The Myth of the Frontier in Twentieth-Century America* (New York: HarperCollins, 1993), p. 173.

32. See Wyatt-Brown, *Southern Honor*, pp. 352–361.

33. Richard Maxwell Brown, ''Legal and Behavioral Perspectives on American Vigilantism,'' *Perspectives in American History*, vol. V, 1971 (Cambridge, Mass.: Charles Warren Center for Studies in American History, Harvard University, 1971), p. 95.

34. See Martín Sánchez Jankowski, *Islands in the Street: Gangs and American Urban Society* (Berkeley: University of California Press, 1991) for a discussion of gangs in American urban society. See also Elijah Anderson, ''The Code of the Streets,'' *The Atlantic Monthly*, May 1994.

35. Anderson, ''The Code of the Streets,'' p. 82.

36. See Robert C. Post, ''Symposium: New Perspectives in the Law of Defamation: The Social Foundations of Defamation Law: Reputation and the Constitution,'' 74 California Law Review 691 (1986).

37. Ibid., p. 742.

38. See Robin West, *Narrative, Authority, and Law* (Ann Arbor: University of Michigan Press, 1993), pp. 121–123.

39. Tocqueville, *Democracy in America*, p. 517.

40. Soifer, *Law and the Company We Keep*, p. 101.

## CHAPTER 3

1. Charles Dickens, *A Tale of Two Cities* (New York: Penguin Books, 1985), p. 35.

2. Hannah Arendt, *On Violence* (1969) (quoted in Martín Sánchez Jankowski, *Islands in the Street*, p. 137).

3. See Wyatt-Brown, *Southern Honor*, p. 367.

4. Lawrence M. Friedman, *Crime and Punishment in American History* (New York: Basic Books, 1993), p. 11.

5. James Fenimore Cooper, *The Last of the Mohicans* (New York: Bantam Books, 1981).

6. Richard Hofstadter and Michael Wallace, eds., *American Violence: A Documentary History* (New York: Alfred A. Knopf, Inc., 1970), p. 3.

7. One aspect of American violence is the violence of our humor. William Keough has covered that subject in *Punchlines: The Violence of American Humor* (New York: Paragon House, 1990). Keough features writers including Mark Twain, Ambrose Bierce, Ring Lardner, and Kurt Vonnegut.

8. Hofstadter and Wallace, *American Violence: A Documentary History*, p. 3.

9. Parviz Saney, *Crime and Culture in America: A Comparative Perspective* (Westport, Conn.: Greenwood Press, 1986), p. 47.

10. Elliott Currie, *Confronting Crime: An American Challenge* (New York: Pantheon Books, 1985), p. 226.

11. Slotkin, *Gunfighter Nation*, p. 13.

12. Ibid., p. 13. Although the statement is generally accurate, the treatment of Native Americans cannot be overlooked.

13. Ibid.

14. Richard Maxwell Brown, *Strain of Violence: Historical Studies of American Violence and Vigilantism* (New York: Oxford University Press, 1975), p. 7.

15. Ibid., p. 4.

16. See Slotkin, *Gunfighter Nation*, pp. 1–21, 651–653.

17. Hofstadter and Wallace, *American Violence: A Documentary History*, p. 7.

18. Ibid., p. 12.

19. Cooper, *The Last of the Mohicans*.

20. Warren, *Night Rider* (New York: Random House, 1939).

21. Slotkin, *Gunfighter Nation*, p. 14.

22. Ibid., pp. 14–15.

23. Ibid., p. 41.

24. See, for discussion of redemption through violence, Olga W. Vickery, ''God's Moral Order and the Problem of Ike's Redemption,'' *Bear, Man & God: Seven Approaches to William Faulkner's ''The Bear''* (New York: Random House, 1964).

25. *People v. Goetz*, 68 N.Y. 2d 96, 497 N.E.2d 41 (N.Y. 1986).

26. Reported in the *Hartford Courant*, December 22, 1994.

27. See, for example, Nadine Klansky, ''Bernard Goetz, A 'Reasonable Man': A Look At New York's Justification Defense,'' 53 *Brooklyn Law Review* 1149 (1988).

28. See *People v. Superior Court*, (Soon Ja Du) 5 Cal. App. 4th 822, 7 Cal. Rptr. 2d 177 (1992).

29. Ibid.

30. Reginald Leamon Robinson, " 'The Other Against Itself': Deconstructing the Violent Discourse Between Korean and African Americans," 67 *Southern California Law Review* 15 (1993).

31. See Richard A. Rosen, "On Self-Defense, Imminence, and Women Who Kill Their Batterers," 71 *North Carolina Law Review* 371 (1993); see also *People v. Aris*, 215 Cal. App. 3d 1178, 264 Cal. Rptr. 167 (Ct. App. 4 Dist. 1989); and *State v. Stewart*, 243 Kan. 639, 763 P.2d 572 (Kan. 1988).

32. Don DeLillo, *Libra* (New York: Penguin Books, 1991).

33. Oates, *them*.

34. Hugh Davis Graham and Ted Robert Gurr, eds., *Violence in America: Historical and Comparative Perspectives* (Beverly Hills, Calif.: Sage Publications, Inc., 1979), p. 265.

35. See Rollo May, *Power and Innocence: A Search for the Sources of Violence* (New York: W.W. Norton, 1972).

36. Mary Kathryn Grant, *The Tragic Vision of Joyce Carol Oates* (Durham, N.C.: Duke University Press, 1978), p. 34.

37. Bronowski is quoted in Grant, *The Tragic Vision of Joyce Carol Oates*, p. 33. See Jacob Bronowski, *The Face of Violence: An Essay with a Play* (Cleveland: World Publishing Co., 1967).

38. Craig Nova, *Trombone* (New York: Ballantine Books, 1994).

39. Richard Bausch, *Violence* (New York: Houghton Mifflin, 1992).

40. See Anthony Chase, "1986 Survey of Books Relating to the Law: II. Crime, Punishment, and Criminal Procedure: In the Jungle of Cities," 84 *Michigan Law Review* 737 (1986).

41. See, for example, "Explaining the Legal System's Inadequate Response to the Abuse of Women: A Lack of Coordination," 8 *Journal of Human Rights* 149 (1990); Barry R. Schaller, "Perspectives on Family Violence: Problems and Solutions," 21 *Connecticut Law Tribune* 3 (1995); and "Proposed Solutions to the Family Violence Problem," 21 *Connecticut Law Tribune* 4 (1995).

42. 595 F. Supp. 1521 (D.C. Conn. 1984).

43. See Conn. Gen. Stat. §§ 46b-38a et seq.

44. Franklin E. Zimring, "Legal Perspectives on Family Violence," 75 *California Law Review* 521 (1987).

45. For discussion of these factors see, for example, "*L. Smith v. United States*: Enhanced Penalties for Using Guns as Barter in Drug Deals," 20 *Journal of Contemporary Law* 295 (1994); Friedman, *Crime and Punishment in American History*, pp. 267, 451, 454, 459.

46. 508 U.S. 223 (1993).

47. 115 S. Ct. 1624 (1995).

48. See, for example, the discussion of gangs in Jankowski, *Islands in the Street*.

49. See Jane Howard-Martin and Derrick Howard, "How OSHA's Response to Workplace Violence Will Affect Health Care Facilities," 11, no. 5 *Healthspan* 21 (1994).

50. See Bruce Porter and Marvin Dunn, *The Miami Riot of 1980: Crossing the Bounds* (Lexington, Mass.: D.C. Heath & Co., 1984).

51. *United States v. Koon*, 34 F.3d 1416 (9th Cir. 1994).

52. Ibid.

53. See, for discussion of violence in riots, "In the Jungle of Cities," 84 *Michigan Law Review* 737 (1986); Carl T. Bogus, "Race, Riots, and Guns," 66 *Southern California Law Review* 1365 (1993).

54. See Terry L. Etter, "The Knock-Down, Drag-Out Battle Over Government Regulation of Television Violence," 3 *CommLaw Conspectus* 31 (1995).

55. See, for example, Steven Bennet Weisburd and Brian Levin, " 'On the Basis of Sex': Recognizing Gender-Based Bias Crimes," 5 *Stanford Law & Policy Review* 21 (1994).

## CHAPTER 4

1. Abram Chayes, "The Role of the Judge in Public Law Litigation," 89 *Harvard Law Review* 389, 402 (1976).

2. Max Frankel, "Out of Focus," *New York Times*, November 5, 1995, S. 6 (Magazine), p. 26.

3. See Anthony T. Kronman, *The Lost Lawyer: Failing Ideals of the Legal Profession* (Cambridge, Mass.: Harvard University Press, 1993), p. 11.

4. See generally discussion and definitions of types of authority in *Encyclopedia of Philosophy*, vol. I, p. 215.

5. The terms selected to designate the two turning points are necessarily oversimplified because many developments occurred during both periods.

6. Ferguson, *Law and Letters in American Culture*, p. 10.

7. Ibid., p. 9 (quoting Anton-Hermann Chroust).

8. Ibid., p. 280.

9. Allen D. Boyer, "Formalism, Realism, and Naturalism: Cross-Currents in American Letters and Law," 23 *Connecticut Law Review* 669, 670 (1991).

10. Graham, *Violence in America*, p. 478.

11. See John Rawls, *A Theory of Justice* (Cambridge, Mass.: Belknap Press, 1971), p. 10, cited in Margaret J. Fried and Lawrence A. Frolik, "The Limits of Law: Litigation, Lawyers and the Search for Justice in Russell Banks's *The Sweet Hereafter*," 7 *Cardozo Studies in Law and Literature*, No. 1 (1995), p. 9, n.22.

12. See *U.S. v. Koon*, 34 F.3d 1416 (9th Cir. 1994); *U.S. v. Milliken*, 769 F. Supp. 1023 (W.D. Tenn. 1991); and *U.S. v. North*, 910 F.2d 843, 285 U.S. App. D.C. 343 (D.C. Cir. 1990).

13. See Ely, *Democracy and Distrust*, pp. 43–72.

14. See theories of civil association in Michael Oakeshott, *Religion, Politics, and the Moral Life*, edited by Timothy Fuller (New Haven: Yale University Press, 1993); and Francis Fukuyama, *The End of History*, and *Trust* (New York: The Free Press, 1995). Negotiation and problem-solving are discussed in Carrie Menkel-Meadow, "Toward Another View of Legal Negotiation: The Structure of Problem Solving," 31 *UCLA Law Review* 754 (1984).

15. James Fenimore Cooper, *The Ways of the Hour: A Tale* (Upper Saddle River, N.J.: The Gregg Press, 1968).

16. Theodore Dreiser, *An American Tragedy* (New York: The New American Library, Inc., 1981).

17. Russell Banks, *The Sweet Hereafter* (New York: HarperCollins, 1991).

18. John P. McWilliams, Jr., "Innocent Criminal or Criminal Innocence," *Law and American Literature*, p. 68.

19. Ibid., p. 69.

20. Ibid., pp. 69–70.

21. Letter to Jack Wilgus, April 20, 1927, in Robert Elias, ed., *Letters of Theodore Dreiser* (Philadelphia: University of Pennsylvania Press, 1959), 2:458, quoted in McWilliams, ''Innocent Criminal or Criminal Innocence,'' p. 88.

22. See *People v. Gillette*, 191 N.Y. 107, 83 N.E. 680 (N.Y. 1908). See also C.R.B. Dunlop, ''Law and Justice in Dreiser's *An American Tragedy*,'' 6 *University of British Columbia Law Review* 379 (1971).

23. Robert Elias, *Theodore Dreiser: Apostle of Nature* (Ithaca: N.Y: Cornell University Press, 1969), pp. 222–223, quoted in McWilliams, ''Innocent Criminal or Criminal Innocence,'' pp. 91–92.

24. McWilliams, ''Innocent Criminal or Criminal Innocence,'' p. 92.

25. Clarence Darrow, *An Eye For An Eye* (1905), cited in McWilliams, ''Innocent Criminal or Criminal Innocence,'' p. 96.

26. McWilliams, ''Innocent Criminal or Criminal Innocence,'' p. 92, quoting Darrow.

27. Ibid., p. 92.

28. *People v. Gillette*, 191 N.Y. 107, 116, 83 N.E. 680, 682 (N.Y. 1908).

29. Ibid., 191 N.Y. 117, 683.

30. See, for background, *Washington v. United States*, 390 F.2d 444, 129 U.S. App. D.C. 29 (D.C. Cir. 1967). See also White, *The Legal Imagination*, pp. 337–358 (on the language of labels, the insanity defense, and the jury's function in determining responsibility.

31. McWilliams, ''Innocent Criminal or Criminal Innocence,'' p. 94.

32. Ibid, p. 93.

33. *Gillette*, 191 N.Y. 117, 683.

34. Ibid., 191 N.Y. 122, 685.

35. *Clockers* is an example of a novel that bridges the gap between legal culture and popular culture, as those terms are defined by Lawrence M. Friedman in ''Law, Lawyers, and Popular Culture,'' 98 *Yale Law Journal* 1579 (1989).

36. See Fried and Frolik, ''The Limits of Law: Litigation, Lawyers and the Search for Justice in Banks's *The Sweet Hereafter*.''

37. Hand, *The Spirit of Liberty*.

38. Ely, *Democracy and Distrust*.

## CHAPTER 5

1. Giamatti, *A Free and Ordered Space*, pp. 95–96.

2. Gunnar Myrdal, *An American Dilemma* (1944; 20th anniversary edition, New York, 1962), chap. 1, quoted in Schlesinger, *The Disuniting of America*, p. 27.

3. *Encyclopedia of Philosophy*, vol. 2, p. 520.

4. Ibid., vol. 4, p. 259.

5. Everett Carter, *The American Idea: The Literary Response to American Optimism* (Chapel Hill: University of North Carolina Press, 1977), p. 7, quoting Jefferson. See Arthur Miller, *The Crucible* (New York: Bantam Books, 1959) for a vivid illustration of ''witch-burning'' in American society.

6. Stephen Crane, *Maggie: A Girl of the Streets*, in *Great Short Works of Stephen Crane* (New York: Harper & Row, 1968).

7. Frank Norris, *The Octopus* (New York: The New American Library, Inc., 1964).

8. John Dos Passos, *The Big Money* (New York: Harcourt, Brace and Company, 1936).

9. Nathanael West, *Miss Lonelyhearts & The Day of the Locust* (New York: New Directions Publishing Corporation, 1969).
10. F. Scott Fitzgerald, *The Great Gatsby* (New York: Charles Scribner's Sons, 1953).
11. Carter, *The American Idea*, p. 5.
12. Ibid., pp. 8–9.
13. Ibid., p. 9.
14. Ibid., p. 10.
15. Boyer, "Formalism, Realism, and Naturalism," p. 673.
16. Ibid.
17. 41 U.S. (16 Pet.) 1 (1842).
18. J. Story, Report of the Commission on Codification of the Law to the Governor of Massachusetts (1837), reprinted in S. Presser and J. Zainaldin, *Law and American History: Cases and Materials* 398, pp. 399–400 (1980), quoted in Boyer, "Formalism, Realism, and Naturalism," p. 674.
19. Boyer, "Formalism, Realism, and Naturalism," p. 677.
20. James D. Hopkins, "The Development of Realism in Law and Literature During the Period 1883–1933: The Cultural Resemblance," 4 *Pace Law Review* 29, 33 (1983–84).
21. Ibid., p. 34.
22. Ibid., p. 37, quoting Holmes in *Abrams v. United States*, 250 U.S. 616, 630 (1919).
23. Friedman, *A History of American Law*, p. 133.
24. Ibid.
25. (Douglas, J. dissenting) 347 U.S. 442, 472 (1954).
26. Ibid., p. 472.
27. Ibid.
28. Ibid.
29. 422 U.S. 490 (1975).
30. Ibid., p. 519 (Douglas, J. dissenting). See also *United Steelworkers of America, AFL-CIO-CLC v. Weber*, 443 U.S. 193 (1979).
31. 505 U.S. 1 (1992).
32. Cleanth Brooks, R.W.B. Lewis, and Robert Penn Warren, *American Literature: The Makers and the Making* (New York: St. Martin's Press, 1973), vol. II, p. 1636.
33. James Nagel, *Stephen Crane and Literary Impressionism* (University Park: Pennsylvania State University Press, 1980), p. 99, quoting Crane.
34. Brooks, *American Literature*, p. 2440.
35. Hopkins, "The Development of Realism in Law," p. 51.
36. *Commonwealth v. Sacco*, 255 Mass. 364, 151 N.E. 839 (Mass. 1926); *Commonwealth v. Sacco*, 261 Mass. 12, 158 N.E. 167 (Mass. 1927).
37. F. Scott Fitzgerald, "Winter Dreams," quoted in Brooks, *American Literature*, p. 2286.
38. Brooks, *American Literature*, pp. 2286–2287.
39. See, for example, Alex M. Johnson, Jr., "Critiquing the Foreclosure Process: An Economic Approach Based on the Paradigmatic Norms of Bankruptcy," 79 *Virginia Law Review* 959 (1993); Linda J. Rusch, "Bankruptcy Reorganization Jurisprudence: Matters of Belief, Faith, and Hope-Stepping into the Fourth Dimension," 55 *Montana Law Review* 9 (1994).
40. See, for example, *Haitian Refugee Center, Inc. v. James Baker, III, Secretary of*

*State*, 953 F.2d 1498 (11th Cir. Fla. 1992); *Haitian Refugee Center, Inc. v. Baker*, 949 F.2d 1109 (11th Cir. 1991).

41. See, for example, *Washington v. Seattle School District No. 1*, 458 U.S. 457 (1982) (action challenging the constitutionality of a statute, adopted through initiative, which prohibited school boards from requiring any student to attend a school other than the school geographically nearest or next nearest his place of residence, but which contained exceptions for purposes other than desegregation.)

42. See, for example, Kim Nobel, ''Demise of a Wonderful Life: The Rise and Fall of Franklin Savings and Loan,'' 60 *University of Missouri Kansas City Law Review* 363 (1991); *O'Melveny & Myers v. Federal Deposit Insurance Corporation*, 114 S. Ct. 2048 (1994) (malpractice action against former counsel of S&L regarding counsel's advice and services in connection with public offerings.); Jan S. Blaising, ''Are the Accountants Accountable? Auditor Liability in the Savings and Loan Crisis,'' 25 Indiana Law Review 475 (1991).

43. See *New York v. United States*, 505 U.S. 144 (1992).

44. 485 U.S. 224 (1988).

45. For other examples of adaptation, see *United States v. Harriss*, 347 U.S. 612 (1954) (constitutionality of the Federal Regulation Act involving lobbyist reporting) and *Examining Board of Engineers, Architects and Surveyors v. Flores de Otero*, 426 U.S. 572 (1976) (due process challenge to statute restricting civil engineering practice.)

46. 505 U.S. 1 (1992).

47. See *Moore v. Ganim*, 233 Conn. 557, 660 A.2d 742 (1995) for a discussion of the constitutional obligation of state government to provide minimal subsistence to the poor. The Connecticut Supreme Court concluded, in that case, that the Connecticut Constitution does not compel the state to provide minimal financial assistance. Consequently, a statute limiting benefits for indigent persons to nine months does not violate the state constitution. A related case, *Hilton v. City of New Haven*, 233 Conn. 701, 661 A.2d 973 (1995), dealing with the city's decision to close a homeless shelter, was decided similarly.

48. Ely, *Democracy and Distrust*, p. 181.

## CHAPTER 6

1. Thomas Jefferson, ''Letter to Samuel Kercheval, Monticello, July 12, 1816,'' *The Life and Selected Writings of Thomas Jefferson* (New York: Random House, 1944), p. 674. Ongoing controversy exists as to Jefferson's opinions concerning change in American society.

2. John Steinbeck, *The Grapes of Wrath* (New York: Bantam Books, Inc., 1966).

3. Wendell Berry, *A Place on Earth* (New York: Harcourt, Brace & World, Inc., 1967).

4. Saul Bellow, *Herzog* (New York: The Viking Press, 1964).

5. *The People, The Press & Politics: The New Political Landscape*, Times Mirror Center for The People & The Press (October 1994), p. 3.

6. Robert Hughes, *Culture of Complaint: The Fraying of America* (New York: Warner Books, 1994).

7. Arthur M. Schlesinger, Jr., *The Disuniting of America: Reflections on a Multicultural Society* (New York: W. W. Norton & Co. 1993).

8. Alan M. Dershowitz, *The Abuse Excuse* (Boston: Little, Brown and Co., 1994).

9. Glendon, *Rights Talk.*

10. James O. Freedman, *Crisis and Legitimacy: The Administrative Process and American Government* (New York: Cambridge University Press, 1978), p. 36.

11. *Mistretta v. United States*, 488 U.S. 361 (1989).

12. Ibid., p. 413 (Scalia, J.).

13. Philip K. Howard, *The Death of Common Sense: How Law Is Suffocating America* (New York: Random House, 1994).

14. Ibid., p. 11.

15. See Teresa Godwin Phelps, ''The Story of the Law in *Huckleberry Finn*,'' 39 *Mercer Law Review* 889, 894 (1988).

16. Ibid., p. 904.

17. Robin West, ''Communities, Texts, and Law: Reflections on the Law and Literature Movement,'' 1 *Yale Journal of Law & the Humanities* 129, 136 (1988).

18. Ibid., p. 191. At one point early in the story, Jim discusses his own value as an item of property. As an example of cases dealing with property rights in the context of adjudicating the emancipation of slaves, see *Tom, A Colored Boy v. Daily and Desha*, 4 Ohio 368, 1831 WL 13 (Supreme Court of Ohio, 1831).

19. *Dred Scott v. Sandford*, 60 U.S. 393, 19 How. 393 (U.S. Mo. 1856).

20. Phelps, ''The Story of the Law in *Huckleberry Finn*,'' p. 905.

21. Martha Minow, ''Words and the Door to the Land of Change: Law, Language, and Family Violence,'' 43 *Vanderbilt Law Review* 1665 (1990).

22. Eusebio L. Rodrigues, *Quest for the Human: An Exploration of Saul Bellow's Fiction* (Lewisburg, Pa.: Bucknell University Press, 1981), p. 183.

23. M. Gilbert Porter, *Whence the Power? The Artistry and Humanity of Saul Bellow* (Columbia: University of Missouri Press, 1974), pp. 152–153.

24. Ibid., p. 153.

25. Ibid., p. 158.

26. Gabriel Josipovici, ''Herzog: Freedom and Wit,'' in Harold Bloom, ed., *Modern Critical Interpretations: Saul Bellow's ''Herzog''* (New York: Chelsea House Publishers, 1988), p. 22.

27. Ibid., p. 24.

28. Ibid., p. 25.

29. 115 S. Ct. 1185 (1995).

30. 115 S. Ct. 1914 (1995).

31. 501 U.S. 808 (1991).

32. 507 U.S. 680 (1993).

33. 114 S. Ct. 2481 (1994).

34. 115 S. Ct. 1624 (1995).

35. 468 U.S. 897 (1984).

36. *Evans*, 115 S. Ct. 1185, 1194.

37. Ibid.

38. Ibid., p. 4184.

39. 501 U.S. 808 (1991).

40. 482 U.S. 496 (1987).

41. 490 U.S. 805 (1989).

42. *Payne*, 501 U.S. at 839–840.

43. 384 U.S. 436 (1966).

44. 428 U.S. 465 (1976).
45. *Withrow*, 507 U.S. 680, 697.
46. Ibid., p. 701.
47. Ibid., pp. 701–702 (internal quotation marks omitted).
48. Ibid., p. 704.
49. *Withrow*, 507 U.S. 680, 709.
50. Ibid., p. 704 (citations omitted).
51. 114 S. Ct. 2481 (1994).
52. Ibid., p. 2494.
53. Ibid., p. 2495.
54. Ibid., p. 2497.
55. *Grumet*, 114 S. Ct. 2481, 2497–2498.
56. Ibid., p. 2498.
57. Ibid.
58. Ibid., pp. 2498–2499.
59. *Wilson v. Arkansas*, 115 S. Ct. 1914, 1918 (quoting *Miller v. United States*, 357 U.S. 301, 313 (1958)).
60. 115 S. Ct. 1918.
61. *United States v. Lopez*, 115 S. Ct. 1624, 1634.
62. Ibid., p. 1637 (quoting *New York v. United States*, 505 U.S. 144, 157).
63. Ibid., pp. 1637–1638.
64. Ibid., p. 1641.
65. *Planned Parenthood of Southeastern Pennsylvania v. Casey*, 505 U.S. 833, 901 (1992).

## CHAPTER 7

1. Bellow, *Herzog*, p. 207.
2. Rodrigues, *Quest for the Human*, p. 173.
3. Thomas Paine, quoted in Ferguson, *Law and Letters in American Culture*, p. 11.
4. See, for example, *The People, The Press & Politics*, p. 6.
5. Alexis de Tocqueville, quoted in Jankowski, *Islands in the Street*, p. 21.
6. See Wilkinson, *The Pursuit of American Character.*
7. See, for example, Glendon, *Rights Talk*; and Alan Dershowitz, *The Abuse Excuse.*
8. Schlesinger, *The Disuniting of America*, p. 134; and Hughes, *Culture of Complaint*, p. 88.
9. *The People, The Press & Politics*, p. 3.
10. Glendon, *Rights Talk*, p. 171.
11. Cass R. Sunstein, "On Marshall's Conception of Equality," 44 *Stanford Law Review* 1267, 1273–1274 (1992).
12. See Herbert Wechsler, "Toward Neutral Principles of Constitutional Law," 73 *Harvard Law Review* 1, 19 (1959).
13. "[T]he Court's legitimacy depends on making legally principled decisions under circumstances in which their principled character is sufficiently plausible to be accepted by the Nation." *Planned Parenthood of Southeastern Pennsylvania v. Casey*, 505 U.S. 833, 866 (1992).
14. See Ely, *Democracy and Distrust.*

15. Ibid., pp. 43–72.

16. See Tribe, *Constitutional Choices*, p. 189.

17. Barry R. Schaller, "Culturally Speaking: Equality, Responsibility and the Social Compact," 14 *Quinnipiac Law Review* 347, 353 (1994).

18. This sector of civil society, which is the subject of considerable renewed scholarly interest, has been widely commented on by Tocqueville and others. See, for example, Soifer, *Law and the Company We Keep*, p. 31; and Fukuyama, *Trust: The Social Virtues and the Creation of Prosperity* (New York: The Free Press, 1995).

19. Kronman, *The Lost Lawyer*, p. 2.

20. Myrdal, quoted in Schlesinger, *The Disuniting of America*, p. 27 (internal quotation marks omitted).

21. Ibid., p. 27.

# Selected Bibliography


Beers, Henry A. *Initial Studies in American Letters*. Meadville, Pa.: The Chautauqua-Century Press, 1895.

Bennett, W. Lance, and Martha S. Feldman. *Reconstructing Reality in the Courtroom: Justice and Judgment in American Culture*. New Brunswick, N.J.: Rutgers University Press, 1981.

Bloom, Harold, ed. *Modern Critical Interpretations: Saul Bellow's "Herzog."* New York: Chelsea House Publishers, 1988.

———. *Modern Critical Interpretations: Theodore Dreiser's "An American Tragedy."* New York: Chelsea House Publishers, 1988.

———. *Modern Critical Views: Joyce Carol Oates*. New York: Chelsea House, 1987.

Bok, Sissela. *Lying: Moral Choice in Public and Private Life*. New York: Vintage Books, 1979.

Brooks, Cleanth. *On the Prejudices, Predilections, and Firm Beliefs of William Faulkner*. Baton Rouge: Louisiana State University Press, 1988.

———. *William Faulkner: First Encounters*. New Haven: Yale University Press, 1983.

Brooks, Cleanth, R.W.B. Lewis, and Robert Penn Warren. *American Literature: The Makers and the Making*. New York: St. Martin's Press, 1973.

Brown, Richard Maxwell. *Strain of Violence: Historical Studies of American Violence and Vigilantism*. New York: Oxford University Press, 1975.

Busby, Mark. *Ralph Ellison*. Boston: Twayne Publishers, 1991.

Carter, Everett. *The American Idea: The Literary Response to American Optimism*. Chapel Hill: University of North Carolina Press, 1977.

Currie, Elliott. *Confronting Crime: An American Challenge*. New York: Pantheon Books, 1985.

Dershowitz, Alan M. *The Abuse Excuse*. Boston: Little, Brown and Company, 1994.

Ely, John Hart. *Democracy and Distrust: A Theory of Judicial Review*. Cambridge, Mass.: Harvard University Press, 1980.

Ferguson, Robert A. *Law and Letters in American Culture*. Cambridge, Mass.: Harvard University Press, 1984.

Friedman, Lawrence M. *Crime and Punishment in American History*. New York: Basic Books, 1993.

———. *A History of American Law*, 2d ed. New York: Simon and Schuster, 1985.

———. *Total Justice*. Boston: Beacon Press, 1987.

Fukuyama, Francis. *The End of History and The Last Man*. New York: The Free Press, 1992.

Girgus, Sam B. *The Law of the Heart: Individualism and the Modern Self in American Literature*. Austin: University of Texas Press, 1979.

Glendon, Mary Ann. *Rights Talk: The Impoverishment of Political Discourse*. New York: The Free Press, 1993.

Graham, Hugh Davis, and Ted Robert Gurr, eds. *Violence in America: Historical and Comparative Perspectives*. Beverly Hills, Calif.: Sage Publications, Inc., 1979.

Grant, Mary Kathryn. *The Tragic Vision of Joyce Carol Oates*. Durham, N.C.: Duke University Press, 1978.

Gwynn, Frederick L., and Joseph L. Blotner, eds. *Faulkner in the University: Class Conferences at the University of Virginia 1957–1958*. Charlottesville: University Press of Virginia, 1977.

Hand, Learned. *The Spirit of Liberty: The Bill of Rights*. New York: The Legal Classics Library, 1989.

Hofstadter, Richard, and Michael Wallace, eds. *American Violence: A Documentary History*. New York: Alfred A. Knopf, Inc., 1970.

Horwitz, Morton J. *The Transformation of American Law, 1780–1860*. Cambridge, Mass.: Harvard University Press, 1977.

Howard, Philip K. *The Death of Common Sense: How Law Is Suffocating America*. New York: Random House, 1994.

Hughes, Robert. *Culture of Complaint*. New York: Warner Books, 1994.

Jankowski, Martín Sánchez. *Islands in the Street: Gangs and American Urban Society*. Berkeley and Los Angeles: University of California Press, 1991.

Keough, William. *Punchlines: The Violence of American Humor*. New York: Paragon House, 1990.

Kronman, Anthony T. *The Lost Lawyer: Failing Ideals of the Legal Profession*. Cambridge, Mass.: The Belknap Press of Harvard University Press, 1993.

Limerick, Patricia Nelson. *The Legacy of Conquest: The Unbroken Past of the American West*. New York: W. W. Norton & Company, Inc., 1987.

May, Rollo. *Power and Innocence: A Search for the Sources of Violence*. New York: W. W. Norton & Company, Inc., 1972.

Nagel, James. *Stephen Crane and Literary Impressionism*. University Park: Pennsylvania State University Press, 1980.

Posner, Richard A. *Law and Literature: A Misunderstood Relation*. Cambridge, Mass.: Harvard University Press, 1988.

Reilly, John M., ed. *Twentieth Century Interpretations of Invisible Man*. Englewood Cliffs, N.J.: Prentice-Hall, Inc., 1970.

Rodrigues, Eusebio L. *Quest for the Human: An Exploration of Saul Bellow's Fiction*. Lewisburg, Pa.: Bucknell University Press, 1981.

Saney, Parviz. *Crime and Culture in America*. Westport, Conn.: Greenwood Press, 1986.

Schlesinger, Arthur M., Jr. *The Disuniting of America: Reflections on a Multicultural Society*. New York: W. W. Norton & Co. 1993.

Slotkin, Richard. *Gunfighter Nation: The Myth of the Frontier in Twentieth-Century America*. New York: HarperCollins, 1993.

Smith, Carl S., John P. McWilliams, Jr., and Maxwell Bloomfield. *Law and American Literature: A Collection of Essays*. New York: Alfred A. Knopf, Inc., 1983.

Soifer, Aviam. *Law and the Company We Keep*. Cambridge, Mass: Harvard University Press, 1995.

Thomas, Brook. *Cross-examinations of Law and Literature*. New York: Cambridge University Press, 1987.

Tocqueville, Alexis de. *Democracy in America*, edited by J. P. Mayer. New York; HarperPerennial, 1988.

Tribe, Laurence H. *Constitutional Choices*. Cambridge, Mass.: Harvard University Press, 1985.

West, Robin. *Narrative, Authority, and Law*. Ann Arbor: University of Michigan Press, 1993.

Wilkinson, Rupert. *The Pursuit of American Character*. New York: Harper & Row, 1988.

Wills, Garry. *Lincoln at Gettysburg: The Words That Remade America*. New York: Simon & Schuster, 1992.

Wyatt-Brown, Bertram. *Southern Honor: Ethics and Behavior in the Old South*. New York: Oxford University Press, 1982.

# Index

**About the Author**

BARRY R. SCHALLER is a judge of the Connecticut Appellate Court. He was appointed to the Appellate Court in 1992 after eighteen years on the Connecticut trial bench. He is a graduate of Yale College and the Yale Law School and has been a Visiting Lecturer at Yale University and a Guggenheim Fellow at the Yale Law School. He regularly teaches courses on law, literature, and jurisprudence to state court judges. Judge Schaller is the author of numerous articles on various legal topics including law and the humanities, constitutional law, complex case management, and violence in American society.